For Pat, Larry, Dev, and Doug

Acknowledgments

The road to completing this book was marked by the timely appearance, or sustained encouragement, of several people. My deepest thanks to the following:

To my friend Larry Stewart, the mastermind behind the inquiries and database upon which much of this work is based. It was his focus, as well as his ability to alternately push and pull me toward technology, that enabled me to develop a much broader view of contemporary dream patterns.

To my family, which takes the eccentricity of my interests in stride, and encourages my enthusiasms without reserve.

To Harold Hansen, for suggesting I contact Sourcebooks and Deb Werksman with this project. That was a wonderful and productive intuition.

To Deb Werksman, for being so efficient and enthusiastic an editor that the process of working with her was filled with happy surprises.

To Kristin Higson-Hughes, the editor of my weekly column in *Woman's World*, who is endlessly diplomatic and a very fine dreamworker. Her writing and focus continue to instruct me on giving readers the goods.

To my own circle of dream friends—Lea Harwood, Marilynne Keyser, Kendra Key, Lisa Medieros, and Tracy Stone—for sharing and exploring dreams with reverence and fearlessness. I am enriched by their wisdom, courage, and humor.

To the students, clients, correspondents, and research participants who have shared their stories and dream adventures with me. These are the teachers who have catalyzed new theories, and the consumers who have demanded more practical information about their dreams.

To my teacher Jon Klimo, who continues to inspire me to look more deeply into the mysterious, and to speak more bravely about what I see.

The DREAM...OK

Discove... ...
ab...

SOURCEBOOKS, INC.
NAPERVILLE, ILLINOIS

Published by Sourcebooks, Inc.
P.O. Box 4410, Naperville, Illinois 60567-4410
(630) 961-3900
FAX: (630) 961-2168
www.sourcebooks.com

Library of Congress Cataloging-in-Publication Data

Holloway, Gillian.
    The complete dream book: what your dreams tell about you and your life/
    by Gillian Holloway.
        p.cm.
    Includes bibliographical references and index.
    ISBN 1-57071-708-7 (alk. paper)
1. Dream interpretation. I. Title.

BF1091 .H58 2001
154.6'3—dc21

2001031334

Printed and bound in the United States of America
BG   10 9 8 7 6 5 4 3

Table of Contents

Introduction: Getting the Most from Your Dreams

Psychologists have long asserted that unforgettable or recurring dreams are related to childhood experiences. Certainly our history has an effect, but I find that these types of dreams are also shaped by the way individuals cope with challenges, and how we respond to problems and stress. People who meet challenges primarily through achievement and excellence often dream of failing examinations or appearing in plays and forgetting their lines. These dreams are shorthand for their worst fear: *I may not be able to perform adequately in this situation to make sure all goes well, or this challenge may not be impacted by my efforts no matter how great they are.* We feel uniquely at a loss when the problems we face are not manageable through the means we like to use, or the way we feel best equipped to respond What appears in your dreams says a great deal about your style of coping and achieving goals, as well as the pressures you may be facing. Anxiety dreams arise when the challenge you face isn't a good match for the coping style you are trying to use.

After the release of my first book, *Dreaming Insights,* I received letters from all over the United States from people who were curious about a particular dream that haunted them. I also did many television and radio interviews, and took call-in questions from the listeners and audiences. I was surprised by how many of the same questions were asked: at midnight in Washington, D.C., and at noon in

Missoula, Montana. People from dramatically different walks of life were worried about the same nightmares; young people were trying to discover the truth about their sweethearts; and bewildered family members were haunted by dreams of deceased loved ones.

It dawned on me that although individual differences are stressed in most work with dreams, there is a need to discuss the dreams we have in common and to address the reasons why this seems to be so. In my work with students, clients, and correspondents, I've studied countless dreams, and have been fascinated by the factors that we share with one another. Informally, I've developed a working personality theory, because certain personality traits seem to coincide with particular dream themes.

With the help of my brilliant website designer Larry Stewart, I've been able to collect dreams on my elaborate dream website, www.Lifetreks.com, and create a database that includes extensive background material and associations from each dreamer. I now have a collection of more than eighteen thousand dream cases that provide excellent information about professions, stress factors, and dreams at home and away from home, as well as the interpretations of the dreamers themselves. Men and women tend to have different dream themes, and their dreams are set in different settings. Men more often dream of watching plane crashes and getting into street fights, while women dream more about houses, possessions, and relatives. Some dreams occur during certain times of life; retired people who worry about a fixed income and being separated from adult children have quite different dreams from those of teenagers falling in love for the first time.

Your dreams are also affected by what you do for a living. All professions seem to trigger dreams about factors that are beyond our control, but which we are often responsible for or affected by. Media people have nightmares about "dead air time" and fire fighters dream about walking onto a floor that has been burned out from underneath them. Nurses dream of being given orders that are not good for the patient, and teachers dream of coming to class without any material to present. These exaggerated themes illustrate the tension between what we must face and what we can control, and can serve as warning signals that we're experiencing a level of stress that should be compensated for if we are to continue functioning effectively and feeling well.

My lifelong fascination with dreams initially sprang from my own experience as a vivid dreamer. During early childhood, I dreamed of an unexpected death in the family that occurred a week later just as I had foreseen it. That early precognitive dream set the stage for my entire life's exploration into a kind of intelligence that is too rarely understood and utilized. I knew irrefutably that dreams have a kind of validity, a language that is worth knowing. As a teenager, I recorded my dreams and found that the parallels to waking life were sometimes quite obvious. At other times, I was delighted by the quirky, almost poetic way that dreams sought to buoy my confidence and hint at talents that would later surface.

In college, I studied psychology because the world of inner life—thoughts, feelings, and perceptions—has always seemed the most exciting and rich terrain to me. By the time I was in graduate school studying counseling methods, I was already noticing the power of understanding dreams to help us let go of the past, negotiate the present, and influence the future. Advice from a friend or even a doctor often doesn't propel us to take action or feel differently about ourselves. But deciphering the raw power and wisdom of a dream changes us by the very act of probing and discovering what it presents. Although I studied numerous approaches to helping people change, heal their scars, and make more productive decisions, nothing proved as potent as the discovery of messages from the wise and undamaged self that speaks through our dreams.

For this reason, I focused my counseling practice and teaching career in the areas of dreams and intuition. These, I feel, are the voices of wisdom, healing, and power that each of us possess and are meant to benefit from on a daily basis. For the past six years, I have taught college courses in dream psychology, nightmares, and intuition. I also facilitate dream study groups, and have a counseling practice devoted to dream analysis and increasing intuition. Far from being "airy fairy," I have chosen these disciplines precisely because this is where I have seen the fastest and most effective results. It is pragmatism, not mysticism, that has propelled me to explore the truths our dreams reveal, and to share the discoveries that have proven most telling.

When I began seriously studying about dreams in college, I discovered it was necessary to cut and paste a great deal of information together from widely different sources. Ancient mythology held certain clues, as did pioneering psychologists like Sigmund Freud. But those kernels of insight were buried amidst volumes of material that seemed to have little bearing on contemporary life. Although I learned as much as I could while earning a doctorate in psychology and exploring history and theory, it was when I began working with large numbers of dreams and dreamers that a more vivid sense of the patterns in modern dreams began to emerge. I came to believe that a more reliable translation of dreams would come from the dreams themselves and the life experiences of the dreamers, not from legends of folklore or psychological theories. Once I began working with dream patterns that sprang from life rather than theory, my students and clients became very enthusiastic about how quickly and accurately they could decipher their dreams. This is not meant to impugn the value of other approaches to dreamwork. Any lens that affords a view into your deeper mind is worthy of respect, and I have seldom explored a theory about dreams that did not have something to offer. But I've also had clients who were scholars on the work of Carl Jung (a famous pioneer in dream theory) who, after researching for ten years, came to me because they were still wondering what their own dreams meant. While I cannot say with absolute certainty what any dream means, I can say what the last hundred people who shared similar dreams were going through, and how their understanding of the dreams helped them. For practical reasons, shared experiences are often the best place to begin a dream interpretation, and that is what this book is all about.

Because this material comes from real dreams and real people instead of abstract theories or historical mythology, the chances are greater that it will strike a chord with you, and have relevance to your life. This is not an attempt to take away your individuality or the uniqueness of your dreams, those are a given. But at this stage in your understanding, it can be very reassuring and valuable to look at what others have discovered in their dreams, and see if similar truths and ideas may be helpful to you as well.

Recognizing Your Most Valuable Dreams

Given that you may dream more than one hundred and fifty thousand dreams in a lifetime and may remember several dreams a week or a night, how do you know when a particular dream is important to delve into? Here is a short list of questions that will help you know if a dream is calling out for a second look.

The seven factors listed below have nudged many people to unravel the mystery of a dream that proved particularly important to them. Use the factors as a checklist; if one of these factors fits your response to a recent dream it is worthy of further investigation.

1. *Strong feelings.* Did the dream shake you up or touch you emotionally? Dreams that come charged with feeling are often loaded with information. Even if they seem unsettling, it can be very satisfying and reassuring to decipher them.

2. *Provocative imagery.* Was there an image in the dream that was so weird, so wild, or so frightening that you can't stop thinking about it? Vivid impressions like this can be a deliberate memory trigger embedded in the dream to make it more likely you'll think about it later.

3. *Recurring dream or imagery.* If you remember having this dream before or the same plot or imagery, it is very likely that you'll benefit from understanding more about this dream.

4. *You can't bear to think about it.* Unspeakable nightmares are among the most useful, valuable, and ultimately healing of all dreams. If something about your dream is too painful to think about, you will almost certainly be relieved and empowered once you understand what it was really about.

5. *You've been in transition or are contemplating a change.* When we're on shifting sands, dreams can be a source of solid ground because they are connected with feelings, memories, values, and intentions. These elements aren't subject to job lay-off, divorce, or other changes. Not only can you learn more about what choices will be best for you, but you can reconnect with the aspects of life that are unchanging and ever-nourishing to the spirit.

6. *It haunts you.* There are some dreams that simply will not be dismissed. They waft through the air around us like an elusive fragrance, rising up when we're driving or doing dishes. If something about a dream haunts you in this way, it is likely that your unconscious mind is gently nudging you to think about it, and is hoping you'll open the message it has sent to you.

7. *You're intellectually curious.* Not everyone awakens from a dream drenched with emotion or riveted by the imagery they've seen. But if you are genuinely curious about your dream and keep wishing you knew what it meant, this too is a signal that it may be particularly valuable to understand.

If at least one of the above factors is nudging you toward exploring a dream, it is very likely that the dream in question is not only worth looking into, but may contain some very helpful insights. This book is designed to give you answers in a direct fashion and to take you through the kinds of dreams people ask about most. By seeing the background that gives rise to these dreams and the kinds of people most likely to have them, you'll see how you fit in. A database of eighteen thousand dreamers was used to collect the data included. Most important, you'll be able to see what meaning others have found in similar dreams. You can benefit from their discoveries by seeing if similar suggestions are helpful to you too.

How Do You Know if It's the Right Interpretation for You?

It is always easier to see what is going on in someone else's life than it is to be certain about your own. Dream interpretation is like that too. It's natural to worry about getting the right answer to a dream, and because our dreams are often composed of unanswered questions or disquieting feelings, it isn't easy to feel crystal clear and confident about what it all means.

There is one school of thought that says when a dream interpretation is correct, you'll feel it all over your body, like goose flesh, and you'll have what therapists call an "Aha" experience of insight. Unfortunately, this isn't true for everyone and it doesn't seem to be the only gauge of whether an interpretation is correct. Different people seem to process information in different ways.

There are actually a number of reliable ways to tell if an interpretation fits for you. When you read about the meaning of your dream or dream symbol in this book, you should experience at least one of these reactions. If you don't, and you honestly believe the information doesn't seem to fit for you, then your opinion may be quite right. Here is the list of reactions you may experience when an interpretation is accurate for you.

1. *You feel a response in your body.* Whether your foot jerks, you break into a sweat, your heart feels funny, or your stomach lurches, the body is often the first responder to a correct dream interpretation. Sometimes the reactions are subtle, like a tingling sensation, other times they're broad, such as having a coughing fit or your eyes suddenly tearing up.
2. *You experience relief of some kind.* Understanding your own dream is, after all, bringing information you already have in one part of your mind over into another part. In this sense, it's a big relief, like finally remembering the name of an actor or recalling where you left something.
3. *It makes sense to you intellectually.* Some of us don't get rushes of knowing or floods of emotion. But we can recognize the logic of a dream's symbolism and see how it applies to our lives.
4. *The situation described fits your life.* If you look up your dream about the Titanic, read that this is common to people who are planning their wedding, and you are getting married in a huge formal wedding next month, chances are good that this interpretation can benefit you.
5. *You experience an "Aha" or sense of recognition.* This is part bodily sensation and part emotional recognition. Some people say there is a sense of something

clicking into place or a fog lifting as if someone had just washed the windows on your world.

6. *You feel upset and unwilling to even consider that the interpretation fits for you.* This is different from giving the idea some consideration and deciding it isn't quite right. A strong overreaction to an idea can be a signal that there's some truth in it.

7. *Your truth detector goes off.* All of us have a sort of psychological truth detector that signals when we've heard something profoundly true. You may have felt it in church, during a lecture, or simply while watching *Oprah.* There is a moment of knowing that what you've just heard was very true, very important, and in some sense *just for you* in that moment.

These responses give you greater control by giving you a way to gauge whether the information you're reading really applies to you. Also remember that the purpose of dream analysis is to discover things that make our lives more successful and happy. The proof is in how useful and helpful this information is for you. This book isn't a journey into labels or mental diagnoses; it's a quick lesson in translating the fascinating wisdom that resides in your dreaming mind.

Why Understanding Your Dreams Is Important

Joni was a senior in high school approaching her graduation with a sense of euphoria. During the school year, she'd already begun sending off for college catalogues and comparing notes with friends about which schools they hoped to attend. Her happiness was only blighted by one thing: at this particular time Joni began having a horrible dream that her mother had died. The dream repeated a number of times with different details. She often awoke with tears in her eyes, worried and confused about what the dream could mean.

Joni had studied a bit of psychology in school and knew that Freud had said some dreams were a matter of our secret wishes finding an outlet. She knew that couldn't be true—she loved her mother very much and certainly didn't want anything to happen to her. She began to worry that in some way her dreams might be foretelling a disaster that was about to befall her family. For this reason, Joni was in the studio audience of a local television program in Portland, Oregon, when I was discussing dream interpretation. She raised her hand and told me about her dream, but not about her background. I was happy to be able to tell her that in dreams, death is often a reflection of change.

It is very common for youngsters moving away from home to dream that one or both of their parents have died. (It is also common for parents at that time to dream that their child has died.) Even later in life, when a core relationship undergoes a change or we move away, that shift may be marked by dreams of death. The "death" refers to the end of an era and usually a change in the roles of a relationship. The connection will remain, but you will never again return to the previous position in that relationship.

After this explanation, Joni grinned from ear to ear and shared the fact that she had indeed been planning her college career and a move away from home. Now that she knew her dreams were marking this rite of passage, she could relax and enjoy planning her future.

All of us can gain confidence from understanding more about compelling dreams because they shed light on our current concerns and decisions and help us better understand loved ones and colleagues. Generally, the more stirring and provocative the dream is, the more you will benefit from understanding it. Unraveling even a frightening or unpleasant dream may present you with a number of very real gifts.

Increased Peace of Mind

Knowing the reasons behind a dream can eliminate needless worry, particularly if the dream has recurred. We may be able to kid ourselves that a single bizarre dream is the result of the midnight movie or too much pizza, but a recurring, highly detailed dream that will not subside is obviously no accident. Getting rid of superstition and misconception about dreams is the first step toward getting acquainted with this level of the mind. Dreams are really just another way of thinking, one that involves a slightly different language and perspective than we use in waking life.

Greater Ease with Making Decisions

A while back, I was offered a prestigious position that would have necessitated placing my teaching and writing activities on the back burner. I was sorely tempted to accept the offer because it would have been lucrative and exciting. The part of my personality that is ambitious surged forward and began chattering mentally about how I could make it work. But I know from experience that my dreaming mind often has a wiser and larger view of things, so I try deliberately to sleep on important decisions in the hope that my dreams will lend me their important council.

That night, I dreamed that I was struggling up the sheer face of a mountain, clumsily juggling the notes for this book along with lesson plans for the university courses I teach. It was tough climbing with my hands full, but since I was so near the top, I decided just to force my way over the summit so I could see what was up there. I literally clawed my way up by my fingernails and looked at the top. I was amazed to find there was nothing there. It was a bare clearing with touches of snow on the ground. Disappointed, I climbed up to rest and catch my breath. I couldn't understand it. "Why does everyone make such a fuss about climbing to the top of the mountain," I wondered, "when there is nothing there?"

My interpretation of this dream was that accepting the position (climbing that mountain) at this time would be a mistake. I had my hands full with projects that I'd put a great deal of energy into and about which I felt particularly proud and passionate. Indulging my ego by trying to reach an illusionary pinnacle would leave me deflated and wondering why I had bothered. I declined the offer and have many times been thankful that I made that decision, since my own work has continued to expand and claim my energy. On the threshold of big decisions and new relationships, our dreams tend to be particularly important and full of deep insights. When faced with a crossroads in your life, one of the most practical things you can do is pay close attention to the perspective offered by your dreams.

Deepened Insight into People

A friend of mine was very excited about a new man she'd met. He was handsome, witty, and seemed to be mad about her. Inundated with flowers and gifts, she savored the attention he showered on her from the first time they went out. But when we sat down to examine her recent dreams, she'd had a particularly troubling nightmare that she was back in a dysfunctional relationship with her former fiancé. The dream finished on a troubling note, with her dashing out of the house to escape from him. "Why would I dream that?" she asked, worried. "I would never go back to Earl in a million years and he's nothing like my new fellow. Earl pushed me way too fast and would never take no for an answer."

Knowing the unconscious mind's ability to see through appearances and to recognize deep similarities, I asked her if perhaps her dreaming mind was providing a cautionary note to balance her enthusiasm. Perhaps her unconscious did see some similarity between these two men already, even though they seemed dissimilar. Unfortunately, my friend did not feel this was a likely explanation for the dream and decided to proceed with the relationship. A few whirlwind months later, she discovered just how similar these two men were. She felt bulldozed and manipulated in the new relationship just as she had in the engagement years previously. Fortunately, she is a wise and powerful person and managed to extricate herself from the entanglement before it became too costly to her.

Because the dreaming mind recognizes patterns, it will sometimes conjure up images of people or situations from the past that hold a similar feeling or presented similar dangers to us. These flashbacks don't arise without reason. Often, as in my friend's case, the dreaming mind is a step ahead, attempting to show us the hazards in the road ahead so that we can avoid trouble and find what we truly want. This capacity for seeing through the surface and into the essence of a person or situation is at times like having psychological X-ray vision.

Increased Self-Awareness

Gary was a bright, young executive whose productivity and ease with people got him swiftly promoted. He was delighted by the progress he was making, but strangely, since his promotion, he'd begun having trouble sleeping. Just when everything was going his way, he was feeling anxious and insecure. When he did sleep, he had troubling dreams about his deceased father. In the dreams, Gary was a young boy again, anxiously biting his fingernails and struggling to avoid the criticism of his demanding father. He would try to do the right thing, and then nervously bite his nails. His father found this habit particularly contemptible, and would criticize Gary for being weak. Since his father had been dead for some time, Gary could think of no reason why he might be dreaming of him at this time in his life, particularly since he was now enjoying the kind of success that his father would never have believed he could achieve.

But when the onset of a dreaming pattern coincides with a change in our lives, there is almost always a connection between the two. As in Gary's case, it is hard to see the connection when the apparent story in the dream bears little resemblance to waking life. We discussed the qualities of his father: demanding, critical, and sometimes punitive. He seemed to be waiting for Gary to make a wrong move so that he could reduce his confidence even more. When we listed these attributes, it dawned on Gary that we were also describing his new boss. A tough leader who was sometimes insensitive in his comments, the man was very unlike Gary's father physically, but he conveyed the same air of impatience with mistakes.

Even though it hadn't occurred to Gary consciously, his unconscious mind had clearly registered the source of Gary's new anxiety and was trying to explain it to him in his dreams. On an emotional level, Gary now found himself working for and with his father every day! And unfortunately, Gary had so many unconscious associations with feeling clumsy and incompetent when he was around this kind of person that he was rapidly losing sleep because he felt so inept and insecure. Fortunately, coming to grips with the nature of the problem went a long way toward allowing Gary to feel better about himself, his job, and his boss.

All of us are multifaceted beings with layers of feelings, memories, and potential. During our busy days, it's often all we can do to stay on top of our scheduled tasks and maintain rapport with others. It falls to the unconscious processes to do the deeper work of making sense of things, deciphering our deep feelings, and offering insights in the form of our dreams. It is ironic that some people tell me they don't want to understand their dreams because they don't want to know themselves that well or are afraid of what they will find out. On the contrary, getting to know yourself well through your dreams is a strengthening process that is full of delightful surprises.

Chapter

1

The Dream You Can't Forget

The dreams in this chapter include themes that are reported to me most often and answer questions that many have asked. Although there are individual variations of these themes, I've tried to include and comment on the general interpretations that are most often meaningful. You will probably recognize several of these dreams as identical to or very similar to your own. This doesn't guarantee that you are going through identical experiences as the dreamers in my practice and database; however, it is likely that some of the same stresses are impacting you or that your own high standards or coping strategies may be accentuating certain aspects of your experience.

With respect to these modern dreams, folkloric interpretations tend to present confusing explanations that don't hold true for large numbers of people. (Many people have heard, for example, that dreams of losing teeth mean that a member of your family is about to die.) Psychological interpretations borrowed from early psychotherapists tend to focus on potential symptoms of illness or dysfunction. The approach offered here is different in that we start with commonly reported themes, the life situations of the dreamers who reported them, and the stresses, feelings, and hopes they experienced. Where certain factors are consistent, I've formulated interpretations that have been widely endorsed by students, clients, and research participants.

Each dream in this chapter is like a road sign with a somewhat universal meaning. Some of those signs say, "Slow down, you're working too hard," while others say "Draw the line and stand your ground." Understanding your dreams is often a matter of reading these signs and considering what they imply in your situation. By recognizing what parts of our lives and feelings dreams reflect, we become better able to cope with challenges and use opportunities to greater advantage.

Each of these classic dreams is described as it is reported most often, followed by an explanation of what it means. Don't be disturbed if your dream is slightly different. After you read the information on the dream, the significance of any differences you notice between the dream described and your dream will make intuitive sense to you. Try on this information as you would a hat: decide how it looks and feels to you and don't let it obscure your point of view.

It is important that you maintain your authority to gauge how well any interpretation matches your situation and feelings. While the most probable meaning of each dream is given, you remain the ultimate authority on your own life—your case may be different. Most people have no trouble discerning when an interpretation makes sense to them because they feel astonished, excited, or relieved when an explanation is accurate. By keeping an open mind and trusting your common sense and gut reactions, you will get the most from these descriptions.

Unprepared for the Exam

It's a familiar theme for many people. You go into an examination room for a test, such as a high school or college final. Upon opening the test materials, you realize that through some crazy mix-up you registered for this class but completely forgot to attend any of the lectures. It's too late to do anything about it and explaining what happened is out of the question. Who would believe this kind of oversight?

Strangely enough, people who dream of being unprepared for an exam are actually the folks *least* likely to go into any arena unprepared to excel. For that reason, I sometimes refer to this as the overachiever's nightmare. It is common for both men and women, usually between the ages of twenty-five and fifty-five. People who have carved out high-profile careers and those who have high standards of excellence in what they do are those most likely to have this dream sporadically throughout adulthood. This theme often arises when an individual moves forward into a higher level of performance or takes on responsibilities that increase what he expects of himself.

Since this person rarely fails at what he does, the dreams are not warnings of impending mistakes. Instead, they illustrate how accountable the dreamer feels for the success or failure of the projects around him. This theme dramatizes the individual's belief that performance is crucial to achievement and preparation is necessary in order to perform well in situations that test your knowledge and judgment.

This perspective is realistic and works well in life; however, there can be an edge of anxiety present beneath the high performance. Sometimes this person expects too much of himself, such as feeling he should know the answers to material he has never studied. Although real-life situations bear little resemblance to the examination chamber of these dreams, positions of responsibility, promotions, and other spotlight situations tend to catalyze this dream.

This dream can act as a barometer of internal pressure. As someone who handles numerous tasks well, you may not always know when to say "enough already." The no win scenario of the test can let you know when you feel you've signed up for too many things at once. Since you set yourself up for dramatic high-pressure situations, you also have the option of taking a more moderate approach to your accomplishments. You are probably so far ahead of the pack that no one will even notice the difference if you set your sights on being a happy mortal instead of a frazzled superhero.

Not Enough Credits to Graduate

You are called back to high school or college because it's been discovered you missed a particular course and have to make it up immediately. This discovery places your status as a graduate in jeopardy, and could also nullify your other credentials. Ultimately, your job and entire lifestyle could come into question. Feeling a keen sense of frustration and embarrassment, you plunge into school again, wondering how things like this happen and hoping you can clean it all up before anyone finds out.

Men and women both have this dream; however, it is most common among people between the ages of thirty-five and fifty who have a definite career focus. This is a dream about progress and the factors that make it tougher to get into the arena where you really want to operate. The graduation represents crossing a mental threshold into another level in your career, a different sort of relationship, or a more satisfying lifestyle. The thing that really blocks the progress is a lack of credit, which translates into lack of awareness of past accomplishments. This dream is particularly common to highly creative people who secretly feel their gifts are flukes. They therefore fail to realize they have earned and are entitled to the results of their efforts.

It is *you* who may not truly give yourself credit for significant accomplishments and knowledge. There may even be some area in which you hold yourself back by doing tasks or staying with experiences you have already outgrown. Although you are likely a risk-taker who can summon the enthusiasm to meet a challenge, it's possible that you come across as much more confident and gung-ho than you really feel.

When we are striving toward a goal, there is often a particular thing that we would prefer not to address or some way that we resist changing. It is almost as if you would do anything but that thing in order to fulfill your goals. This is a time to open up and become willing to do the things you've avoided so far. Use this dream as a checkpoint, like a thirty-thousand-mile tune up, to realistically update your position and options. It's time to dwell not only on your accomplishments, but also on the purpose, passion, and desire that motivate you to graduate to bigger and better things.

Can't Get Your Locker Open

You're back in high school in the hall near your locker. Everyone around you gets into their lockers and grabs their stuff, slamming the doors shut again with a bang. Meanwhile, you twirl the combination to your lock over and over, but the tumblers don't fall into place. Something's wrong. Your skin gets prickly. Although you *know* the number and feel ridiculous, you can't get it open. You stall, trying to avoid attention, because this is really embarrassing. No matter how many times you try it, you can't get your locker open. It's hard to tell what is more frustrating, not being able to get to your stuff, or worrying that someone is going to notice your ridiculous problem.

The two things that make this dream so tense are the inability to do something others do with ease and the sense of being cut off from what belongs to you. Women are more prone to this dream than men, and it can appear between the ages of twenty and seventy. The things in your locker represent parts of yourself that you sense are there but can't always access when you want them. The feeling of being cut off from yourself can happen because of a particular event, like moving to a new city, or it can be a more lasting sensation dating back to an earlier time in your life. Unfortunately for many of us, the very situations that make us hunger to belong and be at ease are the same situations that lock us up. These are the days when we'd like to wear a T-shirt that says, "I am way more charming than I seem today." However, many people who report this dream are also very smooth, successful, and polished. For them social ease is not the element locked away, but something more personal seems to have been lost in the shuffle of their busy lives.

The practice of self-acceptance will go a long way toward putting you at ease and allowing you to retrieve what you're after. If you feel you have lost some vibrant part of yourself along the way, take this dream as a reminder that all that energy and potential is still within you. The things in that locker represent the bright, funny, *real* you that may have been temporarily displaced.

Take a hint from the dream that comparing yourself to others or performing for their benefit only keeps you from getting that door open. No one is really paying any attention to whether you have what you want or not; they are focused on getting to *their* belongings. Avoid scolding or judging yourself too harshly, and when a subtle feeling stirs inside, pay attention. This inner voice is the one that knows the combination!

Forget trying to act as if you already have the world by the tail. The urge to feign perfection is one of the greatest inhibitors to improving our lives. If you can let go of any guilt about the past or embarrassment about the present, you will have more energy and clarity to create what you really want.

Discovering Unused Rooms

You're in your home, although it may be slightly different from your home in waking life. Something makes you explore the house and you discover a room that you haven't used in years. No one else seems to know the room is there, but as you look around, you remember it from the distant past. You had completely forgotten it existed and are delighted by the furnishings, the view, and the atmosphere. Although it's been neglected for a long time, you feel very enthusiastic and decide to clean it up and start using it again. You throw open the curtains and begin making plans to clean and restore it. It seems incredible that you could have forgotten this room all these years, but it's going to be fun getting it back in shape.

This dream is a reminder of something dearly loved that was set aside or shut down earlier in life. The house itself symbolizes you, and the different attributes and rooms within it represent the different interests and capacities you have. The discovery of the forgotten room is a positive image that suggests it's time to rekindle an old interest, talent, or discipline that could nourish you. This dream is more common to women, generally starting after age thirty and becoming more prevalent later in life.

You may have recently undergone a jarring experience or something that caused you to evaluate your life from a different perspective. It could require a little reflection to identify the quality in yourself that you are being reminded of with this dream. But it isn't necessary that you immediately identify exactly what that room represents. It will be enough that you move back toward the things and feelings you love most. You can be sure the timing of this reminder is ideal and meaningful.

Spend some time thinking about your secret ambition or the beloved hobby you gave up years ago. Some dreamers know immediately that the time is right to return to their painting, singing, or college plans. For others, the room represents a return to a value, faith, or wisdom that was central to early life. The image of moving back into that space represents the willingness to embrace and enjoy your true self. So don't make this a worrisome question you must guess correctly or miss out on forever. Instead, use your interests, hungers, and memories like a compass and move steadily in the direction of what you love.

The dream not only shows that something precious has been neglected, it also suggests you will be very happy to discover and restore it to your life. For this reason, it is very likely that if you follow your happiness in small and large ways, you will find your way into the joyous potential that is waiting for you.

Teeth Falling Out

You notice a funny sensation inside your mouth and run your tongue over your teeth. To your dismay, one of your teeth is so loose that it wobbles and comes out. Horrified, you spit it out, and are aghast when other teeth start falling out too. By the time you finish spitting out teeth, an entire section of your mouth is toothless and bleeding. You can't *believe* this is happening to you and can't think what to do about it.

This scene dramatizes the cost of making a compromise. You may be finishing a college degree you're disillusioned with, returning to a relationship that you're ambivalent about, or sticking with a company you've grown to dislike. The people who have this dream are making reasonable choices in situations where their options are limited or even forced. People report this dream most often between the ages of fifteen and thirty-five, and it appears just as common to men as to women. These may be the years when we feel most acutely the pressure to compromise for various reasons but have not yet established sufficient experience or power to permit us greater freedom. Although the dream in itself doesn't necessarily signal that a mistake is being made, it does point out that a deep and highly personal cost is involved in the decision.

The gore of the dream imagery often reflects the severity of the price being paid to keep the peace or stay the course. The person staying in a stressful job may have dreams of teeth crumbling or loosening. The woman staying in an abusive marriage will be more prone to tooth loss imagery that includes gaping wounds and severe bleeding. Lesser versions of this dream tend to occur immediately after a begrudging decision is made to tolerate something for the time being.

Typically, these dreams involve losing a crown or finding that a single tooth has come loose. This kind of post-decision feedback serves as a reminder that a temporary compromise may be strategic, but there are very real costs involved in maintaining this course over the long haul.

Take the long view about the way you want to shape your life and support your core values and ambitions. Don't panic about this dream and feel you must tell off your boss or revamp your career or relationship overnight. A more appropriate response is to review your priorities and put the promises you've made to yourself higher up on the list. If you are near the end of the line with the compromise you've chosen, you can probably finish your stint without much adjustment.

If the arrangement is more long-term, then do everything you can to protect your energy and peace of mind. Schedule more time with people who support you, activities that liberate you, and pursuits that restore your balance. The idea is to get crystal clear in your own mind about what is going on, what you are willing to tolerate for the time being, and how you intend to make life more comfortable and satisfying as soon as you can.

Escaping a Tornado

You're in your home with loved ones when a sudden, horrific tornado appears on the horizon. It's impossible to gauge when it will arrive or what damage it will do, but you launch into action immediately. The others don't seem to realize the danger or know how to respond. You have to handle everything and get them to safety. Racing around the house, you struggle to secure the doors and windows while yelling instructions at others who remain either unresponsive or unhelpful.

The tornado essentially represents an emotional storm. A sudden argument, conflict, or unsettling experience usually triggers this dream and it is often a recurring nightmare that returns periodically from childhood through to adulthood. The image is common for, but not limited to, people who had an unsettling or volatile element in their early years. Later in life, unexpected turbulence in a partner or troubling conditions can trigger a dread of instability. This upset is often accompanied by a sense of hyper-responsibility; you may feel you are the only one who can keep the peace or save the situation.

If you're in the midst of a challenge or relationship that is pushing your buttons right now, realize that you're going to have to manage your own reactions at the same time that you decide what to do about the problem. If you feel unusually shaken by today's challenge, it may be because it is firing off alarms that date back to early years.

Try to be objective about the present, and even if your knees get wobbly, do what you think is right. If you are hurtling into your superhero mode and managing everything with supersonic speed, entertain the notion that the other people involved may have some resources to share as well. Certainly, if you're on your own, then you'll have to manage. But the people who have tornado dreams do tend to blaze past family members who are quite capable of helping without thinking to ask for support. Temper your reactions with realism and share the burden. This will conserve your strength to deal with whatever is on the horizon.

Falling

You are making your way along a path, sidewalk, or stairs. In a slight rush, you put your foot down wrong and it slips out from underneath you. Before you know it, you are tumbling through the air with a powerful sensation of falling.

Dreams of falling usually reflect a feeling of loss of control. The catalyst can be something as terrifying as losing your job or as minor as a day with overbooked appointments. Sometimes these dreams process tension we keep tightly wrapped, letting it unwind like a coiled spring at night. Men and women share this dream and it is more often a signal of current stress and confusion than of an enduring lifelong theme.

When things are most stressful and challenging, we simply don't have time to stop and notice we're getting frazzled. In some cases, a day of physical demands that are unusual for you, such as hiking or downhill skiing, will provoke dreams of falling. People who juggle ten things at once by day may be used to working amidst chaos, yet at night they dream of losing their footing or having everything go out from underneath them.

You may be involved in a situation that carries inherent pressures or hazards. To some extent, we can acclimate to almost anything, but abrupt shifts in challenges or sudden setbacks take a toll on the ability to maintain multiple outcomes. A falling dream can be a signal that you are operating at maximum capacity already and should pause to become acclimated.

Consider what adjustments can be made to spread out the demands on you or at least alternate high-pressure events with periods of ease so the impact on you is lessened. If you are intent on your climb and would never consider cutting back, then make balance part of your strategy for success. Do those little extra things to support your health, enjoy friends and family, and renew your faith and sense of purpose whenever possible.

Flying

You are walking, running, or standing on a high place. It occurs to you to try to fly. You assume your favorite flying position and with a thrill of recollection take off. This is it! You take a moment to recall how to steer by intention and shifts of balance, then enjoy the scenery and the delicious sensation of freedom.

Ecstatic flight is often associated with a recent positive experience, something that made you feel wonderful, capable, and free. People in performance professions have this dream frequently, as do those who engage in a hobby or activity that gives them special delight. Some people report that satisfying sexual encounters evoke flying dreams, while others notice them after a spiritual experience or meditation.

Although more people report flying dreams earlier in life, they can occur sporadically throughout the lifetime and are particularly common to those involved in an activity that allows them to feel liberated or to express their talents.

If you often fly in your dreams, it is likely that you are highly intelligent and enjoy some creative form of self-expression. If there are difficulties in your flying dreams—obstacles, pursuers, or fear of heights—something is impairing your ability to do your best and express yourself fully.

These barriers usually have an objective manifestation, such as a boss, spouse, or authority figure that holds you down. But there is also an internal component—some pattern of dwelling on limitations before you launch an idea so that you never get past the initial stage of early hope.

If you can't do anything to change your situation right away, concentrate on changing your internal barriers. Look into books on positive thinking and mental imagery. When you insist on a clear mental field, the external barriers in your life will show a remarkable tendency to back off as well.

Tidal Wave

You're in a room with several people in a building near the beach. Sitting with others gazing out the window, you become paralyzed at the sight of an enormous wall of water coming your way. Bigger than a huge building, it's bearing down right toward you. There isn't even time to prepare or respond, it's just coming, bigger than anything you've ever seen before.

Tidal waves often represent a cascade of emotion or an impending change. It's not unusual for someone struggling with a rough situation such as divorce, the loss of a loved one, or illness in the family to dream of being threatened by a tidal wave. The ocean is a nourishing part of nature that wreaks disaster when it seems to turn against us.

A tidal wave can depict the emotional devastation we suffer when situations change in unexpected or unwanted ways. It is as if the very fabric of our existence, which formerly sustained us, has become a source of danger so acute we don't know where to turn or how to respond.

Although the dream ends as you are about to be destroyed by the wall of water, it is not actually a harbinger of doom. Whether the wave represents emotion, change, or something else to you, the implication is that you are in the thick of it now, and you have little to gain by trying to deny the situation.

Hiding from reality can inhibit our ability to act effectively because it cuts us off from our survival instincts and true feelings. Whatever the nature of your tidal wave, expect some intense feelings and a few irrational moments to crop up.

Your best approach is to accept that you may feel overwhelmed for a while, but realize this isn't permanent. If you have a strong urge to bury emotions, try going with the flow a bit more. If you can balance your reactions, this storm will run its course and you'll emerge wiser but unharmed.

Naked in Public

You're in a public place, at a party, or at the office. Through some snafu, you forgot to get dressed before you went out today. You're completely stricken to discover you're in the middle of this setting with no clothes on. You make a desperate attempt to conceal yourself behind furniture or a nearby object, all the while trying to seem casual so as not to attract attention to your condition. To your amazement, no one seems to really notice what has happened.

Almost everyone has variations of this dream, usually associated with a sense of unfamiliar exposure due to a change in circumstances. We begin having this dream usually during adolescence when our first social identity and attempts to manage the impressions we make become primary concerns. It will recur in a wide variety of forms during changes in later life that also remind us that we are being "seen" by others. Any situation that puts us on the spot in a way we aren't used to can provoke this dream.

Ironically, positive change is often the culprit because as we excel we are more often asked to step into unfamiliar territory. And because the circumstance is a happy one, there is little chance to discuss or process ambivalent feelings. A promotion, a new romance, involvement with higher management, or other public attention can make us feel we are suddenly on display.

There is a positive note built into these dreams since they almost invariably show that other people are oblivious to the dreamer's condition. You may *feel* naked, but others are more concerned with their own problems than with yours. Take comfort in knowing they are unaware of your situation and you have time to become accustomed to things.

You may feel you have landed in a new situation without your normal defenses, identity, or expertise (your clothes), but in a short time you'll develop an entirely new set that is tailor-made for this situation.

Death of a Loved One (Unrelated to Actual Death)

A close family member has died, and you and the remaining family are attending the funeral. Everyone is grieving and crying; you are particularly sad and somewhat stunned.

These dreams can be terribly unnerving because we worry they mean something is going to happen to the family member or wonder if they indicate hidden feelings of hostility toward that person. Contrary to our worst fears, however, death in dreams is often a reflection of *change*, rather than an image of literal death. Changes that bring some era to a close or cause shifts in family roles are particularly likely to catalyze dreams of death.

Going off to college, getting married, or starting a family often provoke this theme, and it is particularly common for teenagers going through numerous and somewhat confusing changes. When we embark on a new chapter in life, the psyche chronicles the shift with dreams that reflect the end of an era. Such dreams actually lay to rest the past and usher in the future.

If you remember that these dreams are reflections of natural progress and are not harbingers of death, you will be able to accept your own changes with more comfort and confidence. Think of these dreams as signals that you are going through a rite of passage.

Your relationship with the person who died in the dream will not end, but it will be different. When we change, the nature of our relationships also shifts to reflect who we have become, and we must let go, even of the beloved roles we have outgrown.

You Can't Find a Toilet

You need to use a restroom and go off in search of one. You are likely in a public place where there should be a lavatory readily available, but somehow you can't find one. After an absurd series of delays, you locate the restroom and rush in. Unfortunately, there is an unpleasant problem here as well. There are too many people and no stalls available for you. When you finally do reach a commode, it doesn't work properly or is backed up and clogged. Why is this so hard, you think in frustration, and what are you going to do now?

Although men have this dream, it is far more common to women and seems to arise during the early twenties. This theme is about the inability to meet personal needs because of frustrating circumstances and other people. These dreams sometimes occur when we truly *do* need to use the restroom and apparently embark on a search for satisfaction while we sleep. But the specific trials we suffer during these quests represent frustrations in waking life that inhibit the ability to care for ourselves in some personal way. For example, those who place the needs of others ahead of their own often dream of a long line of people in front of them which prevents them from getting into the restroom. People with living situations that diminish their privacy sometimes dream of being uncomfortable because the only available toilet is out in plain view.

The filled or overflowing commode is a theme common to people who are caretakers in some sense—helping others to unload their problems or pursue their goals. They may be a dumping ground for the problems of others and neglect or shortchange their own need for equal time. This dream suggests a need for privacy, self-care, and self-expression.

If you have a tendency to make personal sacrifices and you work or live in a setting that exploits this characteristic, you may feel starved for personal time and privacy.

Try to take a more pragmatic view of your situation and acknowledge that you are more than the patient, giving person who makes everything work. It may not be possible or appropriate to demand more of others right now, but if you begin playing fair with your own needs and maintaining the limits you believe are just, others will become accustomed to and respectful of these boundaries.

Giving Birth (Unrelated to Actual Pregnancy)

You have just had a baby. Other people rally around for the occasion, and you make plans to adjust your life accordingly to care for the child.

When the birth in a dream does not pertain to a real pregnancy, the meaning is most often related to a change in the dreamer's life. Birth is symbolic of new beginnings, such as opening a new chapter in life or launching a creative endeavor. Changes like college graduation, launching a new career, starting or ending a relationship, and moving are associated with birth themes. This dream is almost exclusive to women, starting as early as puberty, and it may appear anytime throughout the lifespan.

There is often something unusual about the child or the birth. These peculiar details may symbolize what part of life is changing or how others will receive this new development.

Be aware that you're going through a *powerful* change, even if you don't see the evidence of it quite yet. We dream of birth when we've created something that is part of us or when we are trying to birth a new life for ourselves. These dreams remind us that trying circumstances are often part of creating a new life—a perspective easily overlooked when we are hurting or laboring to create a longed-for result.

The Impossible Task

You are trying to do something that can't be done. You may be swimming against the tide, climbing a ladder with broken rungs, or trying to put out fires without enough water. Your attempts to correct the situation or fix things only make matters worse, and you're pulled deeper into a complex tangle of obstacles and trouble. Things that should work don't; no matter how you persist the situation is definitely out of hand.

The impossible task represents a strong challenge made worse by the circumstances around it. You are responding in an *old* way to an entirely *new* kind of problem. Any challenge can evoke this dream, but it is most common when you face something lengthy and arduous.

The person working in a system filled with paradoxes will be prone to such a dream, and it may recur with slight variations for some time. If your boss demands results that your organization makes impossible or if you keep trying harder when your approach isn't working, this dream may persist for a while.

Frustration dreams like this one can be valuable allies. The primary benefit of this dream is that it highlights a problem with your strategy. You are probably addressing a big challenge with an approach that compounds the problem or you may be relying on an old strength that is not appropriate to your new situation.

Think of the dream as a problem-solving exercise and identify what it would take to improve the situation if this were a real problem. Should you back off and not try so hard? Get others to pitch in? Work smarter, not harder? Trust the simple solution that comes to mind and try it out for yourself.

Bungling a Public Performance

You are in a familiar setting where you teach, lecture, or work in front of people. Something fairly minor goes wrong; the equipment doesn't work or your usual notes and props are missing. You manage to deal with the problem and are only slightly distracted by having to compensate for it, when suddenly a major problem arises.

There is a power outage, a riot ensues just outside the door, or audience members become ill and leave in droves. Rather than call it off, you carry on with the absurd situation, yelling without a microphone or talking rapidly to the only two people left in the audience.

People who work in the public eye, even occasionally, struggle with the need to do a good job while depending on variables outside their control. The mixture of high expectations, lack of control, and public exposure make for inner tension. The successful program or presentation temporarily relieves stress, but plans for next time serve to activate the cycle again.

This dream usually arises when some factor has served to increase tension. You may be taking on too much work or setting yourself up for failure by lack of adequate preparation. In other cases, accepting more responsibility or taking greater risks can increase tension and trigger these dreams.

Sometimes these dreams release tension by playing out our worst case scenarios. They may also point out areas where inflexible responses contribute to discomfort and increase the degree to which unexpected changes throw us off track.

This type of anxiety is built into some situations but our perspective toward it also has an impact on the toll it takes. People who learn to manage this type of stress tend to look at the long haul, giving their best to each immediate challenge, but never giving any success or problem too much weight. This approach may take some practice, but once it is cultivated some of the craziness will fade from your particular set of challenges.

Runaway Vehicle

There is a runaway object, usually your car, or anything on wheels. It belongs to you, and although it doesn't seem to be your fault, the thing is rolling downhill at breakneck speed. You can't get it to stop by any normal means; the breaks, reins, or other controls aren't functioning. All you can do is try to dash after it or steer it manually so that no one else gets hurt.

The runaway object represents a part of your life that feels out of control, probably something that you used to handle easily or feel quite confident about. These dreams often relate to professional concerns about suddenly going downhill or losing ground. But this theme can also reflect a personality trait or habit that is getting the best of you.

It is likely that you are well aware of the situation that is on a downhill slide but you haven't felt alarmed about it. The dream serves to heighten awareness of the situation and suggests it is time to consider making some changes.

Dreams tend to present us with nasty scenarios when we've been pretty successful at denying there is a problem. By calmly looking this situation in the eye, you'll immediately feel better and be able to evaluate your options. It is likely that this situation won't respond to will power or other control games we play with ourselves.

Instead, you may have to do a little soul searching about what you really want and what your priorities are these days. Being honest with yourself and taking a clear look at where you want to go will set the foundation for natural and relatively painless changes that can correct your course.

Struggling Uphill

You are climbing or driving up a steep incline. The progress is slow and the amount of energy it takes seems more than you or your engine can handle. You may feel dizzy because the incline is so dramatic it's disorienting. You aren't sure if you have the strength or fuel to make it to the top but if you stop now you would only roll backwards or fall. You really have to keep going, but the terrain is uneven, it's hard to get traction or good footing, and you can't think why you chose to come this way.

The uphill struggle represents a challenge you're dealing with right now that feels like it's almost too much. If you make it, the rewards will be great, but you hadn't expected it to be so difficult. The medical resident who never gets to sleep, the programmer who must create software in a week, or anyone who has taken on an enormous challenge may have this dream.

Traveling uphill not only demands strength and courage, it requires a tremendous focus of attention. When dealing with a long-term challenge, we must dedicate energy and orient attention in a similar manner. The situation often contains personal as well as objective challenges that increase the sense of struggle or there may be obstacles that create a sense of fighting against the odds.

There may be little you can do about the nature of the challenge you have undertaken; it is likely that in this instance the only way out is through.

Challenge is subjective; the steepness of the incline is often a measure of how awesome the challenge feels to you. The only way to make it less steep is to focus on the incremental steps of the climb, breaking the task down into manageable parts and pacing yourself. Try to build in some good self-care, including rest, nutrition, exercise, and pleasure. Summon your patience to manage any sense of desperation or entrapment that arises and treat yourself like an Olympic athlete. Taking care of yourself will improve your odds of success and focusing on smaller increments of progress will make the process less overwhelming.

Unable to Move

You have to get out of the way, run from an assailant, or move fast. But you can't get your legs to move at all! The more you try to move, the more panicky you feel because you are simply paralyzed.

You're in a situation that calls for some kind of action you don't feel able or willing to take. You may need to end a relationship that isn't working but don't want to hurt the other person, or you may need to confront a parent or boss about something but feel uncomfortable at the thought of being assertive with an authority figure. Whatever the situation, there's something about it that inhibits you from doing what needs to be done and the urgency in the dream mirrors a growing discomfort you're feeling as a result of this conflict.

Because the source of your paralysis is inner conflict, the only way to relieve the pressure you're under is to make a compromise with yourself. You probably have assumed the most extreme and opposing beliefs about your situation rather than looking at it as an opportunity to walk the middle road. Instead of imagining yourself doing something dramatic and then thinking, "I can't!" consider what moderate action would be tolerable to you and still move you out of immobilization.

By making sensible compromises and taking small steps to get things rolling, you'll shake off the feeling of being stuck and start to see your options more clearly.

The Phone Won't Work

You're in a predicament that requires you to make a pressing phone call. You may be in danger, trying to dial 911, or faced with a dilemma and need to contact someone immediately for help. Maddeningly, the phone won't function! The buttons don't work; you dial the number, but get someone else instead or the operator is too preoccupied to put you through.

You try to explain that the situation is desperate but no one seems willing to help. You try a variety of adjustments to make the call but find it completely impossible. The tension increases toward the end of the dream and the frustration and anxiety cause you to wake up.

Phones in dreams represent our ability to communicate. We usually dream about phone trouble when something we've avoided in real life is coming to a head. If you know who you're trying to get through to in the dream, there may be something quite real you need to tell that person and the dream difficulties reflect the reasons or conditions that prevent you from making your point in real life.

When the dream shows you being put on hold or ignored by an unsympathetic operator, it is more likely that *you* have been ignoring an inner voice that has been trying to convey the need for rest, outside help, or attention to some problem.

Don't think of this dream as an awful signal that something is wrong with you. Instead, consider it a sign that it's time to pay closer attention to something that a part of you already knows. If you've been putting off getting help with some unwanted habit or difficulty, this dream suggests you get started by finding out what options are available to you.

Chances are, if you've been in a bind for a while, you won't be able to tidily dismiss the problem overnight. But getting started by seeking qualified advice and support will take weight off your shoulders and help you get things back on track. If you believe this dream deals with a communication problem with a loved one, don't assume that your next move should be to unload on them or vent your feelings in one big avalanche. That kind of honesty may not be appropriate or even safe in some situations.

Phone dreams are usually signals to be honest with yourself, get help if it's needed, and listen to and honor what you know to be right and good for you.

Being Chased

You are being chased or are attempting to outrun pursuers who mean you harm. It may be a wild animal, a gang of criminals, or a single dark figure with deadly intentions; but, regardless of who or what is after you, it is clear that this is a matter of life and death.

The monsters and villains who give chase in these dreams often represent tensions or issues rather than actual people in our lives. This is more likely to be the case if you have had chase dreams of various kinds for years and if there is a typical monster or evil force that tends to star in them.

Enduring chase dreams are often connected to initial worries learned in early life, such as a fear of instability, the strain of financial struggle, or the wish to avoid conflict. Later in life, adult pressures can trigger the familiar anxiety of earlier times, even though realistically these concerns are no longer a threat.

Chase dreams, by igniting fears brought forward from childhood, help explain why certain current events trigger disproportionate levels of anxiety. Though these dreams are unpleasant, they can be a good barometer of your own stress and let you know whether the compromise or resolution you've made is really working for you.

Chase dreams are a sign that some facet of your life is making you feel pressured or driven. Even if your life is successful and well ordered, this inner tension can perpetuate a sense of feeling off-center and on the run. Make a commitment to try and learn more about the power struggle going on inside you and how it influences you to run away from certain things and towards others. You may decide not to change a single thing in your life but becoming more aware of what drives you will only expand your sense of control and confidence.

The Titanic

You are on a ship very much like the Titanic. Although a fabulous party has been going on, it has become evident that your destination will not be reached. The ship appears to have hit something and is taking on water fast. There is mass chaos. You are as frightened by the ruthless hysteria you witness as you are by the apparent tragedy of your situation.

Those who have this dream are often going through a rite of passage such as a graduation or a wedding. The ship represents something in your life that is considered a big deal. Although the passage should be a positive experience, it has gotten overblown and out of control. Weddings often become the forum for a collection of expectations that must be met, so much so that the private romance and joy of the couple becomes lost in the confusion.

The image of going down with the huge luxury vessel captures the sense of horror and loss at being dragged down by something larger than life. The people going down on the huge ship represent the feeling of being a helpless mortal swallowed up by massive traditions and the numerous expectations of others.

First of all, don't assume that the tragedy of the dream is foretelling a failure in your relationship, marriage, or new career. The voyage you're embarking on isn't doomed but the overblown plans surrounding it are threatening to obscure the happiness you are entitled to feel.

Depending on your situation, you may be forced to follow through with a grand tradition that you'd secretly rather avoid. If that is true, you'll need to buoy your spirits with all the support you can muster. Confide in friends that you're feeling swamped and overwhelmed. Ask them to remind you of the real happiness that lies ahead when they see you start to flounder or lose your grip.

Set up symbols of your success or happiness around your home or room and take time to reconnect with the joy they represent. In other words, while you are forced to wander through something that feels unreal, keep lots of things and people around you that keep you in touch with what *is* real for you.

Finally, talk to people who have gone through what you are going through and get their advice on ways to keep your sanity. They know better than anyone the pitfalls of mass confusion and how to survive with your spirits intact, ready to enjoy the adventure that lies on the horizon.

Smoking

Although you do not smoke in real life, you are lighting up in the dream. You may enjoy the smoke a great deal and wonder how you are going to explain to friends that you have decided to start smoking. Maybe you can do it secretly?

Smoking in dreams almost always represents addictive patterns of some kind. This may deal with unhealthy eating patterns or even addictive relationships. In some cases, the imagery represents an addiction to a pattern of thinking, such as rage, abuse of power, or the insistence that you are always right.

Consider what part of your life might be the stage for an addictive pattern. This does not necessarily mean you must seek professional help for your shopping compulsion or buying lottery tickets. But knowing that your psyche has sent this warning image should be a strong inducement to take a look at the hold something has over you. It may be time to take a step back from a certain habit or situation or at least look at things with harsh honesty.

It will be much easier to change a habit or pattern if you refrain from attaching moral standards to it. People who contemplate change for reasons of health and freedom seem to make choices more freely than do those of us who whip ourselves with guilt or character assassination. Implied in the image of smoking is the potential for eventual loss or harm, so when you do identify the topic in question, simply weigh the downside carefully to protect yourself and reduce whatever risks are involved.

The End of the World

It is the day the world will end. There is mass hysteria and people are fleeing the scenes of disasters to try and escape the inevitable. Some are on rooftops watching rising floodwaters, others are racing in cars across burning highways just ahead of the flames. You are struggling to escape too, but with a greater sense of the futility of the situation. You would like to get to your family members or friends before the end. It is frustrating to know there is so little you can do and horrifying to see everything change so dramatically and suddenly.

This dream shows the effects of a change in the foundation of your life. Often this comes with the death of a parent or spouse because these relationships provide a certain platform of familiar experiences and expectations upon which we build our lives. Whatever has changed in your life seems to have rocked your sense of things on a psychologically global level.

However your life has been up until now, it has changed, and it will always be different. If you have suffered a tragedy, then this makes a certain amount of sense, but even if the change you've experienced has not left you feeling shaken, the psyche will register this as an ending of epic proportions.

Knowing the depth and breadth of the change you're experiencing will enable you to respond with compassion if you feel lost or morbid. It will also remind you that soon after processing the end of something, you can expect the dawn of a new beginning. Your best strategy is to grant yourself compassion and permission to function more slowly.

This adjustment will take time to absorb and transform into something quite different. To whatever extent possible, accept the flow of the current situation even if you cannot help but grieve for whatever has passed. Be gentle, even tender towards the side of yourself that may be disoriented by this change. Make arrangements to have good food, rest, supportive company, and soothing activities.

You will emerge from this ending in a fresh new phase, but don't feel you must force the process or march bravely forward. Be willing to move with love through the place where you are and you'll find soon enough that life is again lifting you up and showing you where the next chapter will begin.

Endless Chewing Gum

You have a mouth full of chewing gum that won't go away! When you try to spit it out, it multiplies right in your mouth. When you try to spit out the gum, parts of your teeth and gums may be pulled out too. Or the gum magically multiplies even though you keep spitting out as much as you can. Although it is not true for everyone, many people report that the gum in this dream is pink bubble gum.

This dream is a picture of frustration and overload. The gum represents an experience that you can't quite accept but can't get rid of either. Objects taken in through the mouth represent things we are trying to assimilate. Indigestible items symbolize experiences that we are unable to process or take in comfortably which have little benefit (or nourishment) for us.

This gum represents an activity that absorbs your energy but from which you derive little except frustration. It also has the quality of multiplying its demands on you, like a mythical task that grows ever larger the more you work at it. The desire to spit it out usually reflects a wish that you hadn't gotten into this mess, but due to various commitments or strong feelings you can't seem to let go of the situation. For some, dropping the problem would seem like a betrayal of their values or promises, yet keeping the gum seems to be an exercise in chewing on something toxic and consuming.

Be honest with yourself. You have not only bitten off more than you can chew—you've bitten into something that isn't particularly good for you. You probably have a code that won't allow you to get out of this mess in a single afternoon meeting, so accept that and begin to think defensively about what you can do to lighten your load. With situations of significant overload there are two ways you can help yourself.

There are always short-term, small improvements that will make you feel better right away even though they do little to solve the ultimate problem. Do them now. Delegate, say no to new requests for your help, and enlist others whenever possible to pitch in. While these things give you some breathing room, turn an eye toward the long-term changes that will ultimately get you off the hook. Talk to a financial consultant, get your business appraised, find out about day-care options. These things won't save you today, but they will set you up for freedom tomorrow.

It may take a little while for sufficient momentum to build up to break the cycle you're in, so be patient and insistent. If you are the glue that holds things together, other people may complain when you draw the line. Let them. Just smile and plow through their objections. Before you know it, the dream and your frustration will disappear.

The Break-In

A burglar is trying to get into the house. He seems to be cracking one of the windows but can't quite get in. Then you hear him at the back door, struggling with the bolt. You frantically get out of bed and race around the house, locking every window you come to and trying to make sure all the doors are locked. In some more horrifying versions of this dream, the intruder gets in the house and there is a terrible stalking game in which you attempt to hide or call for help, usually to no avail.

This dream is a signal that something unusual has penetrated your normal boundaries creating tension in your life. The house in this dream really symbolizes your normal life. The intruder is a symbol for something or someone crossing into your more personal territory and shaking things up. Changes in the workplace and new relationships often catalyze this dream.

Even if the events that usher in this dream seem normal, they often have an edge of some kind that is threatening or disturbing. In waking life, we tend to look positively on the new job, the new friend, or the possible promotion. It is only in our dreams that potential drawbacks or rising concerns are felt, as we race around to lock the doors and try to maintain privacy and security.

This dream does not imply that you must turn away the opportunity that has arisen but the warning elements of the story should be taken seriously. The exciting new partner who provokes this dream may not necessarily have a dark side but his effect on you may awaken destructive impulses or self-doubt.

Proceed in whatever way seems best to you but pay attention to any feelings of being crowded, trapped, or invaded. Being forewarned will enable you to make the right choice on the spur of the moment and avoid getting paralyzed by indecision. As long as you are aware and willing to see, you will make the right choices in the right moment.

The Gifts in Your Dreams

As you have seen, many dreams attempt to point out our tendency to make things harder for ourselves. Sometimes perfectionism or the fear of criticism freezes us; at other times we apply outdated methods to new problems. The dreams we share with so many others are especially fascinating because they not only depict our concerns but also show the way we respond to them.

The prevalence of these dream themes suggests that certain responses to pressure and worry are built into the human condition. Don't worry that a dream is telling you to make a drastic change. Assume instead that it is offering you clues about what attitude to take or what emotional posture to assume in order to get what you want and protect what you love.

Your dreams tell you how to walk with a situation or work through a problem. They show how to look at things more realistically or summon strength when it is needed. By viewing dreams as a fountain of resources rather than directives, you can make the most of their gifts and feel confident in your understanding.

Chapter 2

Recurring Elements in Your Dreams

If you remember dreams regularly, you have probably noticed that sometimes a particular image will crop up in your dreams repeatedly. The more unusual the image, the more likely it will register with you as a recurring element. You may notice a special image, such as a tornado, a tidal wave, or a hidden room in your dreams and sense in a flash that it is significant. Other recurring dreams not only contain a familiar symbol, the entire "story" of the dream repeats in either identical or highly similar forms. These dreams are almost like reruns of a movie.

In folklore and superstition, recurring dreams are sometimes considered signs of impending events; somehow you are destined to live out the circumstances of the repeating dream. In psychological theory, recurring dreams are usually assumed to pertain to real and often traumatic events in the dreamer's past. While any recurring dream may contain elements of the future or the past, they are far more likely to be based on important elements of the dreamer's present life circumstances.

If you have recurring dreams, you will spend the early minutes of your day noticing you had "that dream again," and wondering what it means. Many of us worry about our recurring dreams, imagining they are signals of early childhood trauma or a mental problem that is now rising to the surface. While it is true that abuse, bereavement, and traumatic experiences contribute to recurring dreams, these are only a few of the many reasons why they can happen.

Most people are relieved to learn recurring dreams are quite common. In fact, almost everyone has experienced a recurring dream or image at some point in life. The typical causes of recurring dreams are usually less dramatic than those depicted by the movie of the week. Recurring dreams usually explore the questions and pressure we face and the way our responses impact the situation.

Some recurring dreams take place during particular passages in our lives. The pressures faced by a teenager and the feelings he might have about them are very different from the experiences of a mother whose child is going off to college. Both people might have recurring dreams for a while, but the stories and experience of their dreams would be completely different.

The teenager focused on finding his place among friends will dream of peers, school, and of the girls he is attracted to. The mother might dream of losing things or of deaths and endings because she is faced with the questions of how to let go and what her true feelings are about this life passage.

Developmental Recurring Dreams

Although some dreams are common to many types of people, other recurring dreams are much more typical of a particular age and gender. Because some dreams are so typical of distinct age groups, I think of these as "developmental dreams" that seem to coincide with the stresses and questions we encounter at particular stages of life. Of course, it is possible to have one of these dreams even if you don't fit the profile that typically coincides with it. I am including this information because it may help you understand more about your situation and feelings.

Childhood Dreams

If you are a parent, you may be interested to learn more about the dreams of childhood. If you remember a particular recurring dream from your own childhood, the following ideas may help shed some light on the cause or meaning of your early dreams.

I have noticed that sensitive adults have many more nightmares than other people and I suspect that children who are gifted and sensitive are more prone to bad dreams as well. As in adults, these frightening dreams are not always signs of serious trouble. They may reflect the kind of stress, confusion, and over-stimulation that is part of life during the years before age seven or eight.

Realize that, to some extent, nightmarish dreams are common to children until they reach the age of seven or eight. Your understanding and support may not eliminate the dreams but are very important to your child. It is a good idea to encourage the child to share dreams because simply talking about them dissipates the tension around them. Avoid the instinct to tell your child she is okay because it was just a dream and dreams aren't real.

Responding with the "it wasn't real" approach tells the child she is dealing with someone who is incapable of grasping the gravity of the situation. This may discourage her from confiding in you about future dreams or frustrate her because you don't seem to believe her or understand.

You may also have a child who sits up in bed and continues to see the images from the dream for a few seconds. This seeming hallucination is very upsetting to parents whose experience of dreaming is so very different. When you open your eyes, the dream is over and you're "safe." But a child can open his eyes, sit up, and apparently converse with someone in the dream or seem inconsolable even though you are holding him and trying to get his attention.

This type of phenomenon seems to be individual; that is, some children behave this way while others don't. It may follow a hereditary pattern in the way that sleep walking and talking in one's sleep seem to. In general, these experiences are not signs of trouble but if you suspect a sleep disorder you may want to consult a pediatrician. (To learn more about sleep disorders affecting children or for a list of sleep disorder clinics in your area write to: The American Sleep Disorder Association, 1610 14th Street, NW, Suite 300, Rochester, MN 55901.)

Something in the Bedroom

One of the most common recurring dreams of childhood is that there is something scary in the bedroom. There may be a monster in the closet, something sinister under the bed, or boogie men in the corner of the room. Younger children seem to have fairly simple dreams that there is something coming to get them or something icky or scary in their room. Because these dreams repeat, it is easy to suspect that something is bothering or intimidating the child.

In adults, bad dreams are often the result of feeling a lack of control over our circumstances and it is sometimes the same for children. A new sibling in the house, the separation of parents, or friction among family members can all provoke nightmares in the child. If that seems likely to be the culprit in your child's case, realize that uncertainty and inconsistency aggravate stress for a child.

You may have to be patient and gentle in the short-term and create an underlying feeling of stability as your child learns to adjust to whatever changes are happening around him. Remember, too, that positive change such as moving into a bigger home or bringing home a treasured baby are unsettling to the child, even though the events are happy ones. In my experience, creatures in the room or icky things like bugs in the bed tend to represent situations rather than specific people. Monsters, on the other hand, tend to represent people.

Monsters

Children often dream of monsters, and sometimes a particular creature becomes the "star" menace in a number of nightmares. Some monsters may bear a disturbing resemblance to parents, or appear in dreams after a time of conflict so that we can recognize ourselves in the child's dream. Witches can sometimes represent the aspects of the mother that have worried the child. This doesn't mean the child hates his mother, or is even objectively afraid of her.

These monster dreams show not only the scary side of the parent, but how startling and disturbing it is for the child to encounter this kind of energy. Think about it. Have you ever known a boss, a spouse, or a friend who got into cross moods when they were stressed, hungry, or tired? You probably learned not to try to talk sense with this person until he got back to normal. You may have instinctively developed a special way of coping with this alter ego, and learned to tread warily whenever it showed up. Well, children experience this phenomenon much more powerfully and literally than we do.

The child's psyche is very attuned to when Mommy is replaced by the scary witch, or when both parents become shouting monsters arguing in the front seat of the car. Their dream monsters not only reflect the tension and fear they experience during conflict, but they dramatically show how frightening it is when the people we trust behave strangely.

Some psychologists believe that children dream of these monsters because they are dependent on their parents and dare not dream anything bad about the people they rely on. But I suspect that the dreaming mind uses monsters in dreams not so much to disguise the parent, as to reflect and illustrate the frightening qualities that have disturbed the child.

If you suspect you may be reflected in these monster sagas, then be understanding with the child and encourage him or her to share these dreams with you. You can use such reports to inform you when things have been unsettling to your child, and you can try to provide extra support and confidence during this phase. In some cases, of course, the monster may reflect someone other than a parent in your child's life. This is more common among school-age children who must contend with the expectations of peers and teachers.

Encourage the child to share his nightmares with you, but do not interrogate him about what they might mean. Choose another time to ask whether there are kids at school, teachers, or neighbors that he finds scary. Although it is every parent's immediate concern to worry about abuse of a child, a recurring nightmare is not necessarily a signal of such a serious situation. If you have any reason to suspect a problem, of course seek the help of your pediatrician or therapist. But don't torment yourself by assuming you must unravel the mystery of every nightmare.

If you think back to your early years, you may recall the spooky neighbor lady that all the kids feared or the eccentric uncle whose beard somehow frightened you. Even fairly harmless things can trigger very strong concerns for a child. Their best defense is a parent who listens well and shows consistent support.

Wild Animal Attack

Children dream of wild animals more often after they begin school. Mean bears, wild bulls, lions, snarling dogs, and alligators are among the most common wild animals that chase and stalk in childhood dreams. Wild animals tend to become linked to a particular person or situation that troubles the child, and they become a kind of shorthand symbol of a recurring worry or dilemma.

One boy dreamed of a mean bull chasing him night after night during the year he was assigned to a particularly strict mathematics teacher who put great pressure on him.

Another boy dreamed of a bear chasing him in the woods, and he would have to try and outwit the animal before it caught him and killed him. His family was always struggling financially and seemed to go through cycles of desperation in which he felt his parents weren't "being parents" or taking care of things. Their vulnerability as a family seemed to trigger the dreams of being out in the woods under the attack of something so big that it could not be overpowered; it could only be outwitted.

Something Ordinary Turns Sinister

Another common childhood dream is that something perfectly harmless such as a toy or a cartoon turns menacing and chases them. These dreams can reflect tensions about particular situations that have overtones the child finds threatening. For example, having relatives visit the home is an ordinary event, but along with these visits may come the tension between a parent and in-laws.

A vacation is a treat, but along with it comes the discomfort of traveling with two adults who snap at each other about directions, food, and money. One boy dreamed often of being chased by a maniacal ball of yarn. He would be chased around in circles, and the faster he ran the more the yarn gained on him. In his case, the dream seemed to reflect a tension between his mother (a knitter) and himself. He tried to please her by being as perfect as possible, but the more he strove for an unreachable goal the more pressured he felt.

If your child repeatedly dreams of an object or harmless creature attacking, you may consider whether some very normal aspect of life is carrying an undercurrent that makes him feel uncertain or on the spot.

Dreams of Middle Childhood and Pre-Teen Years

By middle childhood our anxieties and challenges have assumed a familiar shape. We have learned from friends, family, and circumstance what choices and opportunities are available to us. Although our worries are rarely as dire as we believe and the limitations we've learned are not absolute, we are still operating inside a somewhat fixed arena during these years. The tension between what we want to avoid, what we hope to gain, and the rules we must abide by set the stage for the recurring dreams that are produced during these years.

Perfect Monsters

In this dream there is a repetitive task that must be performed, usually at the command of monsters, zombies, or gangsters. The task is something sinister like digging graves, transporting bodies, or sorting parts of bodies to their assigned destinations. The dreamer is horrified by this, but also numbed by the repetition and tedium of the task. During the dream he is more likely to be annoyed by an unfairly heavy workload than by the macabre nature of his task. It is upon awakening from this dream that he feels appalled by the grisly activities it contained.

Both boys and girls have this dream, but it is somewhat more common to boys. Although you might expect this to be the early dream of someone destined to become an axe murderer, you would be wrong. This recurring theme is most common to youngsters who become very successful and appear well adjusted. However, they do have a strong strain of perfectionism to their personalities. This dream may reflect the stress the youngster feels at striving so constantly to achieve and to meet standards that are unforgiving and relentless.

The adults who have shared this dream memory with me have appeared to be driven, but not unhappy or unfeeling. Much of what we feel forced to become or adapt to isn't really crammed into us, it surrounds us like the air we breathe. So children who grow up in a family where everyone excels, or the children of the coach, the school principal, or the minister, experience a sensation of expectation surrounding them. Rebellion is of course an option that some youngsters explore. But those who have this type of dream have made a decision to abide by the rules surrounding them and perform at the levels required of them.

These people choose cooperation and excellence as their basic way of navigating in the world. Since these choices are well rewarded and even considered ideal, these individuals have largely happy lives.

So why does this dream show such morbid imagery? Like other recurring dreams, it shows a question that remains unanswered and a tension that has not yet been resolved. It is as if the dreaming mind expresses a puzzle: "If perfection is the model to follow, then what about the feelings and parts of me that don't fit that model?" At this age, life seems like an either/or proposition. We lack the understanding that life will continue to expand as we grow up, and we don't yet have the skills to support facets of ourselves that don't fit the ideal we've adopted.

It can feel sometimes that the decision to adapt and excel comes with a heavy price tag. The conscious mind and intellect instantly understand discipline, hard work, and maintaining priorities. But there is more to all of us than this task-oriented part of ourselves, particularly when we are so young.

The other desires, interests, and feelings in the youngster may feel like casualties of the regime (and expectations) that have such power during this time. Other dreams during this stage of life will reveal the joy of achievement and the desire for recognition. This dream reflects the less positive feelings and tension that are the flip side of high achievement.

Flying

During late childhood and early adolescence, many people have numerous dreams of flying. Styles of flight vary; some people flap their arms like wings, others run and jump into flight. Still others jump or fall from a high place and discover through necessity that they can fly. During these years, flying dreams are intense and frequent. Many adults tell me the dreams faded out as they got older, and they seldom dream of flying anymore. Many preteens have recurring dreams of flying that contain a specific theme, like flying to escape the pursuit of evil forces on the ground.

Dreams of flight can reflect our relationship to our abilities, talents, and passions. The ability or desire to fly in a dream is very much like the hunger to be free to express, explore, and experience life without limits. It makes sense that we would dream most often of flying during a stage of life when our own talents and interests beckon to us but when we are not yet sure how to take control of opportunities or navigate in life. Therefore, learning to fly is a form of mastering our use of the talents, creativity, and abilities that are emerging in these years.

I have noticed that people who distinguished themselves later in life through intellectual activities or creative endeavors often dreamed intensively of flying in their youth. I suspect that the urge to rise and soar in the dreams may reflect their early awareness of abilities that will take them places in life.

Breathing under Water

Many youngsters report the dream of finding themselves under water. There is some struggle and panic as they try to reach the surface and realize they cannot. There is a truly horrible moment of realizing that drowning is immanent. Then, amazingly, they continue breathing and learn that they can breathe under water. As a nightmare with a surprise happy ending, this is a rare type of dream.

Like the dream of learning how to fly, this too is a story of discovering an ability that has been present all along but which is only discovered during a crisis or while being thrown into a particular situation. Although both boys and girls have this dream, it seems to occur more frequently among girls.

Like most dreams of submersion in water, this one suggests a sense of being overwhelmed, accentuated by the moment when it becomes clear there is no way to get back to the surface. We have this dream during a time when we are most vulnerable to the dominant emotional climate that surrounds us.

One child of a single parent provided emotional support in the years following a grim divorce. She appeared to become an ideal helpmate, almost a junior therapist for her mother; but at night she gasped for breath in her dreams.

Suddenly going from child to emotional custodian was a suffocating and overwhelming change. Yet, in a way, the drowning dream attempted to show that her sense of panic was natural but unnecessary. She would soon discover that she had the ability to breathe (take care of herself and survive) in this new environment (under water). She developed strong interests at school, her mother eventually remarried, and the phase of feeling like a caretaker was outgrown.

Like other dreams of this stage of life, this one is usually outgrown by the time one reaches the age to leave home. It may sometimes recur later in life if you are thrown into another situation that seems foreign or over your head. It can be viewed as a reminder of abilities to survive tough challenges and as a barometer of the subjective stress you are experiencing.

This dream arises among adults who find themselves thrust into settings that are not only tough, but also don't allow them to express their concerns. If you recognize these pressures in your situation, try to find a separate, neutral person in whom you can confide. Cut back on the amount of time you spend as the unofficial therapist of friends, and increase the time you spend at the gym or walking the dog.

Becoming a Superhero

In this dream, the youngster is faced with a terrible antagonist or evil force. Just when the situation becomes most hopeless, the dreamer transforms into a superhero, often a variation on a cartoon or comic strip character. As the superhero they bring their extraordinary powers to bear on the problem, manage to escape from harm, and sometimes get rid of the villain entirely.

This dream seems more common to boys than girls. Although it typically begins at school age, this dream may continue into later years. The youngsters who have this dream seem to be coping with some unusual strain or difficulty. A problem in the family, economic struggles, or a conflict with a stepparent are examples of seemingly unsolvable situations that have given rise to this dream.

This dream, like others of the preteen years, reflects the tension we struggle with at this age. We can feel like captives of our environment, lacking many visible choices regarding ways we might improve the situation. The boys who have this dream may feel a particularly keen edge of distress at this age, and a longing to be equipped to make the problems go away. Yet this is more than just a dream of wishing for magical powers.

Among the adults who shared their memories of this childhood dream were successful entrepreneurs, corporate executives, and other professionals. All were people who had acquired power, overcome early privations, and taken deliberate steps to create better lives for their own families than they had experienced in childhood. In a sense, the dream seems to have done more than reflect the agitation of the moment. It also showed the dreamer reacting to a challenge by summoning and directing his unique powers, protecting his welfare, and often correcting the injustice.

Dreams in Adolescence

Perhaps because adolescence is a time of urgent feelings and some confusion, dreams that repeat during these years can be especially dramatic and insistent. This is also a time when some of the sporadic recurring dreams that will stay with us into adulthood begin. By this age, we have noticed certain abilities and have (often prematurely) decided whether we are attractive, popular, smart, or talented. Abrupt decisions and premature closure of opportunities often produce compelling dream sagas that seem to urge us to stay open to future possibilities.

Burying a Dead Body

This dream begins with the awareness that you seem to have killed someone. Although the memory of exactly how or why it happened is hazy, the body you must dispose of now is all too real. Often, the body is buried in the basement or backyard of the home, but there are usually complications that make discovery a terrifying threat. Despite the horror of this dream, the main concern is avoiding discovery and the need to conceal the evidence of the crime.

Although both men and women have this dream, it seems more prevalent among men, who report that their earliest memory of it dates back to teen years. People who experience this dream have it frequently until the age of twenty-five or so, then less frequently into their thirties. By the late thirties, its recurrence is usually rare.

This dream is connected with the need for acceptance and the decision to do away with things in ourselves that we believe (or have been taught) are undesirable.

The murder victim represents the part of the self that has been deemed a liability to the plan we have mapped out. That is why there is typically no remorse about the killing at all, only a concern that these actions will be brought to light and cause trouble. The panicky fear of discovery is due to the desire to conceal (or preferably erase) the existence of the qualities in ourselves that are being set aside. Although this may sound like an irrational or unhealthy process, this is very much the type of sorting and defining that occupies teenagers. They are in the process of deciding what is okay, desirable, or possible, and what would hold them back, reflect badly on them, or make them appear less grown up.

When you have developed the body of a man or a woman over the course of a summer, the things that recently marked childhood would indeed become hot evidence that you couldn't ditch fast enough. However, the urge to be a cool, desirable adult is not the only force catalyzing this dream. Many of us at that age were hit hard by parental expectations about appearance, conduct, attractiveness, and the future.

One boy who longed to be an artist was prodded toward a career in law school. He learned repeatedly that his artistic urges marked him as somehow weak or impractical. Dutifully, he developed a kind of scorn for his early hunger. As he lived more in his mind and less in his aesthetic sense, he dreamed about where to bury the body of the person he had killed.

While this dream marks the ending of one era and the expedient dismissal of certain parts of the self, the story does not end there. The bargains we make with our potential and our energies are never final or absolute. This dream begins when we make a shift in identity. It marks our decision. But it stays with us through the years as a reminder that what we left behind still exists and can be redeemed when the time is right.

Although it is popular to advise people that change can happen any time we want, I have seen from the rhythm of our dreams that certain points in our lives are more ripe than others for reclaiming our energies and old loves.

In early adulthood, this dream seems to haunt us as a reminder of the choices we've made and the potentials we've left behind. By the late thirties, most of us have recovered from the illusion that we must sacrifice our authentic awareness in order to become successful or admired. We may have climbed partway up our chosen hill and been struck by the knowledge that something essential was left behind. This dream recurs at important junctures in our lives, times when we have the chance to retrieve old friends from exile without disrupting our lives or creating imbalance.

Many people who share these dreams with me feel strongly that this interpretation fits their experience. But some cannot immediately identify what specifically they cut off in that time period. I believe the willingness to reclaim these aspects of the self is enough to create movement in the psyche and in your life. The dreaming portion of the mind has evidently kept meticulous records about the "self" that was put aside. All that is needed is the official decision that you are ready to reinstate and utilize lost energy. If you make this decision, be prepared to feel your way through a series of marvelous coincidences and tugs at your heart. Books will leap out at you, friends will introduce you to contacts or courses of study, or you'll sign up for a class. Many different things will seem to conspire to bring you back in touch with the parts of life you are now ready to enjoy.

Celebrity Friends

During teen years, both boys and girls begin to dream regularly of hanging out with celebrities. Although it would seem reasonable for young people to have fantasy dreams about a different actor or rock star every week, that is not usually how it works. Typically, the teen will seem to feel a connection with a particular star, or even the entire cast of a television program. She will then dream repeatedly of being among the close circle of people surrounding the star or of being a member of the cast or band.

The basic recurring element of these dreams is that of being part of a group of talented, admired people. Within that context, an assortment of episodic adventures may take place. Although some sexual and romantic interludes may occur, the majority of these dreams don't seem like sexual fantasies or Cinderella stories. Instead, the focus is on group solidarity, creative projects, and supporting the movies, music, or activities for which the celebrities are famous.

These dreams seem to serve a number of purposes. They allow the teen to be part of an interesting, tight group and to have a sense of playing an important role within that group. They also give the dreamer a vivid sense of participating in an ensemble effort, including the necessity to gauge when to support the needs of the personalities involved and when to stringently pursue artistic goals. Finally, these dreams seem to provide a practice ground in which unique abilities fit with collective goals, and talents find new channels for expression.

I believe many of these recurring celebrity dreams arise during adolescence because of the strong urge felt at that time to find a place within a group that is emotionally secure and also creatively satisfying. These dreams suggest that the teen's hunger to belong is not merely a matter of peer pressure, but is related to a deeper urge to use personal gifts within the context of meaningful group goals and purpose.

Death of a Parent

It is usually during teen years that youngsters begin to have dreams that one or both of their parents has died. This dream usually is set either at the site of the funeral or just outside a hospital room when the dreamer is told the bad news. These dreams are both startling and upsetting to most people. Concern can be intense if the teen has never dreamed about death before and now wonders if the recurring dream is foreshadowing a real event, or if in some mysterious way it suggests that they wish harm to the parent.

Neither of these concerns is likely to be behind the dream.

At this age, many of us are undergoing such rapid changes that we seem to be hurtling forward into the self we are about to become. This free-fall into adulthood is accompanied by numerous forces making us feel we should make it happen faster; other people wish us to slow down, and however we're handling it, we're probably all wrong. The sudden death of the past is reflected by the image of a parent dying. This is likely to be the end of the line for the youngster's existence as a child, and his relationship to his parents as it once was is over. This does not mean that the connection will disappear or even become negative. It simply means that the end of an era has arrived, and a new parent-child relationship will be part of the future.

Although death may appear in dreams for a variety of reasons, among adolescents, this type of dream almost invariably marks a powerful and unalterable change. The onset of puberty is a time when these dreams may begin or repeat a few times, then again in later teen years when the youth goes to college, joins the military, or moves out of the family home. A few people notice the dream most prominently just prior to moving out, others experience them once they are settled into the dorm or are transferred away from home.

Dreams During the Twenties and Thirties

During the years when we are going to college, finding a place in the workforce, or perhaps choosing a mate and beginning a family, one of the ongoing challenges we face is keeping everything on track. Though there are exceptions of course, many people find that their dreams during these years take a turn toward the frantic and the frustrating. In these dreams, tasks are urgent and time is compressed. The focus of anxiety is around split-second mistakes in timing, wrong turns, or carrying so many objects that you can't find your keys or wallet.

Missed Flight

In this dream, you have crammed too many things into your luggage, fumbled to get to the airport, and rushed into the terminal. Just when you thought you were over the hump, there is trouble with your ticket, seating assignment, passport, ID, or finances. Everything that can go wrong does, but you manage to handle each consecutive hassle and break free to run for the gate. Unfortunately, it is too late and the flight has just taken off without you.

This dream is common to both men and women who are juggling responsibilities while trying to make connections they believe will advance their careers or happiness. Despite the disorganized frenzy on the way to the airport, the people who report this dream are typically well-organized realists, *not* the kind of people to arrive late for a flight without a ticket and hope for the best.

The plane in this dream represents the ability to move to the next level, either by getting more of what you want in life or experiencing the sensation of fulfillment. The inability to catch that flight reflects a continuing frustration that the experiences or satisfaction you are striving for seem elusive. In some cases, real opportunities have been lost. One executive who was passed over for a promotion dreamed that everyone in his office made the flight while he was held back at the gate.

Others who report this dream appear to be successful in objective terms. The frustration and disappointment in their dreams seems to reflect an internal experience rather than their measurable results. They are in a race against the challenges they've taken on, and they tend to agree to additional tasks and responsibilities like a gambler raising the stakes in the hopes of winning.

The implication of this dream is that racing faster, striving harder, or carrying more is not the solution. The dreamer is struggling against time constraints and seems out of harmony with everything and everyone he encounters. He tries to solve the problem by straining harder at an approach that is clearly failing him. Given a choice, most of the people who have this dream would not wish to step off their treadmill entirely; for them the benefits outweigh the problems. But it is possible for them to shift their style in minor ways and experience noticeable changes. Anything that can move you away from the formula of "too fast, too much, too late," will have a positive impact on this type of tension.

Strategies like planning farther ahead, completing things in advance of their deadlines, and tackling smaller pieces of a task at a time can bring a dramatic change in how compressed your life feels. If you have a tendency toward heroically taking on more than is manageable all the time, being watchful for this pattern can help you avoid sabotaging your deeper priorities. Although you may believe that taking time to savor your accomplishments is out of the question, it may be an important antidote to getting lost in the mirage of endless striving for the deal that is always around the corner.

I Forgot the Children

Most young mothers are familiar with the nightmare of leaving their child in the high chair of a restaurant and going off to run the thousand or so errands on their list. One reason movies like *Home Alone* have been so popular is because they allow us to laugh at a fear that we've all had at one time or another. But dreams of this scenario are no laughing matter. These recurring nightmares feel very real when we have them, and many women worry that a repeating dream is a signal of some tragedy about to unfold.

These dreams tend not to be warnings of actual events. But they *are* signals of overload and the possible consequences of stretching beyond your limits for too long.

One cost of juggling too many details is the risk that sometime, somehow, you're going to drop one of the balls. Although overloaded attention has become the norm for most of us, recurring dreams like this one act as an early warning signal that your system can only handle so much without increasing the odds of accident or misfortune.

The second drawback to our rushed lifestyles is the potential for getting caught up in minor details that seem urgent and neglecting the things that are more important. The small, compelling details that capture the dreamer's attention here are obviously not as important as her children. The shock she feels upon realizing she forgot the children is like a wake-up call reminding her not to get so caught up in details that she forgets what is most precious of all.

If you have this dream, consider whether you could adjust your routine so that your attention isn't so continually overloaded. If you've been missing out on the joys of your family life by focusing too much on mastering your schedule, think about where you might compromise in order to savor this time with loved ones more fully.

Dreams at Midlife

By the time we're in our forties, many of us are taking a pause from the all-consuming push to establish careers and families. Like explorers returning from a jungle adventure, we emerge into a clearing and, possibly for the first time in decades, have an opportunity to notice where we are and what we have learned. At this time, we also can become profoundly disturbed by the things we haven't done or tried and by the aspects of our natures that have not yet found expression. The dreams that arise during this part of life can be confusing because they have a particularly haunting quality and stir up deep feelings. Yet they can appear to be completely illogical and without any connection to the dreamer's current life experiences. What makes midlife dreams compelling is that they reveal the parts of ourselves that have been subsisting on bread and water for too long. Earlier decisions made in the service of survival and necessity can now be reviewed. Pleasures and interests that were relegated to the shelf labeled "someday" now clamor for a fair hearing. This need to look back at the early promises we made to ourselves often prompts dreams of high school, old friends, or the search for a lost vehicle.

Can't Find the Car

In this dream, you have parked your car in a normal fashion, but upon returning from work or your errands you find it isn't there anymore. You wander anxiously around the area trying to retrace your steps and determine what has happened. The situation is made more embarrassing by the fact that other people seem to be having no trouble finding their cars. Although you're becoming more desperate, you feel a need to try and conceal your predicament from other people. Rather than ask for help or call the police, you continue to wander back and forth covering the same ground without results.

This is a dream about getting lost by following all the rules.

People who have this dream have typically made choices based on reasonable guidelines rather than personal preferences. They may wake up one day and realize they haven't gotten what they bargained for, or they may discover that the realization of their plans brings little satisfaction.

One woman worked feverishly at a high-tech company and surged ahead until she reached her goals. Only then did she have the time to notice how bored she was by her job and with the entire field she'd mastered. Much earlier in life she'd longed to become a teacher, but had been advised that her computer skills would earn her more money in a technical field. Although this was true, she became inexplicably depressed by her most recent promotion and was short-tempered and irritable with her family.

Her dreams of the lost car reflected her confusion and sense of loss, as well as her embarrassment at having a problem she considered irrational and unusual. In the dream, she is as concerned with her wish to conceal the problem as by her need to solve it. Many recurring dreams imply that the ability to respond constructively to a problem is badly impaired by our disapproval of it. Many high-functioning people feel embarrassed or confused when their feelings are in contrast to the measurable facts in a situation. We look at what we've accomplished and conclude that we "should" feel differently. But refusing to admit that something is missing makes it all the more difficult to recognize what has been lost and where it may be found.

If you have had this dream, the implication is that some part of your life feels unsatisfying, and you may have a sense that something precious has been lost or misplaced. The lost car is like the hope, meaning, and satisfaction that are mysteriously missing right now. When a feeling of discontent arises, one response is to argue against it; make a case for the most reasonable option (staying put, ignoring your feelings). But this dream illustrates how important and valuable these missing elements really are. Not only are you distraught because they're missing, but your life comes to a standstill without them.

This dream often points out trouble with work or a vocational choice. You may not be doing what you would really like to do, or you may enjoy your work but feel you're involved in the wrong industry or with the wrong company. A wise response to this dream is to get clear about what is off track in your life and what you'd like to change. Because this is a dream about personal satisfaction and meaning, the solution will likely be something that enriches your experience and happiness.

For some, this may mean a change in careers, but for others, it may mean adjusting the way you work or the focus you hold, rather than a change in what you do.

Forgotten Baby

This disquieting dream is most often reported by women with grown children or by those who do not have children. In the dream, you are going about your day when you hear a child crying. Following the sound, you go into the closet or bedroom and are horrified to discover a baby that has been placed in a drawer or on a shelf. It is still alive, but in a flash you recall that this baby has been left here without care for several years! *How could you have forgotten it?* You rush to gather up the infant and tend to it, fighting back tears of shock and guilt at the neglect it has suffered.

This dream is very upsetting and some women tell me they awaken from it in tears. It is usually a sporadically repeating dream that comes a few times a year. Sporadic recurring dreams act to spotlight a condition of an enduring nature that is largely correctable. The problem is usually something we've learned to live with so skillfully that we've entirely forgotten that we have a choice about it. When a dream like this begins to repeat more regularly, it is usually because the time is right to correct the mistake we've made or to get a fresh start with something positive.

The baby in this dream represents a part of the woman herself; such as an idea, interest, or project that was initiated and then abandoned. For one woman, the baby represented her college education which she barely started and then postponed for marriage. For another dreamer, the baby represented a career she began after college and then abandoned to work in her husband's business. For yet another woman, the baby represented a book she had started to write.

The babies in these dreams seem to represent things we have created ourselves, through labor and love, which we set aside, believing we would return to them when circumstances allowed. Long after we have forgotten our temporary compromises and the things we loved so much, these dreams begin tapping on the door to remind us that it isn't too late to take care of those potentials and interests.

If you have had this dream, it is probably time to retrieve a beloved idea from your past and follow through on it. Consider your early career plans, interests, and ambitions. Remember that taking care of this forgotten baby many not mean quitting your job or doing something radical. One woman returned to her serious study of music and began doing volunteer work with music training for youth groups. The dream does not seem to be saying, "Your life is all wrong." Instead, it is reminding you that something extremely precious is still awaiting your promise to return to it when you have the time. The time may be now.

Dreams of Later Years

In the later years of life, our dreams may become more intense and memorable. Many people report an increase in anxiety dreams and nightmares in later life. There are many variables such as health challenges, shifts in sleeping patterns, and medications that increase troubling dreams and make sleeping more difficult as we age. Two dreams that are common to later years are losing your purse or wallet and getting lost.

Lost Purse or Wallet

In this dream, you are out somewhere, perhaps shopping or walking through town. You discover that you've lost your purse or wallet. In a sudden panic, you try to remember where you've been and where you may have left it. It is confusing to try and determine whether someone took it or if you left it somewhere. You race back to the last place you remember, but it isn't there. Now what? The problem is compounded because you have no money or car keys now.

This dream reflects frustration and anxiety. The loss of a purse or wallet suggests that a change is occurring in the dreamer's life which is experienced largely as a sense of loss, confusion, and threat. For some, the dream is related to changes in lifestyle related to aging, but for many, the dream arises after the loss of a spouse, a move away from familiar surroundings, or after retirement.

If you have this dream, do everything practical to amplify the sense of connection and support in your life. Get involved in activities that enhance your sense of community and contribute your expertise to the groups and individuals who can benefit from it. Whenever changes have created a sense of disorientation, we can all help to get our bearings again by dipping into the reservoirs that we find personally interesting or rewarding. Return to the faith, studies, or interests that have supported you in the past. Remember this dream is not usually related to actual financial loss or misfortune; it reflects the internal worries associated with change and uncertainty. A wise response is to increase the stabilizing elements in your life and to reconnect with the constants that bring reassurance and joy.

Getting Lost

In this dream, you have gone into a city or a strange neighborhood. Somehow you've gotten into a scary neighborhood and it doesn't seem wise even to stop for directions now. If you do stop, people will either give you wrong directions or set you off on a circular route so that you wind up even more hopelessly lost. At this point, the original purpose of your journey has faded away and you just really want to get home. Getting home becomes a dominant and panicky thought, amplified by the lack of help and conflicting suggestions you receive. Usually, this dream becomes so frightening toward the end that you awaken out of sheer discomfort.

This is a dream about trying to find your way through a situation that seems unfamiliar and insecure. The advice of others may not only be unhelpful in this context, but it may actually make matters more confusing. The "strange neighborhood" in this dream often represents a situation that is unsettling because it is new or it lacks the kind of clarity you are accustomed to. Things that once acted as landmarks or deciding factors in your thinking may not apply to the specifics of the choices and desires you now have. The goal of getting home actually represents the wish to know what is best and to feel connected with what makes you happy. For some, this may be as deeply personal and haunting as clarifying spiritual beliefs. For others, getting home represents a more practical concern such as determining whether to make a move to be closer to grandchildren while losing the reassuring familiarity of their hometown. Whatever the individual situation may be, it is almost certain to be something that only you can determine and resolve for yourself.

If you have this dream, take time to sort through your priorities in this situation before you try to decide what you should do. Bear in mind that the path you choose may not be one that another might take or recommend. This is a situation in which the more closely you follow the dictates of your heart and preferences, the easier it will become to find your way home.

Recurring Life Themes

While many recurring dreams are linked with stressful conditions or life passages, others depict our struggle to answer enduring questions. These dreams reveal the invisible theme song playing in the background of our relationships, careers, and choices. Bringing this "life theme" into awareness can be empowering because it helps us understand the question we have been trying to answer all our lives. And though these questions have distinct differences, they share in common a certain paradox. They generally cannot be answered or "solved" unless we become willing to alter our perspective. Because the feelings involved in these questions are central to our being, most of us cling stubbornly to a certain style of reacting or compensating for the discomfort they arouse. When recurring dreams reflect and identify these life themes, we have a unique opportunity to understand what drives us at a deep level, and also to view the central question of our lives from a more effective and healing perspective. Recognizing these themes does not mean we automatically find the answers, but it does bring a new level of peace and compassion to our search.

Discovering Treasure

Dreams of finding treasure and valuable objects have numerous variations. The one constant element is the discovery of something precious, magical, or valuable. Often the object itself is something ordinary which happens to have magical properties. One woman dreamed of a cup which was never empty no matter how much she drank from it. A young man dreamed of a tree that was all-wise and spoke to him comfortingly when no one else was around. A young woman dreamed of a luminous jewel long buried which she unearthed accidentally during an outing on the beach.

People prone to these discovery dreams tend to have special artistic or creative abilities. They are sensitive and empathetic toward others, and quick to reach out with kindness to someone in need. Although anyone can dream of finding treasure or magic occasionally, these people do so regularly. They are forever discovering magic pens that write automatically, sunken chests of gold, mystical tablets, or artifacts that solve the questions of the ages. Despite the joy and success of their dreams, however, they often struggle with more than their share of challenges in waking life. They have a hard time discovering what kind of work suits them and often spend years in a field painfully antithetical to their talents and temperament. Their diverse talents, broad-ranging interests, and easy understanding of another's perspective make it difficult for them to focus on areas that would be a good match for them in the long-term. Often they are accustomed to feeling out of place and mismatched with their environment or the people around them, so it may not occur to them that it is possible to have a different kind of life.

The life question these people struggle with is how to transform their uniqueness from a painful condition into a fulfilling expression. This person has an assignment in this lifetime to weave straw into gold. Their dreams imply they are more than equal to the task and that there is treasure beneath their feet. Yet after years of compensating for "not fitting," they often feel disconnected from their real power and sense of certainty. Previous disappointments may have created a kind of psychic bruise over their gifts and interests. When they approach or even think about what they would truly love to do or create, the first experience they have is immediate and familiar pain.

If you have this type of dream often, realize that at least one of your major life themes involves the discovery of how you fit in the world and where you can share your gifts. As life themes, these questions are not going to be answered in one instant or by one success; they will run like a river through the course of a lifetime. But waking up to them will alter the way you experience them, and the progress you make will be richer, sweeter, and saner than before.

As with all life questions, there is a strong element of paradox in this theme. The very way in which you don't fit in the world will probably turn out to be your greatest strength, your passport into the life you want. Give up trying to reshape your essential nature. Instead, consider how you may have something to offer precisely because of your uniqueness. Your task is not just about discovering your talent and "making it." The magic here involves focusing on the way your talents reconnect you with the world by helping or healing others. Finally, look close at hand. The treasures you have are lying haphazardly around your closet, strewn through your history, and jotted down in your journal. Once you stop expecting the secret to be a distant or exotic one, you'll see the first sparkles of magic in the things you've been taking for granted.

Life and Death Battles

Life and death struggles occur in dreams for all of us at times. But for some people, battles and survival are the central concerns of most dreams. Every adventure ends with a combat scene or a struggle to avoid catastrophe; and almost every stranger turns out to be an enemy. Even the landscape of their dreams is laden with quicksand, sharp ravines, wildfires, and dangerous animals.

People extremely prone to life or death dreams make ordinary choices and decisions as if their very survival were at stake. They are usually excellent businesspeople and tend to be successful at whatever they undertake. Small disappointments or minor annoyances may upset them, and this may seem odd in such a powerful person. But this is because whether they are dealing with ten dollars or ten million dollars, they are really fighting for their survival. They may have strangely vehement preferences about food and be upset when they cannot have exactly what they wanted. Unconsciously, it is almost as if they fear they will die if the food is not right, the point is not gained, or the argument is not won. They are often high achievers and excel in settings where vigilance and defenses are needed. They are frequently dissatisfied, as if some invisible inner standard has not been met. This inner standard can make them discerning critics capable of making very fine distinctions or innovators who can bring dramatic improvements to a creative or business project. They often have an almost feudal sense of family and friends, and can be unmoved by the plight of those they consider to be outsiders. However, they are fiercely protective, generous, and loyal to those they consider to be a part of their group or community.

The life question these people are wrestling with is where to find the safety and certainty that cannot be taken from them. They are good at acquiring things, keeping defenses strong, and anticipating and controlling circumstances. Though these tactics are effective in helping them maintain their guarded stance successfully and giving them a measure of security, they seldom feel contented or at peace with their achievements. They are sometimes haunted by a hunger to do things differently or to embrace something new, but they usually have so many survival rules in place that they don't allow themselves to experiment.

If you are extremely prone to life and death dreams, realize that one of your life themes has to do with finding a kind of security that cannot be taken from you. The natural tendency is to work a lifetime to try and acquire, fix, and control enough circumstances so that you can finally have your security cemented into place. As a realist, you know there is nothing wrong with this plan, except that it hasn't provided the feeling of permanence and certainty you crave. To find security that can't be lost, you will have to look at things that are intangible because everything else is always at risk. The things that can never be lost reside in your spirit, emotions, soul, and humanity. This does not imply that you should give away your property and read philosophy. It wouldn't suit you. The answer you're after involves keeping and enjoying all you've built but shifting your emphasis so that you now can find contentment and peace as well.

The key to working with this theme is to complement your considerable strength by developing greater flexibility and tolerance.

Avoid the tendency to view your choices as either strong or weak or to fear that compassion toward others might water down your considerable power. The paradox you must face is that greater tolerance and acceptance of others will not weaken your position. Instead, greater acceptance will catalyze a depth of understanding in you which is the real key to finding lasting peace and security. You do not need to discard or sabotage the achievements you have fought so hard to win. Keep them and savor them. But conduct experiments in tolerance and suspending judgment, and permit others to do things differently or imperfectly. It is in the unexplored territory of acceptance that you will encounter the contentment you've always hungered for. Use your powerful will to decide to explore tolerance, because you won't be able to feel it at first. Just practice thinking more gently about others, resisting the urge to judge, and avoid condemning events from the past that cannot be changed. After using your volition to practice these changes in your reactions, peace will well up from inside you.

Rejection

Dreams expressing the theme of rejection take many forms. One of the most common follows a dramatic story line set in World War II. You have struggled to reach the border in order to escape persecution by the cruel leaders who have taken over your country. A small band of friends in the underground have helped you reach the gates of the border. Just as it seems all will be well, the friends turn out to have another plan. You have only been used for their purposes and now they shoot or stab you brutally and leave you in a crumpled heap to bleed to death, just yards away from the land that would have given you asylum.

Another variation on this theme involves catching a train to safety amidst a crowd of struggling, panicked people. Again, trusted friends deliver a deadly blow and leap aboard the train while you slide dizzily to the ground, as horrified by their betrayal as by the certainty that you are about to die.

These grisly and apparently depressing themes of rejection are extremely memorable. The people who have rejection as a life theme will have experienced dreams of this type fairly early in life and will tend to have numerous dreams that involve being an outcast or being left behind.

Individuals prone to rejection themes are remarkably loyal themselves and tend to put a premium on relationships of all kinds. These people are extremely intelligent and kind; friends may have cautioned them about the hazards of being so altruistic. They work at their jobs with a sense of a mission and what is now a rather old-fashioned pride of workmanship, expertise, and service. Often there is something exceptional about these people: they may be quietly involved in heroic efforts to correct injustice or save the planet. You will find this person in a field or setting that generally provides little recognition, but it will be common knowledge that he or she is the best there is at whatever they do. In relationships, this person has suffered numerous disappointments of varying forms and intensities. However, this person is not a professional victim; instead, he or she has learned to function with higher levels of emotional pain than most of us could, and those around them often have no idea of the sadness or grief they carry. People with themes of rejection often carry themselves with remarkable grace and unselfishness. They understand the nature of surrender and acceptance, and despite some rather unfair experiences, remain unresisting toward life itself.

The life question these people face is how to enter the flow of life more fully. They crave harmony and the sense of being connected in an emotional and a spiritual sense. Almost everything they do is in service of this impulse toward harmony and synergy. Without thinking, they tend to acquiesce constantly because they feel this is "going with the flow." These people are not doormats, they genuinely feel themselves as part of a larger whole. Their hunger to increase the sense of connection causes them to put the needs of that whole above their own. At the workplace, they recognize the ideal level of functioning or the purpose behind the operations and stay focused on that. In relationships, they honor what they believe to be the connection or the other person's needs. The paradox of this theme is that self-sacrifice can actually prevent the kind of connection and synergy this person is trying to foster. The balance and flow of life will be experienced in full force when this person can practice saying no to what is inadequate or dissatisfying to them. They need to practice rejecting some of the things they are accustomed to flowing with, and supporting their own standards and preferences more often.

If you are prone to dreams of rejection or recognize this as one of your life themes, realize that the goal you constantly strive for really is as wonderful as you think. It is merely that the choices you've made to achieve a sense of flow in your life have had the reverse effect. Having suffered rejection, you may have vowed never to make anyone else feel that way, to always listen, understand, and love. You have probably become more kind and wise throughout the years, and have quietly been polishing your craft with quiet acts of courage and generosity. What you don't realize, though, is that too much surrender and acceptance actually separates you from the flow of life. While other imbalances such as hatred and prejudice tend to create blockages that hold us in place, too much acceptance allows us to move freely and travel far, but never to flow with the current in a comfortable, rewarding way.

The key to working with this theme is not to change your goal but to shift the way you go about creating it. This involves changing the way you think about rejection and negativity. Instead of viewing negativity as something inherently cruel in opposition to everything you stand for, begin to consider it as a neutral presence in nature. Like all parts of nature, it too is necessary to the whole. The artist could not sculpt effectively without the chisel, just as the surgeon saves lives with the use of a scalpel. The power to reject what is counterproductive or misplaced is necessary to the flow of life. When we deny ourselves the use of that power, we shackle our ability to create and sentence ourselves to labors without results. We also tend to magically draw into our experience people and events that reject us. The more consistently we deny our ability to say, "No, I don't enjoy that," "No, I prefer something else," or "No, I won't do that," the more pronounced this imbalance becomes. Well-meaning friends over the years may have suggested that you be more assertive or have hinted unhelpfully that you suffer from low self-esteem. But neither of these ideas is true. Your actions and decisions have stemmed from the belief that acceptance and endurance will ultimately create a sense of fluidity in your life. You have more than enough courage and power to create the experiences and relationships you want; self-esteem is not really the problem. A more effective approach is to consider your life as a work of art which you are constantly shaping, crafting, and sculpting. You need sometimes to say no to colors, shapes, or designs that are not consistent with your vision and destiny. Sometimes this will mean firing someone, leaving the lover who isn't right for you, or informing your boss that you need a schedule that will permit you to return to school. You will not need to pump yourself up to confront anyone, nor will you feel particularly uncomfortable about expressing your decisions. Once you view rejection as a neutral element that has its place and function, it will cease to have a hold over you either as a source of pain or as a forbidden power. Oddly enough, by being loyal to the vision of your life and to your own needs, you'll begin to experience the sense of effortless flow and connection that you value above all else.

Overcoming Barriers

The barriers in our dreams have many qualities, but they all express the feeling that something is blocking access to goals or progress. Some people dream of castle walls barring their passage inside, others come to the edge of a canyon and realize their destination lies across the other side. Some of us dream of locked rooms that we are forbidden or too frightened to enter. Still others dream of bridges that go straight up instead of across the water. Not only are these bridges impossible to cross, they create a sense of panic and disorientation that turns the dream into a nightmare.

People who are prone to dreams of barriers have diverse interests and abilities. They may work three part-time jobs instead of one, or have split lives, pursuing a career in music by night while studying accounting by day. They have the ability to get along well with very different personalities and can shift gears upon entering a particular environment. Because they can adjust almost seamlessly to changes in their surroundings or coworkers, they are often popular and admired. Few people realize that the polish and adroitness they show have been developed in response to the obstacles that have prevented them from traveling a straight path toward their goals. They have learned to walk in a curve, adjusting their trajectory depending on what appears on the horizon. Often this person will be employed in a setting that forces them to work around a particular person, or they will have a spouse or other close family member who seems to thwart them or block their freedom.

The life question these people are struggling with is how to dissolve the limiting factors in their lives. These people have often experienced a number of restricting factors in early life and have developed a coping strategy of diplomacy, flexibility, and thinking on their feet. They have usually developed an amazing ability to anticipate problems and recognize impediments on the horizon long before the rest of us. These skills are invaluable when dealing with people or settings that have power over us, but too great a reliance on adaptive strategies and flexibility can make us forget what it is like to move through an obstacle rather than to work around it. They have so often faced impossible people and situations that they almost reflexively begin to plan their way around the roadblocks they encounter or begin too quickly to scan for alternative goals to replace the one that now seems out of the question. They know how to change plans at a moment's notice, but the result of honing that ability can be a deficiency in knowing how to confront, penetrate, or master a problem by moving toward it. Like all life questions, this one tends to foster reliance on a response that ultimately makes resolution impossible.

If you are working with the theme of obstacles, realize that the events you've experienced and the reactions you've had to them are perfectly natural. You are not at fault. You may sometimes have felt as if you've taken a wrong turn in life or tried to second guess your early decisions. But the strategy of adaptation, compromise, and changing plans was probably a lifesaver for you in certain situations. You are not a quitter, nor do you lack the character or substance to make your plans gel. You can speculate endlessly about good or bad fortune and wonder whether you gave things more power over you than they warranted. At this point, the best approach is to admit that events sometimes do arise that seem outside our control and that we may never understand their causes. What we can control and work to understand is the way the belief in obstacles affects our experience.

The key to working with this theme lies in attacking your own belief in obstacles and the internal equivalent of barriers in your own mind. This certainly doesn't mean all your problems are in your head. But the inner landscape is the only one over which you have control, and it is astonishing how dissolving the belief in barriers also diminishes the effects that real life obstacles hold over us. One way to do this is to become skeptical about your ready acceptance of "impossible" situations when they arise. Begin to attack that certainty with doubts and scratch away at its façade. Also, realize that there is a kind of magic that unfolds when we are ready to move through a situation rather than adapt and reshape ourselves around it. Many roadblocks are vaporized by our willingness to tackle them or do battle with them. The good news is that your arsenal of skills enables you to choose your battles wisely and to swiftly calculate the effort and odds of success in any situation. When you do decide to lean into the storm, you may find the whole thing disappears in response to your energy. If it does not disappear, your combat with it will result in the stripping away of an inner obstacle or your belief in it. You will discover the power of being willing to penetrate walls. As you practice this way of responding, the obstacles in your life will become much less solid, and your own energy and confidence will take on a new focus.

Other Life Themes

Don't be concerned if you didn't recognize your life theme in one of the descriptions you've just read. Many people are able to gain a sense of their life themes and questions by reflecting on their most memorable dreams and the themes that are common to them. Keep in mind that life questions drive us to resolve imbalances. The way we respond to pain, fear, or imbalance is usually effective within a particular setting or span of time. Later, however, we continue to react to our discomfort or strive to answer our question by behaving in a fashion that makes the imbalance worse. The rigid defenses become more rigid or the flexible adaptation prevents us from creating lasting results. If and when you discover a life theme or question you are working with, simply consider whether your way of responding to it is serving to resolve the problem or to lock you into it. For most people, recognizing this pattern is enough to help them change it and begin to find the answers they've been looking for.

Recurring People

Many of us wonder about the people who appear repeatedly in our dreams. It makes sense that we would dream of our family members and perhaps a close friend or co-worker who is part of the rhythm of normal life. Why then do most of us also dream quite often of a particular acquaintance we barely know, a childhood friend we haven't seen in years, or even someone who is no longer living?

When a recurring character appears in our dreams, it is sometimes because the image of that person is associated with a particular feeling, set of experiences, or way of relating. Even if our connection with that person is over, they can still appear in our dreams whenever we are affected by the types of feelings, fears, or hopes that we dealt with when we knew them.

David dreamed of his ex-wife Julie whenever there were concerns or undercurrents in his new marriage. Although his present wife Claire was very different and their relationship was a happy one, he experienced a similar sense of confusion when there were communication problems between them. During his first marriage, he'd found Julie's emotional tirades draining and alarming. He developed a habit of withdrawing and becoming intensely rational as a defense against them. Although life with Claire was less stormy and much happier, when things got a little emotional or uncertain between the two of them he unknowingly became remote and cold. He often dreamed he was back in the first marriage, struggling again with the demands and volatility that had been so unpleasant to him. On the surface, these dreams made no sense to him since he was completely over his first wife and was very much in love and happy with Claire. The problems with Claire were so mild and transient that David didn't see any similarity to his first marriage at all. David assumed that a repeating dream of an old partner must mean he either missed her or felt he was in a situation that was identical to the old one. But for him, neither of those explanations made sense. The recurring dream of being married again to Julie wasn't really about her as a person, nor was it about Claire being similar to Julie. Instead, these dreams showed that David was having a button pushed which had been formed and sensitized during his first marriage. Dreams often recognize the similarity between a current situation and something from our past, even though the intensity and qualities of the two situations may be quite different. In this situation, the repeating dreams served as a warning to David to be aware of his automatic withdrawal from Claire as a hangover from his early turbulent marriage to Julie. This awareness was enough to permit him to respond with the support and affection he truly intended to share with Claire. Characters borrowed from unhappy past experiences are often pictures of patterns that are operating in our lives today.

Pointing Out Hidden Resources

Sometimes dream characters represent qualities we possess but have forgotten to use. Dana was a boisterous woman who spoke first and thought about it afterward. Her forthright manner and gutsy spirit served her well as a manager and single parent, but she often fought with friends and found dating a nightmare. As a child, Dana had been best friends with a quiet, serious girl named Teresa who always knew how to get them out of scrapes. Although she hadn't seen Teresa in decades, Dana often dreamed they were together again and that Teresa lived right next door. In these dreams Dana was thrilled that her girlhood chum and chief problem-solver was so close at hand. She had good friends and a full life, so it made little sense to Dana that she would continue to dream of someone she had lost touch with so long ago, and whom she seldom if ever thought about. But Dana's recurring dreams were using the image of Teresa to represent all the qualities that Dana attributed to the girl, which in fact she herself could stand to use. She described Teresa as someone who thought about the implications of her words before blurting them out, someone who considered the possible ramifications of her actions before leaping ahead. Like many recurring images of childhood friends, Teresa was borrowed from the past to remind Dana of the qualities she herself possessed but seldom put to use. In fact, most of her friction with coworkers and dates could be reduced if she practiced some measure of the consideration and gentleness that Teresa might have exercised.

People from early childhood and best friends are particularly likely to represent characteristics of the dreamer that have been forgotten. The point is not to try to become someone different, but to remember and reclaim your version of those qualities to enhance your current life.

Illustrating a Quality in Someone Else

Some recurring characters are not people we have known in real life, but are borrowed from fairy tales, headlines, or Hollywood. Repeating dreams of actors or famous murderers are mysterious on the surface, but can provide important clues about qualities in loved ones that cause conflicting feelings.

Kathy's husband Charles was successful and powerful. Their marriage was essentially happy, but sometimes Charles could be dominating and surprisingly unbending in his opinions. Kathy became increasingly uncomfortable during any conflicts between them, and rather than express herself honestly, she began to feel it was more important to be careful of Charles and to avoid doing anything to make him angry. During this time, Kathy had a series of dreams in which she found herself married to a Mafia leader. In the dreams, she was always surrounded by her husband's henchmen and felt oppressed by the control they exerted over her movements and freedom. In waking life, neither Kathy nor her husband had anything to do with organized crime or illegal activities. But the dreams of having married into the Mafia served to illustrate Kathy's sense that she was living in a power structure that was uncomfortable for her. The dreams did not mean that Kathy's husband was as implacable or evil as a criminal, but they served to help Kathy understand that it was in the area of control and power that she was becoming increasingly unhappy. Although they have not resolved all their differences yet, Kathy feels knowing more about the problem has been helpful. She feels she has a better chance of reacting constructively and enlisting her husband's cooperation than she would have if she were simply working from her sense of uneasiness.

Providing Reassurance

People from the past who served as mentors, guides, or sources of encouragement to us are likely to reappear in dreams periodically whenever we need a similar boost of faith in ourselves. Ron had a wonderful teacher in middle school who encouraged him to become involved with computers and radio. Although they have not been in contact for virtually decades, Ron still dreams of Mr. Crane periodically, usually when he is feeling doubtful about tackling a new project. These dreams show how powerfully we respond to faith and belief in our abilities; years after an early experience of support, we continue to dream of a particular teacher, friend, or relative when we need to be nudged beyond our doubts or hesitation.

Guidelines to Recurring Characters

Here are some guidelines to use to help you discover the most probable meaning of the recurring character in your dreams.

1. *Is the person someone from your distant past, such a best friend or acquaintance from childhood?* If so, this character is very likely to represent qualities that you can activate in yourself to make your life more enjoyable.
2. *Is this character someone with whom you were once involved and have painful memories about?* If so, it is likely that this character is a reminder of a pattern of relating that is affecting you today.
3. *Is the character someone you have never met, such as a celebrity or notorious criminal?* If so, it is possible the character is illustrating a particular quality that is operating in someone you know.
4. *Is the character someone who was supportive and encouraging to you in the past?* If so, it is possible that this character is reminding you of what can be accomplished if you believe in yourself.

These are just a few of the reasons we dream of particular people repeatedly. If they don't seem to apply to your situation, trust your instincts and borrow the reasoning that you've seen here. Remember that a character can represent a pattern such as a trigger and reaction, a quality in yourself, a characteristic in someone close to you, or serve as a reminder of hope. For the most part, people we feel positively toward tend to represent qualities that we can apply in our current life experiences to make them better. Those people we associate with painful memories tend to reflect entire patterns and feelings that are affecting us in new experiences and relationships today.

Recurring Symbols

There are few things as unsettling as repeatedly dreaming of a very odd or highly specific object. It can be particularly hard to understand what this means when the item seems to have nothing to do with your normal life. Generally, symbols appear because of the quality they illustrate, the specific way they function, or because of the association we have to them. A jungle is lush and teeming with life, but it is also filled with hazards and it is easy to get lost there. People who dream repeatedly of jungle settings are often dealing with something that offers them tremendous growth potential but also comes with hazards and confusing side effects. Most exotic and specialized settings illustrate the *qualities* of a current situation and its effects on us. Other symbols are incorporated because they function in a particular manner that aptly captures the essence of something we're dealing with. Roller coasters are predefined rides that provide distraction, entertainment, pleasure, and fear. They control us while we ride them and give the illusion that unexpected twists and turns are spontaneously arising so we must hold on tight. However, they function by following a track, and every nuance of the ride has happened before and will happen again for the next batch of passengers. The odd blend of high adventure and rote repetition may be one reason why people struggling with difficult relationships are so prone to dreaming of roller coasters. This symbol captures the sense of being involved in something that is out of your control, but it also conveys the sensation of repetition, that feeling of "here we go again."

Still other symbols appear because they are so closely connected with a particular time or situation in our lives. One man dreamed of sitting down to dinner with his family dressed in the military uniform he'd worn during the war. Everything else in the dream was realistic, including the dining room and his family members. Only his clothes were unusual. This image suggested to him that he was operating within his family in a manner that was unsuitable or out of context. He knew immediately that his reactions to his teenagers had recently become more authoritarian as he felt less in touch with their interests and habits. He suspected the dreams were repeating this image precisely because an increase in military discipline around the house was only worsening the growing gap between them.

Symbolic images repeat in our dreams because they express something significant about the way we feel or because they offer a key to understanding a particular problem.

Settings and Scenarios

Settings and scenarios tend to reflect the way something affects us. A sinking ship or a flood is an image that illustrates a sense of being swamped or overwhelmed. Many people report this recurring dream during a time of change such as graduation, a time of intense planning, like the months prior to a wedding, or a time fraught with worries, like during a move or divorce. The image is not a portent of doom or failure; rather the sinking image and rising waters seem to depict the sensation of dealing with something bigger than you are that cannot be escaped or controlled. Although understanding this does not eliminate the stress that accompanies a new chapter in your life, being aware of your own feelings and the pressures you're juggling can help you feel more stable and less frightened by the ups and downs of your experience.

If you have a particular setting that is recurring in a dream, define its most notable characteristic and then consider what portion of your experience can also be described by the same adjectives. The prison camp with its cruelty and confinement may immediately remind you of the corporate setting in which you work. The storm on the horizon that rises quickly and then passes may be very much like the temper of someone close to you. The Civil War scene with its bloody battles may illustrate the painful conflict you're dealing with, either in your family or within yourself. Recognizing the deep emotional undercurrents of your situation can help you have more compassion toward yourself, and evaluate your long-term choices with greater awareness.

Objects

While the setting of a dream can reveal how a current situation makes you feel, a recurring object can sometimes point out a valuable perspective or a new approach toward a difficulty. Try to make note of the *functional characteristic* of the object. Tools, instruments, and devices all operate in a particular manner and serve a purpose. Dreams that feature specific tools tend to show how our response to a situation is either working or would work better. One woman dreamed of trying to use a sponge to soak up some spilled milk from a sandy beach. The more she worked to clean the beach, the more covered with sand she became. The implication of these dreams was that her response to a situation was creating a worse problem than the initial incident (the spilled milk). She was involved in a conflict with a coworker that was escalating into a significant challenge. As soon as she stopped trying to fix things, the conflict diminished and eventually was forgotten.

Another woman, faced with an enormous project, began to dream of various construction sites. It wasn't difficult to recognize that the imagery of building something was related to the large project she was involved with. In a number of these dreams, she was handed a fine pair of embroidery scissors and informed that they were just what she needed. Although she didn't do any embroidery in waking life, she felt the fine-edged scissors were capable of very close, detailed work. She realized that her sense of being overwhelmed at her large assignment would be improved if she paid attention to details and to the quality of her work. She began focusing on smaller portions of her project at a time and in this way was able to function more effectively and with less anxiety.

If you have a number of dreams featuring a specific object, you may be able to unravel its meaning by noticing what purpose it serves, how it functions, or in what kind of situation you would be most likely to find it. Here are a few questions to ask yourself about the recurring symbol in your dreams.

1. *Does the setting or scenario reflect the quality of your feelings?*
2. *Does the object have a particular function?* If so, then define it with a word or two.
3. *Does the object date back to a specific time in your life, or does it belong in a very specific setting?*

These questions will generally help you identify what the image represents and give you an idea of how the dreams may be helping you understand more about a particular situation.

General Rules about Recurring Dreams

Although movies and certain ideas about psychology have fostered the notion that recurring dreams are signs of hidden trauma or premonitions of disaster, I feel it is important to broaden these preconceptions. Recurring dreams more often coincide with particular phases of our lives, and are particularly likely to arise when we are moving through significant transitions, or are forced to deal with situations that are new and unknown.

Bereavement

If you have gone through a trauma or are in the throes of bereavement, you can certainly expect to have dreams about your experience and the feelings that go with it. These dreams may seem obsessed with what has happened, but a number of researchers believe that dreaming about painful incidents actually helps us cope with what has happened. These dreams help us absorb changes, they strive to make connections with past experiences that may have similar qualities we could draw upon, and they struggle to make sense of questions about the nature of life and death and the afterlife. The fact that you are having distressing dreams is not in itself a sign that you are not coping well with what has happened to you. However, in the wake of a shocking or painful loss, it is a good idea to connect with support that you might not otherwise consider necessary. For some, this means confiding in family members and friends more regularly and devoting time to discussing and sharing feelings. For others, it is a time to lean upon your spiritual practices and beliefs and take advantage of the trained personnel who are available for support and prayer. And for many people, this is a time to explore a short-term therapy option with a professional who is familiar with the territory you are moving through. Whatever feels appropriate to you, make an effort to connect with some additional support during this time.

Recurring Dreams as Signposts

Most recurring dreams are not symptoms so much as they are signposts. Like the markers along mountain roads that inform you of falling rocks or steep downgrades, recurring dreams provide signals about what you are going through and how it is impacting you. By looking at the recurring elements in your dream and noticing how long you have been having it, you will be able to identify what part of your life is being reflected. It is up to you then to consider what the implications of the dream are and how you can benefit from them.

Chapter

3

Sex, Romance, and Relationships in Dreams

Our dreams of romance, sexuality, and relationships are often thought-provoking. People have told me they've awakened from a dream in tears because it touched them so deeply. Some feel a brief but intense heartbreak upon awakening from a night of true love when they realize the perfect partner they found exists only in the dream realm. Although people are often embarrassed about the depth of feeling involved, I assure them that the wrenching loss of such dream lovers is briefer but no less profound *in that moment* than the loss of a waking-life relationship.

Some psychological theories interpret romantic dreams as episodes of wish-fulfillment or opportunities to get close to people we cannot reach in waking life. While this view is correct in some instances, I believe it doesn't apply to many of our romantic and sexual dreams. Instead, the dreaming mind seems to use the metaphor of sexuality and closeness to represent a number of different kinds of connection.

Dreams with romantic and sexual themes strive to answer our questions about relationships, sexual satisfaction, and the nature of love. This is no small order. In the search for answers, the dreaming mind will scan past relationships, try on acquaintances and celebrities as lovers, and give us a taste of how things might be different.

The Relationship Imperative

There is a portion of the psyche that seems devoted to the health and survival of our relationships. It is as if a perpetual computer program on relationships operates throughout our lives, scanning for trouble, running hypothetical scenarios, comparing and contrasting options. Even if you move on or close the door on romance for a while, this portion of the psyche continues to mull things over and figure out what went wrong, what might have worked better, and what would be nicer next time. The number of dreams we have that address sex and romance is a testimony to the importance of this part of our lives. But the focus of our erotic and relationship dreams shifts throughout the life span and also depends upon our circumstances. The dreaming mind is always trying to generate ideas and warnings on our behalf, but the goals change slightly over time.

Adolescence

In teen years, we dream a kind of loves-me, loves-me-not story line that continues into early adulthood. The goal of these dreams seems to be to recognize subtle cues of attraction, figure out how to win love and pleasure, and understand our sexual feelings. In these dreams, we are thrown together with someone we find attractive and the opportunity presents itself for sex and declarations of love. Upon awakening, the question then becomes, does this mean that your crush is really interested in you? Or was it just one of those dreams that tries to make you feel better by giving you an outlet for your desire, like a dieter dreaming of chocolate? The truth is, sometimes the unconscious mind really does tune into the true feelings of someone you're interested in and it tries to get the point across in a dream. In other instances, these dreams are expressions of your own feelings and have virtually nothing to do with the object of your affection, except borrowing their image for your story. I'll explain how to tell the difference between the two in the section on the top ten romantic dreams to follow.

Twenties

By the mid-twenties, our dreams go a step beyond trying to determine if someone is interested in us and begin to explore what does and does not suit us in a partner. These dreams focus not only on how to get love and sex, but also on going after the kind of experiences and love that are likely to make us happy. This is a time when strangers and acquaintances guest star as lovers in our dreams with great frequency and apparently little provocation. There is also a tendency toward dreams of sexual encounters with partners you would not choose in waking life, such as friends, family members, or even animals. During this age, many of us are bewildered by the erotic pageantry of our sexual dreams and make a private decision not to discuss or even think about them. It is unfortunate that we take these dreams literally, since in most cases the exotic or inappropriate partners represent *qualities* we are sampling and evaluating and have little or nothing to do with the actual person in the starring role.

Thirties and Forties

During the thirties and forties, our sexual and romantic dreams focus on protecting the connections we've forged or upon finding healthier and more authentic alternatives to the relationships that disappointed us in the past. It is common during these decades to have dreams flashing back to times of great passion, intense feelings, and even desperate pain. The psyche begins to offer up dreams that explain how our hearts got broken and what to go after or avoid in the future. Women and men also report many dreams of their partners being unfaithful during these years. It is as if the psyche says, "Now that you have a partner and a family, your primary goal must be to safeguard it. Look out!" Although these dreams are always meaningful and hint at some kind of anxiety, it should be remembered that every time of life has its focus. When the focus of a particular time is safeguarding what you have, then dreams about loss-prevention are almost inevitable.

Fifties and Sixties

During the fifties and sixties, sexual and romantic dreams tend to be preoccupied with a kind of value clarification. That is, we dream of the things we have neglected to cultivate in our lives and also of what we have learned to value most. This is a time when we are off the hook in many ways and have the freedom to acknowledge what truly does and does not make us happy. By this age, the dreaming mind has isolated a few characters from the past that stand for particular traits or patterns in relationships. The partner you "had to leave" will appear in dreams whenever you are frustrated with current conditions or have been cornered by circumstances, and the urge to leave is simmering beneath the surface. The "first great love" appears in dreams when you are wrestling with questions about a current love relationship. Our romantic partners become shorthand symbols for the quality or experiences we had with them. Although you may be dreaming of someone you knew years ago, it is likely that your dream is actually sorting through the relationship you're in right now and how that quality or experience is playing a part in it.

Seventies through Nineties

In the seventies through the nineties, relationship dreams tend to zoom in with exquisite clarity on the nature of love itself. During these years, the search for meaning and understanding experiences can be intense, and the dreaming mind seems to function like a jeweler's lens to reveal the various facets of the way love has run through the lifetime. It is common during these years to have recurring dreams of an early relationship that was filled with promise, but was never allowed to play itself out. In the dreams, this romance may blossom, be lived out in an entire lifetime, or be like a kind of second life in which that relationship grows to fruition. These dreams seem to suggest that no matter what choices we make, unselfish love never dies and is never truly lost. These romantic scenarios also show how important it is to us to understand the nature of love. The dreaming mind zeroes in on these stories, not in an attempt to recapture youth, but in an attempt to distill a deeper understanding. When we graduate from this lifetime and go on to whatever may come next, it appears we want most of all to bring with us a spiritual and emotional understanding about matters of the heart.

Dreams that Highlight Imbalances

Not all of us find ultimate fulfillment in romantic love or marriage. The more I work with people seeking happiness, the more convinced I become that we are like unique plants, thriving and blossoming under the conditions that harmonize with our particular natures. Living in a style that goes against the grain, we are like plants dying from the wrong type of care or conditions. There is a slow but definite loss of vitality and hope that occurs when we live according to what we believe we *should* want, if it is not what we really need. Awareness of our needs can be clouded by societal directives, parental programming, concern about appearances, and also by the notion that in order to be spiritual, one must strive toward an imaginary ideal relationship. None of these filters are inherently bad. But when they obscure the awareness of our authentic needs the dreaming mind seems to rear up and protest. When this happens, we experience disturbing and pointed dreams to remind us that we have neglected an important part of the equation.

Rescuing Fish

Sheila wrote to me about her recurring dream of trying to rescue her fish from her husband's neglect. In the dream, she had gone out of town for a few days, asking him to care for and feed the fish in her aquarium. When she returned, she found that the tank was almost out of water and the fish were lying at the base of the aquarium gasping and trembling. Horrified, she began replenishing their water and offering them food, hoping they would somehow survive. Since they did not have an aquarium in real life, she suspected the dream was offering some special message to her. Because the dream was emotionally upsetting, she felt driven to try and find out more about it.

Although this might appear to be a dream about sharing household responsibility rather than romance, it follows one of the most prevalent themes of romantic disappointment. Translated, it goes something like this: "I entrusted you with the care of something very precious within me which requires special love and attention. You have neglected it to the point where it is almost dead. I am left to repeatedly try to bring it back to life on my own." In this case, the fish represent the dreamer's emotional nature and faith in the relationship, which she had to tend alone. When she called on participation from her partner, he not only ignored her request, but also had no idea that an emotionally supportive environment (water) was necessary for the health of his partner and their relationship.

Clients who are dreaming about their relationships often do not realize that their other dreams are also focusing on the same questions. When there is a deep imbalance in the lifestyle or a difficulty in a relationship that impacts the constitution, dreams take on a feverish, warning quality and become haunting and strange. Plants, trees, animals, and fish tend to appear as symbols of the dreamer's vitality. You may dream of trying to repair a damaged tree, repotting a plant that is root-bound, or rescuing an abused animal. The plant or creature in need of care represents the essential aspect of the dreamer that is being starved or killed off by present conditions. People like Sheila, with naturally fluid emotions who live in a setting where emotion is discounted, will often dream of needing to put more water in the fish tank. This is because their innately emotional spirit is being slowly dried up by the lack of emotional support in their lives. This does not mean that the dreamer will literally die from their lifestyle, but it is a signal that a part of them which is most essential is already gasping and struggling to survive.

Invisible Nutritional (Emotional) Needs

Other signals of this kind are dreams of houses on fire, bombs waiting to be exploded, or people who have been tortured or beaten. These images tend to be warnings that something fundamental is out of whack in your world or that a part of you feels emotionally battered by the struggle to make something work. Although I strongly disagree with theorists who pronounce that clients are in denial when they do not understand a dream, I do find that often people are disconnected from this level of themselves. So when a dream illustrates that your essence is being mortally wounded, you may not understand it because you are unfamiliar with the notion of having a certain essence. Many people stay with relationships or conditions when their dreams are screaming for them to rescue themselves. We never want to believe a connection is irretrievable, and we have been taught that it is selfish to leave or insist on change just because your life depends on it. But the most common reason for these dreams' obscurity is that in modern society we have no expressions, no words with which to describe the essence that is most our own. Everyone knows that each wood has a certain grain, that fish need water, and pets need love. Yet we have no sense of ourselves as possessing a similarly intangible and definite essence with requirements of its own. This may be one reason why we intuitively enjoy theories that explain what type we are, from astrological sun signs to body-type diets. It isn't that we long to be categorized, it is that we know on some deep level that we are made from a particular kind of material and that we have invisible but critical needs because of it. I call these invisible nutritional needs because they can't be seen or even articulated well, but they nourish us perhaps even more than food nourishes the body. Without them, we flounder and suffer enormously. When they are well-tended, we are able to meet immense challenges and endure things that a casual observer might think overwhelming.

Each month I receive more letters and email correspondence about romantic and sexual themes than any other kind of dream. Despite our differences, many of the concerns are the same around the world. I've selected the ten most common questions to answer here.

The Top Ten Questions about Romantic and Sexual Dreams

1. *Does my dream of a sexual encounter with an acquaintance mean that he or she is really interested in me?* We cannot help but wonder about a friend, schoolmate, or coworker after a remarkably convincing sexual dream about them. Some people even feel a bit awkward the next time they see the person they've

dreamed about in this way. Many teenagers and young adults are especially hopeful that such dreams reveal a previously well-concealed interest on the part of the acquaintance. He or she may have been too shy to hint at the secret passion they harbor towards the dreamer. Unfortunately, this interpretation isn't always accurate. Sometimes these dreams have more to do with your own feelings than with any hidden passion coming from the other person. These dreams allow you to see what it might be like to be close to the object of your affection and the dreaming mind tends to use attractive partners to test drive relationship skills and erotic responses. It's quite normal for very young people to dream of a first kiss long before it happens. Teens tend to dream of their first sexual encounter with an idealized partner or their current crush some time before becoming sexually active. Nature seems to provide dreams of romance to come in order to help us better handle the real thing when it arrives. But this does not mean that the lover of your dreams is necessarily meant for you. There are several telling factors that will help reveal the truth about your romantic dream life. Ask yourself these questions to decide what the odds are that your dream lover is also dreaming of you.

a. *Is he or she already married or involved with someone else?*

As tempting as it is to fantasize that your dream has revealed a hidden yearning to be with you, if the answer to this question is yes, then your dream probably has nothing to do with their feelings at all. Enjoy your experience for what it gave you and taught you, and focus your attention on finding someone who is available and right for you.

b. *Has this person exhibited signs of interest in you in real life?*

If the honest answer to this question is yes, then your dream may be trying to make subtle clues more explicit. You are safe in making a respectful overture to the person to see if they are interested. If they don't respond, don't chase them because of your dream. The very fact that you are having romantic dreams and trying out appealing partners suggests that your radar will be working very effectively in finding romance if that is what you want right now.

c. *Are you involved with or married to someone else?*

Strangely enough, sexual dreams about other people generally have more to do with your existing relationship than they do with fantasy encounters. If your dream highlighted experiences you'd like more of or qualities in a relationship that you value, focus on building these in the existing relationship. Don't make the mistake of thinking the grass is greener over the horizon. Dreams often try to help define what we need and want so that we can foster those qualities where they are most likely to flourish—with the love we already have.

Don't get too caught up in trying to psychically tune in to the person you're attracted to or in trying to reel them in. Remember, the dreaming mind is focusing on giving you enriching experiences and in teaching you about love and passion. Behave responsibly toward those you desire and don't be outraged or disappointed if they don't respond in waking life as they do in your dreams. One of the great tricks to finding love is in letting go of the potential partners who aren't quite right for whatever reason. Insisting on something that isn't working seems to block the right person from finding you. Letting go and trusting life seems to attract genuine relationships and happiness like a magnet.

2. *Why would I dream of being intimate with someone I'm not even attracted to?* It may be a celebrity you like but don't find attractive or it may be someone at the office you don't particularly care for, but it's fairly normal to have sizzling or romantic dreams about people we would never choose for a sexual fantasy.

There are four possible reasons for dreaming of a romantic tryst with someone who isn't your cup of tea.

 a. *The person represents a quality.*

The lover may symbolize a quality or characteristic that you are having encounters with in waking life. Sex and romance sometimes symbolize closeness and connection, particularly in terms of getting acquainted with some part of your own personality. A man who was studying public speaking dreamed of getting engaged to Oprah, who for him represented an excellent communicator who is never at a loss in public. A woman who was cultivating her sense of humor dreamed of having a fling with Robin Williams. A girl who decided to embark on a graduate program in psychology dreamed of running away with Frasier Crane (the television character of a radio psychiatrist.) For these people, their dream lovers did not reflect their taste in sexual partners. However, each person embodied a quality which they had recently decided to connect with in themselves. If your dream partner doesn't attract you, consider whether they have a profession, talent, or trademark that is closely aligned with a quality you're exploring in yourself these days.

b. *You're doing something that isn't right for you.*

You may be getting in bed in the metaphorical sense with something else right now that is also not in your normal style or taste. Women particularly are prone to dreams of saying yes to a partner whom they cannot respect and do not want when they have also said yes to another kind of offer in waking life. One woman was considering accepting a job that paid well and allowed her to travel, but which required her to schmooze powerful clients and dress up corporate meetings. She was tempted by the offer, but recoiled when she dreamed of getting engaged to an older man she knew whom she found particularly lecherous and distasteful. She awoke feeling soiled by the dream and realized her mind was warning her not to make a bargain she would find unpleasant to keep. If your dream partner was particularly unsavory to you, make a mental note of what specific characteristic made them so. Now consider what activity, option, or person near you has a similar quality. It may be time to reevaluate your choices and be willing to say no to something that isn't right for you.

c. *There really is an unconscious attraction.*

There are instances when we feel a spark of attraction toward someone, but by day it is well concealed for one reason or another. We don't like to feel attracted to someone who does things of which we disapprove or who belongs to a friend. Nor do most of us want to acknowledge feelings toward a coworker with whom we will be working closely for some time. There are all kinds of scenarios in which it just doesn't work to have the tingles over someone and we can't even let ourselves think about it. But the dreaming mind has no such compunctions and will happily provide you with a sample of forbidden fruit from time to time. Generally, after such a dream, it is pretty easy to recognize that indeed there are some undercurrents towards the dream lover. When this is the source of such a dream it's particularly easy to discern. Another clue is that these types of dreams tend to be quite sensual and realistic. Sexual dreams that are hot, tactile, and realistic tend to have more to do with actual attraction than do dreams in which you remember running off with someone or having an affair but you cannot really remember any of the action. Men appear to be slightly more prone to this type of dream than women, but all of us can learn to recognize these dreams by their tangible qualities and by being honest with ourselves about those hidden feelings. Although hidden desire is the motivation most people use to explain their dreams with unexpected partners, this is not the real explanation as often as we believe. Trust your perceptions on this one. If you honestly don't find the other person attractive, then one of the other explanations probably applies to your dream.

    d. You may be connecting with this person in some other important way.

A woman whose male friend invited her to join his church immediately had a dream that they became sweethearts. She honestly didn't find him attractive, but appreciated his friendship. She did, however, fall in love with the church he attended and immediately joined the congregation. Another man was assigned to do a radio show with an attractive and witty female cohost. Their partnership gained popularity and resulted in an increase in ratings and an upswing in both their careers. He was embarrassed that at times he had sexual dreams about this woman when he was very happily married to a lovely wife. However, he did feel his partnership with the cohost took his career to a different level and that their banter on the air was a kind of connection that was important. They were, in fact, forging a bond professionally that changed their lives—in some ways, a partnership that was as important as a romantic one. Remember that connections of all kinds tend to be depicted in dreams through the imagery of romance, sexuality, and intercourse. Don't panic or feel guilty about these dreams. Consider whether you are connecting with the dream lover in some important way which the dream is depicting in physical terms.

3. *What does it mean if I dream I'm a member of the opposite sex?* A dream like this can be a bit of a shocker when you wake up. But remember the principle that dreams tend to take emotional and psychological elements and symbolize them in physical ways. In most cases, gender-shifting dreams deal with changes in perspective or exploring different aspects of the self, not with a change in sexual orientation. In a common variation of this dream, you may still be yourself but discover in the lavatory that you somehow have the genitalia of the opposite sex or of both genders. Be careful not to judge yourself or these dreams too harshly. Almost everyone has such dreams at times, and they appear to be markers of psychological development and maturity more often than anything else.

4. *What does it mean if I have a dream that involves incestuous scenes?* Foremost in our minds is the worry that we are recovering a hidden memory when we

have a dream of this kind. Close on the heels of that worry is concern that one interpretation of the dream is that we dream about what we wish for. Both of these interpretations are upsetting and largely unacceptable. Fortunately, most dreams of this type have nothing to do with suppressed memories or wish fulfillment. Instead, there are a number of more complex reasons why we have dreams of this kind.

a. *Someone you are involved with has qualities similar to your relative.*

Psychologically, if you are involved with someone who has similar traits to a family member, you may expect some dreams to depict you as "involved with" that family member. This doesn't mean you chose your partner because they remind you of Dad or Mom (although it's possible). It may mean that you are responding to this person with some of the same patterns that you learned in that earlier relationship. One woman who was dating a man could not figure out the cause of their friction until she had a dream that she was romantically involved with her father. Immediately, it became clear that much of the hostility and suspicion she felt toward her partner stemmed from her earlier disappointment when her father abandoned the family. Just being more aware of this pattern enabled her to see her situation more objectively and spend less time reacting from programmed fears.

b. *You may be involved in something that is unwholesome with a family member.*

Incest can symbolize love that is too close, too enmeshed, and confused. One woman dreamed that she was performing sexual favors for her father. In waking life, she had embarked on a serious romantic relationship but was pretending to her father that she wasn't seeing anyone at all because she sensed he would disapprove of her choice. This particular lie felt uniquely unwholesome because of the depth of feeling she had for her partner. In deciding not to acknowledge the relationship to her father, she was trying to do him a favor and not upset him. However, it was a favor that violated her personal code of emotional honor. Hence the imagery of an arrangement between them that seemed to gratify him but dishonored them both. Eventually, she chose to confide in her father and found that she had underestimated his ability to accept her choices.

c. *You may be picking up that there is something tainted, unwholesome, or contaminating about a current relationship.*

One woman dreamed that her child was involved in an incestuous relationship with her husband. She felt convinced that this was not literally the case, but as she looked at the dream symbolically, it was easy for her to see that her lifestyle was potentially harmful to her child. There were many things about their current situation that put the child at risk, created uncertainty, and forced her to live as though she were much older than her years. When the emotional fallout of our struggles to be happy hits children, it can be like a toxin loose in the home. This dream (as it was intended to be) proved upsetting enough to provide the catalyst for her to make changes to create firmer boundaries in the home.

d. *You may have experienced a kind of emotional incest growing up, a violation of boundaries that still proves confusing.*

Incest is an obvious violation of trust and a confusing one. For that reason, it can be used in dreams to depict the kind of emotional confusion that overly enmeshed families sometimes create. While some dreams of incest may indeed prove to be surfacing memories of abuse, many dreams of this kind are memories of psychological boundaries crossed and violated. If you have recurring dreams of this nature that feel as if they have a basis in memory even though they do not match what you recall of early life, assume that some kind of disrespect of your boundaries has taken place. Many therapists believe that it is less important to retrieve the actual memory of what did or didn't take place than it is to seek support in cultivating healthy boundaries in your present life.

5. *Are dreams of a partner's infidelity warning signals of real trouble?* Dreams of this type need to be considered against the background of the overall relationship. True, some people have glimpsed the awful truth in a dream which was apparently pieced together from a number of clues that were overlooked during waking hours. But for the most part, dreams of infidelity are not in themselves an indicator of actual cheating. Instead, these dreams are often metaphors for a kind of emotional abandonment or having a loved one show more attention to their job or hobby than they do to you.

6. *Do repeated dreams of an old flame mean I have never gotten over them?* Old flames tend to be human symbols of romantic love. This means that your first significant romance tends to become imprinted, so that person will act like an emblem of love in many of your dreams. It is likely your dream is actually trying to work through your current relationship with someone entirely different. But when issues with romance are the subject of a dream, the file that

comes up has your old flame's face on the cover. Don't be deceived by this, in most cases your heart and your dreams are focused on current issues.

7. *Why would I dream of being back with my ex when I feel lucky to have left them behind?* If you've been through a tough relationship, you may tend to dream about that person more often than you'd like. This certainly doesn't mean you still want to be with them! Instead, it probably means that psychologically you are still removing shrapnel that you collected during your stint in that war zone. It takes a long time for emotional wounds to heal, and, unfortunately, even long after you've found happiness with someone new, you may still have periodic dreams of a painful ex. In some cases, these dreams can warn you not to react to your new love as if they were your ex. It's so easy to lash out or put up walls as you did in an old relationship. If you have any dreams about your current love morphing into the ex, be warned that you may be going through some confusion with old issues. Sometimes, too, new partners do similar things or make similar requests of us that seem to set off a cascade of reactions that are inappropriate to our new situation. This usually doesn't mean the new person is guilty of the same crimes as the ex, but it may well mean they are triggering a preset group of responses in you. One of the best ways to counteract this cycle is to confide in your current partner about the dynamics at play. Demystifying these monsters goes a long way toward creating lasting freedom from them. If you are not currently involved but still have dreams about a past you're glad to have left behind, it suggests that you are still recovering from that time in your life. Repeated dreams occur in part to heal trauma and assimilate new experiences. They are your way of getting over it so don't feel you are failing when they crop up. Accept them and realize your deeper mind is doing important work through these dreams to move you forward into a more positive present and future.

8. *When I'm on a break from a relationship and I dream of my sweetheart, does that mean I was wrong to break it off?* There is a theory that the course of true love is rocky, and that frequent splits and reconciliations are a sign of profound feeling. For this reason, it is easy to interpret dreams about someone you've parted from as signs that you should rush back into their arms. As with other romantic dreams, these should be evaluated along with all that you consciously know about the relationship. The dreaming mind seems to feel that relationship is about as important as it gets, and rightly so. After any breakup, there is a need to dream about relationships in general. Your deeper mind is

delving into memories, feelings, hopes, and fears. It is creating many dreams that are all an attempt to make sense of what will work for you in a relationship. You are, in a sense, getting ready to love more successfully and find deeper fulfillment in the future. The dreams that are setting the stage to make this happen tend to use your most recent partner as the actor who represents the love interest. He or she will appear in your dreams and you'll have all kinds of adventures and disasters with them as your mind unravels mistakes and gains understanding about the things that make real love work. It's important to give credence to the lessons these dreams have to offer; but don't assume that the appearance of your latest ex is a sign that he or she is the one, unless that coincides with your conscious understanding of the relationship as well.

9. *If I have a great new romance but still dream of my previous partner, does that mean I'll never really love the new person in my life?* Dream flings usually don't indicate any lack of fulfillment in your current relationship. Sometimes, these dreams are just for fun and don't appear to have profound meaning. At other times, the inner mind is busy sorting through what works and doesn't work in a relationship, and it will quickly refer back to other relationships to compare strengths and weaknesses, or to try and make sense of patterns.

10. *If you have a perfect dream lover, is there any hope that he or she is somehow really on their way into your life?* Surprisingly enough, there is hope of just that. Many feel that we have a perfect romantic or sexual dream as a kind of relief from a romantic dry spell, like a dieter who dreams of eating chocolate. But this is not really so. It is far more typical of our dreams to mirror our current circumstances. So if you are lonely, misunderstood, starved for affection, or feeling amorous, your dreams will tend to show you that, with a lack of, rather than a fabulous, relationship. So when a perfect relationship shows up in dream form, pay attention. In some cases, this is the psyche's way of warming us up, reminding us we are not robots after all, and that we can still fall in love. Don't elope with the first person you see the next day, but do open yourself up to the possibility that a romance may be on the horizon.

Common Sexual and Relationship Dreams

Nowhere to Make Love

In this dream, you take off with your partner and decide to have a lover's tryst. You go to the selected location but there are too many people around.

Annoyed but adaptable, you head off for a more secluded location but it is unacceptable for other reasons. In fact, everywhere you go, there are people, circumstances, or problems that make it impossible to make love. You awaken feeling like you spent the whole night searching for a place to make love!

This isn't really a dream about sex so much as it is about trying to salvage intimacy itself. It's typical to have this dream after a break up or whenever you and your partner are feeling estranged. The frustrating circumstances that serve to keep you from making love in the dream represent the different forces and obstacles in the relationship that prevent you from feeling close and intimate.

Become conscious of the fact that there are two factions in this relationship—the parts of you and your partner that want to be together, and the aspects of you both that are keeping you apart. This means you're likely to have some confusing moments as you sort through your options and find your thoughts and feelings in conflict at times. If you've already left the relationship, just relax and let your psyche do its healing work. If you are in the relationship and want to make it work, you may want to get some support to help open up communication so that there is some psychological place where you two can meet and rekindle the spark.

The Interruption

You're in the midst of a passionate embrace when your parents, your boss, or some other intruder barges in. This person speaks to you as if you are not in the middle of something so private, and although you're upset and embarrassed, you conduct a brief, logical conversation with them.

This dream suggests that there are outside forces intruding on your relationship, specifically in the areas of sexuality and private time. Some people find it easy to admit that the appearance of the boss in their bedroom shows just how often their career interferes with their love life, invading even those moments when they'd really like to forget about the office. For others, the implications are more subtle. It may not be real-life parents who intrude with phone calls and suggestions, but rather the opinions and expectations we absorbed from them that interrupt.

These dreams show how completely an outside element can spoil a moment of passion. In the case of things we absorbed from parents, it may not be our libido that is inhibited, but rather our ability to deeply connect and trust that is impaired. The source of the intrusion is usually a clue as to what kind of energy is disrupting your intimacy. It is vital not to blame your partner or yourself, but to look objectively at how you can bolster psychic boundaries so that you can enjoy a romantic sanctuary with the one you love.

Making Love in Public

You and your sweetheart are in an improbable place for a sexual encounter, but, overcome by the moment, you decide to indulge in a few minutes of passion. What begins as an innocent impulse turns out to be a major display as you realize the place you've chosen is more public than you'd realized. You may be in a store display window, in the orchestra pit at a major symphony, or on the sound stage of a TV show. Although no one seems upset by this, you and your partner freeze like two deer caught in the headlights of a car as a major audience forms around you.

This is a dream that exaggerates a sense of your relationship being in the public forum. People whose private lives are made public may have this dream, and so do people who feel conspicuous for some reason. If you select a partner your friends or family find provocative for some reason, you may have this type of dream. The public intercourse simply represents the sense that people are speculating about your private life and, for you, this knowledge is quite uncomfortable.

By understanding the sense of vulnerability this dream reveals, you have a distinct advantage. These days it's fashionable to pretend you feel comfortable with almost everything; thus, if you do feel some sense of exposure, you may not give yourself permission to have those feelings, learn from them, and gently let them subside. Recognition will allow you to own your feelings and process them in a more healthy and effective way than will denial and pretense. In addition, you have a perfect opportunity to discuss this with your partner, or if that doesn't feel right, with supportive friends who may understand and have suggestions. Finally, the dream itself lets you know that although an audience may indeed be observing your relationship, they aren't really sitting in judgment. They are simply watching the show. This provides a hint that if you and your partner carry the energy and intention that "there's no show here folks, go home," others may pick up that psychic signal and lose interest.

The Case of the Vanishing Partner

You're carried away by passion in the arms of a lover who knows how to do everything just the way you like it. You feel uninhibited, safe, swept away. Just as your thoughts seem to melt and you're losing yourself in the feelings, the intensity lessens. You reach for your partner and try to move into them again, but they seem to be disappearing. In fact, the partner, like a ghost, is just vaporizing. He or she is turning into fog and disappearing, leaving only traces in the air.

This dream is a picture of passion that is frustrated due to lack of an adequate partnership. This doesn't mean necessarily that you are alone in life, but that at the times when you most want to connect or be spontaneous, the answering response just isn't there for you. Women report more dreams of this sort than do men, and they appear to have more dreams that reflect sexual and romantic frustration than do men.

This is more than a report on frustration. This dream can offer profound clues about what you need to feel fulfilled in a relationship. Whether it's spontaneity, respect, being known for yourself, or being found desirable, this quality is something you need to foster in the connections you form. Being aware of what really matters to you, what allows you to feel connected, is important. Not only does it motivate you to help create this in relationships, but it may help you to recognize and treasure connections in which this experience is present.

The Faceless Stranger

You're involved in a delicious romantic encounter with one of the most satisfying lovers of your life. This is someone with whom you feel close, yet free to experiment. The dream is filled with realistic and delightful sensations that leave you breathless and very pleased. It is only upon awakening that you look back on this dream and realize that your wonderful lover was perfect in every way except that he or she had no face.

This theme allows you to experiment with passion and to learn more about what pleases you physically and emotionally. Because the partner has no identity, you are absolutely free to simply have the experience without any thoughts or constraints. The mental baggage that attaches to an identity is enormous; even if one is with a handsome or beautiful stranger, the pleasure that creates is laced with self-consciousness and concerns of the ego. This scene allows you to be free and to recognize what you are capable of experiencing when the mind is free of chatter and the ego is free of concerns.

Dreams like this are a gift because they create an unforgettable sample of the type of pleasure your system is wired to create. They let us know what can happen when we get out of our own way, so to speak. Repeated dreams of this nature are signals that you can enhance your intimate pleasure by learning to leave mental chatter, hard feelings, and power struggles on the doorstep. This is easier said than done, certainly, but when the dreaming mind repeats a message with such conviction, the prescription for happiness is well within reach if a bit of intention is applied.

Interpreting Your Sexual Dreams: Avoid Judgment, Seek Understanding

Our sexual and relationship dreams, like their real life counterparts, are fraught with emotion and desire. We awaken from them moved, frustrated, aroused, and confused. Sometimes we're appalled or embarrassed by the choices we made in the dream or the pleasure we found in bizarre circumstances. In most walks of life, it's difficult to discuss any dream intelligently without being teased or taken lightly. When dreams deal with delicate or controversial subject matter, it's almost impossible to find anyone to talk to about them. So we wonder and worry.

Points to Keep In Mind

When you're confused about a sexual or romantic dream, keep these general rules in mind.

1. *Avoid labels.* Don't interpret the dream according to how you judge it when you are awake. Disapproval and fear only keep you from understanding the dream, and once you do understand it, you'll probably find that your fears were unfounded.
2. *Be receptive to lessons.* Consider whether the dream has anything to teach you about love, romance, or sexuality. Does it permit you to understand intimacy from another person's perspective? Does it take you outside your habitual self-concept and let you experience things differently?
3. *Don't feel guilty.* Now that you understand the tendency of your dreams to use physical symbolism, you don't need to feel guilty about sexual themes. Look at these dreams as metaphors or as opportunities to learn about yourself.

4. *Be tactful and respectful of others.* Your partner will probably not enjoy hearing about your dreams of another lover. There is no moral code of openness that requires you to share these dreams unless you know absolutely that he or she is interested in them as a learning experience. I receive hundreds of letters each year from spouses who are worried sick that they are losing the love of their mate because he or she disclosed such dreams to them. Don't share these dreams if you suspect they will be misconstrued or a source of worry. In the same spirit, do not share your sexual dream with the person who was the star of that dream unless your friendship with that person renders that type of conversation appropriate. Men find such confidences confusing and many women find them downright creepy.

5. *Trust your dreams.* Stay open-minded and positive about your dream experiences. As quirky as they may seem, there is always an underlying positive intention involved. There is a lesson, an insight, or something healing and inspiring being offered. By keeping a wholesome and accepting attitude, you'll be able to understand and benefit from even your most provocative dreams.

Chapter 4

Who's Who? Understanding the Characters in Your Dreams

Have you noticed that sometimes you dream of great friends, soul mates, or life-changing creative partners, people you love and have seemingly known forever? You know them and they know you, right down to the bone marrow. The only trouble is, they don't exist in your waking life. Still, other times you may spend the night hanging out with Cher, Oprah, or Albert Einstein, and feel so close to them that you *miss* talking with them for the rest of the day after the dream. And who are all those extras: the people who seem to come right out of a Hollywood production about the Mafia, the Gestapo, or the Wild West?

One psychological theory of dream characters is that at all times and in all dreams they represent elements of the dreamer's own personality. In folkloric circles, dream characters are considered to sometimes represent spirit guides, demons, or even ghosts. In my experience, these theories are not diverse enough to be universally helpful in understanding our dreams. I believe that certain kinds of dream characters tend to represent elements of the dreamer's own personality, while other characters tend to be quite literal—your husband or your child are probably just themselves in your dream.

Types of Characters

The characters in our dreams come in five general categories. Generic characters, fictitious characters, core connections, celebrities, and soul connections, each serve a different function and offer a different kind of gift. Regardless of how strange some of your dream characters may seem, make no mistake about it, the people and creatures in your dream are not appearing at random. Each one is deliberately selected by your psyche because it best captures a kind of energy that is being dealt with in the dream. We'll discuss the types of dream characters you're mostly like to encounter, and what they have to offer.

Generic Characters

Some dream characters bear no resemblance to anyone you know in waking life but are familiar as stereotypes or people who look like extras in a movie scene. These include doctors in a hospital, police, gangsters, and soldiers. Any character who could provide background in the location shot of a movie or who is instantly recognizable for their role may be a generic character. For years, clients and I would have long conversations trying to identify who or what these characters represented. When I finally said, "Okay, was it just a cowboy, a generic cowboy?" the client would nod excitedly as if that described it perfectly.

These characters appear in our dreams precisely because they have such general and obvious associations. Spies are subtle and covert, police have authority and play by specific rules, gypsies are free, nomadic, and mysterious. Of course, the associations you have to the characters are most important in determining precisely what these people represent. But for the most part, the general associations toward these types of characters are pretty widespread. Just as you recognize the outlaw or the hero when they come on screen in a film, you can recognize the role of the generic character in your dream.

They have an obvious role, bear no resemblance to anyone close to you, generally have a costume or other marker that makes them recognizable, and don't exist in waking life.

Generic characters are what I call *intrapsychic* symbols. This means they don't usually represent anyone in your waking life, they actually represent a part of you!

Their broad, stereotypical traits reflect the part of your personality that serves a similar purpose in your life. The rebel in you, the martyr, the vamp, or the inner policeman all play a part in your choices. These facets of the personality contribute to your sense of responsibility and the things you want in life. Specific situations cause us to have encounters with these facets of ourselves. They blossom and come to the forefront or give us odd yearnings at times. Pressures to perform and philosophical conflicts are likely to give you dreams about your inner Mafia, Olympic coach, or supreme court. Many people who ignore their own needs dream of visiting a hospital and finding the emergency room nurses and physicians ignoring their requests for help and information. In such dreams, they are both the person asking for help and the one who has the answers but refuses to acknowledge their need. I believe the frustration and disapproval they feel toward the healer's callous attitude is intended to goad them into responding more compassionately and swiftly to their own neglected needs.

Realize that the generic characters in your dreams will be somewhat one-dimensional exaggerations of the parts of your personality being represented. They are almost like a cartoon of a facet you possess, and may be unflattering or quite different from your overall self-concept. Don't slow your progress by making judgments about these characters. Instead, consider whether you can recognize that inner dictator or inner critic. Although it sounds like a self-help cliché, I find it helps dreamers to recognize the meaning of their generic characters by trying them on in this way: *"I was minding my own business, when my inner show-off volunteered me to lead the reunion committee."* Or, *"I went to the mall and my inner vamp talked me into buying her three new outfits, and then she presented me with the bill and walked away with the shopping bags."* When you summarize a scene in this way, it's easy to see if a generic character is representing a part of yourself and just how the differing forces in your personality are operating with regard to current conditions in your life. Don't fall into the trap of deciding that some dream characters are just bad news. Understanding these inner qualities helps you own their energy. And what you understand and accept about yourself becomes a resource that is potentially useful.

During the time I attended graduate school, I worked three part-time jobs and had a demanding hobby. I was also involved with a troubled man who demanded extensive attention and energy. During that time, I dreamed repeatedly of indentured servants of all sorts. These dreams took place in many settings and time periods, but always the servants were featured in the background. I felt wrenched by their plight and angered by the unfair and cruel people who held them in bondage.

They worked endlessly, suffering and enduring hardship, hoping for some kind of relief or rescue but never receiving any. After a while, it dawned on me that my own belief in being selfless was a misunderstanding of a nobler and healthier ideal. I was, in a sense, enslaving my possibility of a more enjoyable existence because I was so focused on enduring my life from day to day. Also, beneath the surface, I felt obliged to do something significant in the world and toward that end I took on too many things and gave my energy unthinkingly as if this shotgun approach to humanism would accomplish something. Once I realized that the unfair imbalance in my dreams reflected an imbalance in my waking life, I was empowered to make other choices and became much freer in many ways.

Fictitious Characters

These characters usually have an important role in your dream, but do not exist in real life. For example, you may dream of taking a trip around the world with your beloved sister although you don't have a sister in waking life. A wise, elderly neighbor may give you advice in a dream but you have no such neighbor in real life. Or you may be one of the many people who dream quite regularly of other people's lives and who seem to watch dreams as one might watch a movie. It seems puzzling to think you only dream about other people, and many people mistakenly believe that their dreams have nothing to do with their own lives. Nothing could be farther from the truth. All our dreams are connected with our own lives, at least on some level, even if none of the people or settings bear any resemblance to our lives.

Fictitious characters tend to operate in two ways. They sometimes magnify qualities in someone close to us so that we might better understand the dynamics in a relationship or situation. And they often reflect a particular aspect of ourselves that has relevance to our happiness. One woman who was dating an extremely extroverted man dreamed she was engaged to a stand-up comic who insisted on giving impromptu performances at every family gathering—even funerals! The dream was a graphic illustration of how uncomfortable she felt with him at times, even though she was also drawn to his flamboyant style. She'd felt ashamed of her own more introverted style and had tried to suppress her feelings of discomfort by telling herself not to be uptight. But when the dream dramatized the insensitive side of her boyfriend by using a loud comedian to play the role, she felt better able to sort through her feelings without condemning them or her friend.

When characters who have no real-life identity appear in your dreams, you can be sure they are there to convey some quality that has direct bearing on your current circumstances. When fictional characters represent aspects of someone close to you, they are often so exaggerated or one-dimensional that it can feel disloyal to recognize them. Dreamer's often protest: *Well, my boss has a mean streak, but he isn't as cruel as the playground bully!* This is because the dream character is highlighting a specific quality within that person which is having an impact on your current circumstances. It isn't saying: *Watch out, this person is a bully.* It is saying: *Understand that this person has a side that is like a childish bully. A part of him feels more comfortable and in control when those around him lose their normal confidence.* Dream characters exaggerate qualities that help us understand the mechanics involved in relationships and they can clue you in on traits that impact you, even though the other person may be unaware they even have them! When fictional characters represent qualities within yourself, they usually do so to let you know the source of a recurring pattern or to remind you of a resource you didn't know you had.

A powerful woman executive was forced to retire from her fast-track position at the pinnacle of her career. She was suffering so many symptoms of stress that she knew, along with her physician and family, that continuing to work as she had would wreak havoc with her health. She quit and found it difficult to deal with the fallout from her loss of status and identity. Shortly after leaving work, however, she dreamed of taking a joyride with Peter Pan. They flew through the night sky, visiting interesting places and observing the world from a higher perspective. They also played with the ability to fly, swooping and cavorting through the sky with gleeful freedom. For this woman, Peter Pan represented a childlike attitude of enjoyment and irresponsibility— a thing she had never really allowed herself to experience. Yet this dream suggested that she did have the potential to feel these things, and that embracing this part of herself would allow her to view things from a higher perspective. Over time, she came to relish her freedom to travel, to explore intellectual territory that intrigued her, and the luxury of not having to always act grown up.

Core Connections

When you dream of your spouse, your child, or your best friend, you are probably not dreaming in symbolic terms. These people are what I call *core connections* and they typically appear in dreams representing themselves. Although there are exceptions to this rule, it is easiest to understand most dreams by accepting these characters at face value and seeing how well the dream makes sense.

When you dream about family members, you have a chance to learn more about their point of view, what motivates them, and how your actions may be affecting them. One working mom was unaware of how cranky she'd become until she dreamed of responding to her young son's questions by biting his head off! A man felt guilty for resenting his wife's insistence that he change so many things about himself until he dreamed that she was forcing him to wear women's clothes around the house. Not only were these clothes embarrassing and unwanted by him, they were far too small and he felt suffocated and constricted by them. This dream helped him realize that to some extent his wife was unwittingly trying to get him to behave more like a woman. Clearly, his sense of constriction in this role indicated that despite both of their good intentions, some kind of more realistic and tolerant compromise needed to be struck between them.

Take for granted the exaggerations and physical symbolism in these dreams. Physical actions and violence usually reflect emotional hurts and psychological forces. Costumes and funny clothes hint at where that person is coming from, just as weird pursuits reflect motivations that are sometimes difficult to understand through logic alone. Sometimes your dreams will reveal more honestly and clearly the feelings you've been struggling to understand by day. This can give you the opportunity to see a pattern in one night that has been baffling you for years, or to recognize a growing rift before it has time to solidify and do damage. Concentrate on the gifts these dreams bring in terms of understanding and healing relationships. Take the spirit of the dreams to heart while you forgive and accept the eccentric forms they take.

One woman was upset because her best friend at the office was subtly turning against her. There were odd moments of rivalry that had never been there before and the camaraderie they'd enjoyed for years was replaced by tension and jockeying for power. Although the woman continued to behave generously, her friend responded to every gesture by taking advantage of things as much as she could. Heartsick, the woman wondered what she could have done to set her friend against her. One night, she dreamed that she and her friend put on giant, spongy boxing gloves and set upon each other for several minutes, slugging it out with harmless flailing. At the end of their boxing match, the friend said: *Look, the reason I can't stand you anymore is because I'm jealous of you. You're going back to finish your college education and you're marrying a man you love. I'm not doing either of those things and it's burning me up. Just stay out of my face with all your happiness, will you?* The woman awoke stunned but calm. It would never have occurred to her that someone could dislike you because you went to night school and finished college or because you were planning a wedding. But the truth of the dream was crystal clear. Although dismayed by the situation, she was relieved to know that it was nothing she had done wrong that had driven a rift into what she'd considered a friendship. She avoided discussing her happiness around the woman at the office and they eventually built a less personal level of friendship that worked well for them in professional circles.

Celebrities

Famous people carry a great deal of symbolic energy. Movie stars, musicians, authors, inventors, and entrepreneurs appear in dreams frequently. Princess Diana, when she was alive, was one of the common celebrities reported in women's dreams. For many, she epitomized a fairy-tale princess, golden with promise, who did not seem to be really recognized or loved by her prince. During the first term of his presidency, Bill Clinton was also an extremely common dream figure in the United States. His vitality and obvious leadership abilities seemed to strike a chord with men and women alike. As they sorted through power issues in themselves and others, dreams of the president offered a forum in which to encounter and explore the dynamics involved. Celebrities are usually emblems of the quality or activity for which they are most well known. Just as generic characters are stereotypes of personality traits, celebrities are often shorthand symbols for outstanding talents and attributes. The meaning of any given celebrity seems to be a combination of the thing the dreamer most identifies with them and their overall public persona. In some dreams, a celebrity may represent someone close to you who has a similar quality or interest. More often though, celebrities tend to reflect resources within the dreamer that are ideal for applying to current goals or problems.

So if you dream of getting on stage with Madonna to sing a duet, what does that imply? If the duet goes well, it suggests that you may be calling on a part of yourself that is resilient, feisty, and highly artistic. This may be the side of yourself to trust as you audition for the school play or buy the new outfit to wear on your blind date. Although most celebrities became famous for a talent or activity, they may actually represent something that is even more meaningful to you. One man who had experienced only brief initial success in his career kept dreaming of running into John Travolta. Since there was no one in his life who seemed to have similar traits, he sensed that the actor was representing a quality in himself. He had absolutely no interest in the theater or in acting. But John Travolta is also a person who experienced real success and stature in his profession only after his peers had spent several years underestimating him and diminishing his talents. Travolta's astounding comeback and popularity in the second phase of his career made him the ideal image to represent the dreamer's own ability to make a greater contribution despite his years of disappointment and frustration. Some people actually ripen psychically during long dry spells and build up incredible skills and assets they put to good use when they encounter the right opportunity. Although he has not yet fully realized all his ambitions, the image of Travolta has brought this man surprising encouragement.

To receive the gift from a celebrity character, you'll have to hone in on the quality they represent and decide whether it pertains to someone in your life or some aspect of yourself that might come in handy.

1. *Identify the trait.* Consider the outstanding trait for which the celebrity is famous. Now consider what personality characteristic you associate with that person. What is their magic? What makes this person different from others in their profession? If you dream of comic Rodney Dangerfield, why did your dreaming mind choose him rather than, say, Jerry Seinfield? Is it because you're feeling you're not getting any respect? When you can spell out in a word or two the qualities this person stands for in your mind, then you shouldn't have any trouble with the second step.

2. *Decide whose trait is being shown.* If you feel Meryl Streep is the greatest actress in the world, then you may easily recognize that you've been dreaming about your fascinating but demanding roommate who is something of a drama queen. If you're trying to work on your social skills and ask thoughtful questions during conversations, then you may recognize that Larry King appeared in your dreams to underscore and inspire your blossoming conversational potentials.

3. *Consider the implications.* Celebrity dreams may seem short and sweet or even corny, but they convey powerful energy and inform us about our hidden qualities and those of people we care about. If you determine that the celebrity represents a quality in yourself you'd like to foster, don't assume this means you have to try to follow their career path or emulate their precise style. Remember that dreams have an uncanny knack for depicting the essence of something. The way you choose to put that energy to work and what form it will take in life is up to you.

Soul Connections

Over the years of working with so many dreams, I've slowly come to the conclusion that some dream characters are actually linked to us through our spirit. Many people have ongoing relationships with a dream character who seems to operate as some kind of guide or protective presence. Others have had dreams of deceased relatives over the years and feel convinced in their minds and hearts that these were not only dreams, but actual communications from loved ones. While it is important not to jump to conclusions every time a mysterious character appears in a dream, I feel it is also important to remain open-minded about the possibility that we are multidimensional beings. Perhaps we do have friends, guides, angels, and loved ones who visit us in our dreams. Perhaps most important of all is the fact that these types of dreams usually bring such healing and uplifting gifts. While the jury is out trying to capture proof of our spiritual nature, you can proceed to accept the blessings and encouragement that may come to you through these fascinating dreams.

If you dream of a departed loved one or a spiritual support coming to give encouragement, try not to obsess about whether or not your instincts about the origin of the dream are correct. Whether a dream guide is a guardian from the universe or a part of your own psyche, the guidance and support you receive is the important thing on which to focus. Someday we'll understand more about the nature of these dreams and our connection with the big picture, but for now you can evaluate the meaning of your dream by the implication provided. Are you being shown the way, encouraged to sustain efforts despite disappointment, or reminded to call upon your faith? One typical theme of this type is the appearance of a wise elder or sage telling you to face your fears or let go of an old grudge. Another common theme is that of an animal leading you through precarious terrain into safety. In the latter case, the meaning of the dream suggests following your intuition, allowing the less glamorous side of yourself to navigate through current challenges. Whether the loving creature is a symbol of your instincts or is indeed a spiritual helper, the advice is sound, wholesome, and often of immediate benefit.

These types of dreams usually have a prominent message or implication. Draw your conclusion about the point of the dream and then run it through your own filters of discernment. These should include: common sense, personal values, spiritual faith, and psychological wholesomeness. If the dream message is meant to be taken seriously, it will generally be a match with your existing ideals. In some cases, these dreams challenge us to transcend our fears or to become better people. But even when that occurs, these special dreams usually pull us back into our center, returning us to what is important in life. The underlying message is usually about being more true to yourself and your ideals. In other words the message of the dream should make you feel more like yourself, not pulled off your path. If you have doubts about how to apply the advice you've received or whether or not to follow it, ask for some follow-up insights. Be open and honest in your request and you will find coincidental signs cropping up that help give you an indication of the lessons behind this experience.

Working with Dream Characters

If you ever have trouble determining what or who a dream character is representing, keep in mind that the dream as a whole should have some internal consistency. That is, even though it may appear chaotic from a logical perspective, there is an internal logic to your production and those characters were not just thrown in willy-nilly. When you properly identify the meaning of a character, your understanding of the entire dream will fall into place. If you're on the wrong track about a character, you'll have to bend over backwards to come up with any reasonable motivation behind the dream.

A young man working at a high-pressure position in a busy company began having nightmares about a vicious badger that was breaking into his home and attacking his dog. One way to interpret this dream would be to say that the badger was a part of him that was very self-critical and hardworking. However, this really wasn't true. He was an easygoing young man who worked hard to please his supervisors but was not overly self-critical. With this interpretation of the character, the dream doesn't make sense. This is always a sign to back off, let go of that theory, and try another. In considering the qualities of the wild creature, he described it as violent, invasive, hostile, and domineering. This aptly described a new supervisor he had who'd recently been placed in charge of a project that was understaffed. Everyone was a bit intimidated by this man's temper, rough style, and insistence that people toe the line before there was much sense of a team developed. In fact, this man seemed to always be badgering the dreamer to accomplish the impossible to meet an unrealistic deadline. When the dream character was viewed as representing the hostile boss, the entire dream made sense. The young man felt invaded, threatened, and to some extent violated by the way this supervisor walked through boundaries and threatened people's sense of autonomy over their work.

Your sense about what a character represents should fit the plot and mood of the dream. When this happens, you'll understand more about your genuine reactions to the events in your life and about the motivations and agendas of those around you. Life will become easier to navigate and interpersonal relationships will become much easier to understand and enjoy.

Dream Symbols

Although more has probably been written about symbols than any other aspect of dreamwork, they remain a challenging part of deciphering dreams. One reason for the confusion and difficulty surrounding this area is that many sources of information about symbolism come from ancient texts, different cultures, and historical perspectives. There is usually a kernel of truth in most ideas about what symbols represent, but it's difficult to get a satisfactory answer to today's puzzles by using those sources exclusively. And rarely does one interpretation of an image have universal application.

The information in this chapter comes from actual dreams—large numbers of them—and the lives of contemporary people. Most people working with dream analysis agree that we're just beginning to grasp the way dream images represent complex factors in our lives. So ideas about the meaning of any symbol should be considered to be what we believe so far.

Tornadoes

The weather conditions in a dream tend to reflect the emotional climate of the dreamer or the forces with which the dreamer contends. Tornado dreams are extremely prevalent throughout the United States and they seem to represent some kind of emotional storm that is threatening. The storm can represent something as real and recognizable as a recent argument or as subtle as unconscious anxiety or anger.

Often the tornado represents someone in the dreamer's life who is prone to fits of temper or verbal blasts. For others, the tornado has represented a sense of crisis about a specific and unwanted situation.

Teeth

At their most fundamental level, teeth seem to represent fidelity to self. That is, the degree to which we uphold our decisions, respect our inner preferences, and remain loyal to what we love and value. In an age when we are taught to hedge our bets, go along with the majority, or stick with situations that are a poor fit because of potential rewards, many of us dream of losing our teeth or finding they are misshapen or unhealthy. This often occurs when the reasons for a compromise are powerful indeed and our awareness of more individual needs has been pushed aside.

Threat or harm to teeth often reflects a compromise that is exacting a high (but private) cost to you. Teeth that return to health or wholeness often symbolize the emergence into a situation that permits you greater freedom to be yourself.

Snakes

Snakes are incredibly prevalent in dreams, and they often have special significance. There are four quite different meanings associated with snake imagery.

1. *Snakes symbolize trouble.* This is the most common association I find with this image. The snake pit, the snake in the grass, or the threatening snake is usually a symbol of a situation that holds tricky and worrisome potential. The situation is usually difficult to grasp or control, and has an off-putting or repelling element.
2. *Snakes can operate as a phallic symbol—most notably when the dream has a sexual nuance, takes place in the bedroom, or involves penetration or embrace with the snake.*
3. *Snakes can represent a situation that offers the potential for transcending a limiting pattern (sometimes referred to as transformation).* This is most often the case when the snake bites you but it is not fatal, or when you are forced to face the snake in an encounter that is almost ritualistic.
4. *Snakes can be references to the passage into the afterlife.* People who are dying or who have recently lost a loved one will often dream of snakes.

The varying interpretations of this image make it necessary for you to check the plot of your dream for verification. If the snake is merely frightening and troublesome, it is likely to represent a tricky problem you're dealing with. The snake that makes contact with your body or climbs in bed with you may be a reference to sexuality. A snake that challenges but doesn't harm you may indicate a situation with the potential for surprising growth for you. And finally, if you have recently lost a loved one, you may dream about a snake in the initial stages of grief.

Guns

Guns are associated with power, aggression, and in some cases masculine energy or sexuality. Sometimes in dreams we are threatened by a gun, or frightened by someone who is carrying a gun. In such cases, it is likely that the gun represents the power of a particular person or situation to intimidate or harm us. In some cases, the armed assailant represents a portion of the psyche that may be "gunning for you," in some sense. If the gun is a weapon you carry in the dream, it may be a symbol of personal power for you.

Guns represent directed force in most instances. A threatening figure may represent someone in your life who is exerting undue influence or a portion of your psyche that is operating like an inner bully trying to force you to follow a certain agenda. If you are having trouble finding, keeping, or using your own gun in the dream, this implies some confusion and conflict about wielding power in a current situation.

Knives

Cutting instruments tend to represent experiences that are hurtful or make us feel separate. When there is an injury from a knife in a dream, it usually reflects a recent cutting remark or experience that wounded our feelings. Many women and teenage girls dream of a lone man chasing them, brandishing a knife. In many cases, this dream is associated with sexual pursuit of some kind and there is usually an unsettling quality about the relationship or the pursuit involved. Men are more likely to dream of a fight in which a knife is pulled. In these cases, there is usually some conflict between opposing forces or agendas.

The physical threat or harm in the dream usually represents an emotional hurt or a threat to feelings in some way. A lone man with a knife is more likely to represent a man who is pursuing the female dreamer sexually and evoking ambivalent feelings in her.

Clothing

Clothes tend to represent either the persona we are presenting to others or the identity we're living in at the time. In this sense, a goofy costume may reflect where you're coming from with regard to a current situation, such as letting your vampy side show or acting the clown to gain acceptance. Clothing that is incongruous to the situation reveals the mindset you're using in that situation or the profile you are striving to present. Inadequate or inappropriate clothing that makes you embarrassed suggests that in the current situation you may feel ill-prepared for the role you're in or uncomfortable because you can't put on the kind of show that may be customary in that context. Clothing that is too small, dating back to childhood, or too constricting suggests that something in a current situation is restricting you or holding you back. It is common to dream of being unable to find your suit or outfit for an important occasion and then searching frantically to locate it, or at least to improvise some makeshift ensemble. These dreams reflect anxiety about being adequately prepared and able to meet the obligations of current demands and expectations.

If you are aware in the dream of a problem with the clothing, then this suggests you are already conscious of the tensions that are affecting you in waking life. If you are unaware in the dream that you are dressed in a bizarre manner and only notice this oddity upon awakening, then it is likely the dream is explaining the source of feelings you have not yet understood.

Food

Food typically represents a kind of experience or a type of energy to be taken in. One such dream is that of being at a banquet yet being unable to eat due to some restriction. This suggests that the rich experiences of life are somehow being held at bay, either by an inner restriction or due to circumstances beyond your control. Other themes involve searching for or consuming specific foods. Generally speaking, proteins and meats represent strength while sweets represent gratifying experiences that may or may not be good for you. Fruits and grains are associated with fertile, generative capacities and greens symbolize new potentials and the promise of ideas and impulses that are now beginning. Unwholesome or rotten food reflects an experience that is foul or toxic to you which for some reason you may be inclined to accept or take on. If you are dieting, it is true that you may dream of eating a favorite food you crave, but more commonly the food in dreams can be considered a representation of different types of experiences.

The preparation of food represents the formulation and creation of something important, either an experience for others or a creative project of your own. The consumption of food represents the taking in of an experience. If you eat a foreign object or something that cannot be digested, the implication is that you've tried to swallow an event but are having trouble accepting it or making sense of it.

Elevators

Elevators tend to appear in dreams featuring some kind of bizarre malfunction. You push a button and go sideways or fly hurtling upward through the roof. Others report that the elevator crashes and they are either killed in the dream or emerge shakily from a horrifying fall of many stories. As with all symbols of movement, elevators tend most often to reflect our progress with a current question or problem. One young woman, promoted into a stressful position that left her rattled and bewildered, dreamed repeatedly that no matter what floor she requested the elevator soared upward uncontrollably at breakneck speed. She had the giddy sense of being forced upward, unable to control her speed or destination. People who are experiencing a sudden increase in power, responsibility, or recognition report this dream, which I call The Upward Fall, rather frequently. It seems to matter very little that the circumstances they are struggling with are positive (except perhaps in the sense that we tend not to give ourselves permission to feel negative emotions about positive events and thus our responses are less well processed). As with all dreams of elevator malfunctions, this one highlights the sensation of loss of control and the disconnection between what you ask for and what you get. In dreams of sideways movement, the individual is usually going through a concerted effort to make progress that is essentially futile or inappropriate. The implication is that even if your current plan works, you may find that you've only succeeded in prolonging your stay in a situation that cannot possibly fulfill your needs. Rather than pursue the carrot that is in front of your nose, or the relationship you are trying repeatedly to mend, take a step back and consider what you want for the long-term. Then set out to move in a manner consistent with what you really want to have. Most people dream of elevators crashing or falling when there is something causing a sinking feeling in their lives or when a particular habit, relationship, or problem seems to be slipping out of control. I do not find these dreams to be predictors of danger, but in one sense they do serve as signals that it is time to stop pretending that nothing is wrong. If you are getting into debt, eating everything that isn't nailed down, or letting things slide at work, these daytime signals say the same thing as the falling elevator. Something is getting away from you and it's time to pay attention and at least be honest with yourself about it. The good news is that getting clear and conscious in your own mind about the situation is the most empowering step. From there you will start to see options differently and you will have a hunch about the most painless and effective way to correct whatever has gone off track.

Elevators' movements reflect how well your conscious attitudes and actions are serving to move you toward the conditions you desire. If the elevator malfunctions, then you are not getting what you bargained for or you may be contributing unwittingly to a pattern that is no longer in your best interests.

Colors

The colors in your dreams are like emotional tones, reflecting not only how you may currently feel about a certain situation or issue but also what potential it holds for you. In this respect, it is worth our while to learn more about the symbolism of color. It has the capacity to reveal nuances about situations that we are unaware of consciously.

Color in dreams can be highly significant, particularly when the item in question appears to be colored in an unusual manner. For example, a red wedding dress, a purple sky, or a blue elephant are not only symbols in themselves, but are encoded with additional meaning because the dreaming mind has gone to the trouble of creating them in an unusual (and meaningful) color. In addition to having certain relatively universal symbolic values, colors also carry positive and negative potentials. In this sense, red may represent powerful feelings and vitality on the positive side, but it may signal danger on the negative side. For this reason, it is necessary to consider the qualities of the symbol in question, whether it appears in a positive or negative light, in order to be sure what the color implies. A red rosebud would almost certainly suggest strong feelings, vitality, and the promise of future growth; it would not be difficult to determine this as a symbol carrying the positive energy of the color red. A knife blade dripping with red blood which looked like a murder weapon could also easily be recognized as carrying the negative energy of the color red, conveying some kind of warning to consider. In cases where the symbol is not obviously positive or negative, such as in a red sports car, the overall plot of the dream sequence in which it appears will usually clarify whether the color is conveying its positive or negative potential.

Green

Positive Potential: The color green is associated with life and growth for obvious reasons. New grass, plants of all kinds, as well as trees (a powerful symbol of life) are all green. If the image in your dream is some kind of plant life form, then it is most probably reflecting your own potential for future growth as well as your current subjective state of vitality. People who are going through transitions often dream of repotting plants, caring for trees, or working in their garden with fledgling starter plants. This kind of imagery serves to underscore the sense of newness and potential that is present during times that can feel uncomfortable and uncertain. Others considering new careers may dream of working in a green office building or buying a new green car. Several women have told me their dreams of going out to buy themselves a new green dress. In most cases, these women were embarking on a new relationship or a new job at the time they had the dream. The sense of starting fresh, being filled with possibilities, and experiencing a sense of renewal was reflected by the color green.

Negative Potential: When the hunger for growth and fulfillment is neglected or distorted, this drive can take on a toxic, compulsive quality. Think of the green sludge on a stagnant pond or the mold on food left in the refrigerator too long and you will see the negative side of the color green. It is usually easy to discern when a dream image is made more specific by its negative green color because there is usually something repellant about it. A moldy sack of food, a big, slimy, green monster, or a green ring around the bathtub all suggest growth that is rampant but going in the wrong direction. The emotional qualities reflected by the negative side of green are envy, jealousy, insecurity, greed, and a compulsion to change and try new things before giving the old ones a fair shot. It's been my experience that this negative aspect of the color green is actually an erroneous attempt at finding happiness and progress which has been prevented from finding a healthy outlet, now sprouting up and taking control from another direction. If you have something green in your dream which you determine to be reflecting a negative potential, consider what corrective action you should take. There are usually bills that have been postponed, dietary changes you know would be healthy for you, or a relationship or environmental condition draining your vitality. In addition to considering how to clean up any messy situation in your life, give some thought to what potential, talent, or healthy appetite has been held in check so that it was forced to transmute into the negative green energy shown in your dream. One woman who dreamed of wearing a very sickly green dress when she met her lover confided to me that she'd been involved with this married man for a number of years. Over time, she'd grown almost sick with jealousy and frustration because he refused to leave his wife as he'd promised and she became constantly preoccupied with the situation. In her case, the negative green dress showed that her whole being was clothed in these compulsive thoughts and feelings. Yet on a deeper level, her hunger to love and be loved, to have a home and family was a natural manifestation of green energy, of the need for life to fulfill itself. Ironically, the situation of being involved with someone she could not have had slowly turned her normal feelings into unwholesome, troubling ones that seemed to have a life of their own. It was some time before she could bring herself to end the relationship that couldn't bring her the fulfillment she wanted, but the dream had planted a seed of recognition that eventually strengthened her resolve to create space in her life for a more complete relationship.

Yellow

Positive Potential: Yellow is associated with sensitivity to feelings and subtle influences. In its positive form, yellow sunlight, flowers, or a golden beam of light can symbolize a kind of intuitive certainty that your hunch or instinct is correct. This is a kind of knowledge that doesn't have to come piecemeal, as with logical deductions, but comes over you in a wave. Typically, if the image in your dream is bright and positive, the implication is that your take on things can be trusted and you can expect to be able to feel your way through the current situation.

Negative Potential: In its negative form, yellow carries the energy of being compelled to feel or behave in ways that are not necessarily desirable to you.

One woman dreamed of driving an ugly yellow car that her parents had given her because she was reluctant to tell them she didn't want it. She was dealing with a problematic situation through the programming and expectations of her parents—in this sense, being driven by expectations that diminished her capacity to make authentic choices for herself. Another woman dreamed of being at a family gathering dressed in a bright yellow dress with matching yellow shoes and purse which she would never have chosen for herself in waking life. She was struggling with an important decision and part of her difficulty lay in her habit of viewing her choices through her family's eyes. If the object in your dream is colored a striking yellow and it doesn't suit the occasion or your taste, you may consider whether the negative compulsive energy of yellow is being reflected. Consider whether you are being too sensitive to the preferences of others or if you may be operating out of empathy and need to draw more specific boundaries for yourself. I believe that our traditional folkloric reference to yellow as cowardly is associated with this sensitivity. But in truth, it has nothing to do with moral courage, but is instead a by-product of psychic and intuitive overload. An influx of too many impressions and concerns makes it difficult to think clearly or know your genuine preference. If your dream has highlighted something in yellow that strikes you as wrong, take time to sort out what is your genuine preference or in your best interests before making a decision. By weeding out the urges that come from the attitudes and preferences of others, you'll feel much freer to make a solid decision.

Blue

Positive Potential: Blue is a symbol of authenticity and truth. The color has a certain spiritual overtone because it hints at a level of honesty that comes right from your soul. During a time of personal upheaval, I dreamed of riding a blue elephant out of the jungle to safety in a nearby village. The dream suggested that my best tactic for finding my way in the current predicament was to stick with what I knew to be true and trust that I would come out all right. That turned out to be excellent advice, and I often dream of some blue creature coming to guide me when I have forgotten that the simple way is often the best. Blue is also a color associated with teaching and speaking your truth, or the particular wisdom that is unique to you. People often dream of a special blue object or creature when considering career moves or a change in a relationship. This symbolism implies that your decision will be wiser if you keep track of your personal truth—what you need, want, and value most of all—and the side of life that is most sacred to you. It is fine to weigh other factors as well in your decision, but do not abandon or overlook this true-blue part of life.

Negative Potential: Almost everyone is familiar with the idea that blue is a symbol of depression or sadness. In dreams, you may find yourself in a blue room, wearing blue clothes, or visiting a blue house if the color is presenting its negative potential. One woman who was having difficulty dealing with a very cranky supervisor dreamed that she visited his house and found it empty of furniture and the walls and floors all colored blue. This dream clued her in that her boss's grouchiness was not merely a petty problem or a nasty personality streak but that he was genuinely having problems with depression and felt empty inside. This knowledge enabled her to respond differently to him and to be supportive of his needs rather than take the situation personally. When the color blue depicts this negative potential, there is usually a palpable feeling of sadness in the dream or a haunting quality about the image in question. It is useful to note that the negative side of blue usually can be traced back to questions or issues with authenticity. That is, it deals specifically with the loss of sense of identity or with feeling depressed due to over-identification with external roles. With the great emphasis we place upon success and achievement these days, it is all too easy to misplace your center, the part of you that is most essentially yourself. This leads to the baffling sensation that although everything you can point to is good, everything in your life feels wrong. If this applies to you, here is one way to retrieve your inner compass. Beginning with small things first, start choosing what is right for you, telling small truths, and evaluating things according to your gut response. Decline invitations to events that you really don't like, and make time for the things you really care about. Bit by bit, practice making choices that suit you deeply. Before you know it, your center of gravity will be back in place and you'll automatically make choices that expand your life into greater expressions of who you really are.

Orange

Positive Potential: Orange is associated with vitality and feelings, particularly human emotion. In its positive form, orange denotes the ability to identify with the emotions of others and to be at home in the world of human passions and needs. Most often, the positive orange symbol in a dream will be in some natural form such as changing leaves, fruit, or in the sky. One woman dreamed of replacing her blue dress with a flowing embroidered gown of orange and gold. This dream came at a time when she was ready to make some profound changes in her life and was more accepting of both her own feelings and those of others. This hearty acceptance of the feeling nature of life is a healthy shift for most of us, and I find that orange crops up in the dreams of those who are making changes that are more profound than they may realize. This may come at a time when you are leaving behind a structure (such as graduating from school, or moving into a larger sphere). The robust orange color supports this move into an expanded life, suggesting that you are steady and sure enough to create your own boundaries in the world and to enrich those with whom you come in contact.

Negative Potential: In its negative form, orange represents strong emotions that have a toxic or draining quality. One woman who worked in customer service dreamed of a large orange spider weaving a deadly web around her. She was so kindly and sensitive that customers took advantage of her capacity to listen and dumped their assorted tales of woe on her in addition to their business complaints. This accumulation of problems that were not in her power to solve was building up, leaving her disoriented and oddly anxious all the time. This dream helped her take her discomfort more seriously and she eventually accepted a transfer into another department where she was not inclined to serve as the toxic waste dump for others. When orange appears in its negative form, there is an uncomfortable quality about it like the jarring sensation of a wrong note in a song or mismatched colors. It may strike you as ugly, tacky, or an ill-chosen item. Consider whether you may be the recipient of someone else's drama these days, and if so, whether the role you've taken on is really appropriate and helpful. If you yourself are embroiled in an overly emotional problem, consider whether there is any way to steady things or reduce the tempestuous quality in the situation. Sometimes just accepting what has already occurred and admitting that you'll have to proceed from precisely where you are can help to calm the stormy emotions enough for you to navigate again and make wise choices.

Red

Positive Potential: Red represents life energy, a strong force of vitality that is truly dynamic. In its positive form, red is associated with a zestful approach to life, a sense of exhilaration, and excitement. In some dreams, red signals passion, often romantic in nature, but also in the larger sense, a passion for life and an appreciation for the physical and earthy side of life. Women often dream of wearing provocative red gowns when they are enjoying a loving relationship that is particularly satisfying and stimulating to them. Men tend to dream of driving bright red sports cars that are high-powered and responsive when they are feeling appreciative of their vitality, success, or a relationship. I have noticed that a hunger for a red item, such as a car, red shoes, or another possession often coincides with a readiness to step into your power more fully. Conflict over a choice of colors in a dream, when red is the color you want implies that someone in your life or some part of your-self is attempting to hold you back from making straightforward decisions and assuming your full authority over your life.

Negative Potential: When dynamic energy runs amok, there is the potential for danger. In its negative form, red is an almost universal warning signal. It implies the presence of a threat to your physical well-being; the danger is immediate and usually intense. This does not mean that if you dream of a red stain you are about to die, but images in red should be evaluated carefully and with a certain respect. Usually, as with other negative forms of color, there is an unmistakable aura of dread, danger, or harm involved so it is relatively easy to recognize the presence of a warning signal. (The exception to this rule is that women often dream of blood or red stains just prior to or during their menstrual period and these dreams do not appear to be warning signals, but rather a recognition of the menstrual flow.) Many dreamers report with some dismay how real their wounds were in a nightmare and how realistic the sensation was that they were bleeding to death. In many cases, such dreams appear to use the image of blood as both a warning signal and a metaphor for the loss of energy and autonomy that can occur in troubling situations or relationships. If you have a dream involving something you feel is a red warning signal, evaluate whether there are sensible steps you can take to slow down, increase your safety precautions, or stop hurtling through life at such a breakneck pace. If there is an issue that is bleeding you or taking your energy away, take whatever steps you can physically and mentally to prevent it from taking such a drastic toll on your life force. You may not be able to alter the situation itself, but at the very least you should be able to set your intention to guard your personal energy and do what you can to replenish your spirit. As with stop signs and traffic signals, if the red warnings in our dreams are responded to with care, they can serve to help us navigate safely in waking life.

Black

Positive Potential: When the color black arises in dreams, it can be an indication of tremendous readiness to explore territory that has been previously off-limits or unknown. People will often dream of a black forest or flying through a darkened sky when they are ready to examine life questions in a deeper way. Even in its positive form, the color black carries with it an aura of mystery. You may be drawn to a handsome fellow dressed in black while at the same time you wonder vaguely if he is safe. I once dreamed of a visit to hell in which I was surprised to find the ground was exceptionally fertile, so that all things, good and bad, grew there very quickly in that black soil. This let me know that although I was feeling a bit lost regarding a particular issue at that time, I was also in a place of immense possibilities and that the choices I made then would take hold quickly and have far-reaching results. The image of rich soil captures the fertile quality of the color black because it symbolically contains the seeds of all other colors, and therefore all potentials. In some cases, dreams remind us that even our time in unknown territory, with problems that resist our best efforts, can result in creative breakthroughs and immense growth if we will meet them with greater awareness of these possibilities.

Negative Potential: The negative form of black speaks more eloquently about our attitudes toward a problem than about the difficulty itself. When a symbol or place is black in a dream, it usually suggests that the issue in question is still very much outside our conscious awareness. We cannot see well in the darkness, and I find that dreams taking place in the nighttime or in black settings depict questions that carry heavy unconscious programming or have not been consciously explored. This need not be a cause for dread or fear, but instead can be used as a cue to begin opening yourself to intuitive impressions and helpful coincidences that may shed light on the real reasons for a predicament. An animal or object that is black also suggests that there is an element of unconscious material at work in the current situation. Many dreamers have found a kind of uneasy comfort in assuming there is more to their current challenge than meets the eye and in striving to take a balanced approach to help them tolerate the sense of something just beyond their reach. When dreams go to the effort to present black imagery to bridge the gap to consciousness, you may assume it is a sign that you are ready to explore the potentials and the fears that are resonant in this color.

White

Positive Potential: White is featured in many dreams with spiritual overtones. People find themselves in radiant, white homes surrounded by beings dressed in white robes, eating or drinking from gleaming white dishes. In this form, the color white is associated with light, illumination in both the visual and the conceptual sense. Similarly, a lovely, white flower or an airy, white butterfly are easily recognizable as emblems of hope and lightheartedness. White clothes, homes, or animals all suggest an openness and a faith in something good that is yet to come. Some people who have felt they'd seen it all and been through so much that they'd lost all faith and innocence have been surprised by dreams featuring the restorative nature of the color white. It is not uncommon after a nasty, tumultuous passage to dream of wearing cool, flowing, white clothes, resting in an airy, white home, or being in a tranquil, white room so soothing it seems to bathe you inside and out. These images are conveying the capacity for renewal and cleansing that is inherent in the psyche and which comes to the front when needed. In this sense, the color white doesn't always suggest that the situation you are in is brand new, but that you possess the capacity to be renewed and soothed no matter what has happened or where you have been.

Negative Potential: In its negative form, the color white suggests a kind of positive veneer over more complex issues and conditions. In the desire to be positive thinkers or to convey the impression of being a winner in life, some have developed a strained positivism that involves the denial of a more sophisticated or earthy view of conditions and life. White plastic items in dreams often reflect this pattern, as does white paint, shoe polish, and makeup. One woman dreamed that her white car could no longer be kept clean no matter what she did or how often she washed it. It continued to collect grime from the road and the weather conditions. Her frustration at this lack of perfection reflected a growing uneasiness with a similar approach that she took to life itself. As most of us do, she had outgrown the constructed life that was now getting rough around the edges and was frustrated and hungry for something more real. If the white item in your dream strikes you as tacky and artificial, or if some other color or fabric is showing through, you may consider whether it is time to withdraw your energy from maintaining some presentation or mode that you have outgrown. Should the item belong to someone else in the dream, the implication is that you may want to take a second look at someone or something in your life that is being presented as pristine and pure but which may have ulterior motives or a quite different agenda.

Man-Made Colors

It is less typical for dreams to feature man-made variations of colors such as neon red, hot pink, or iridescent lime green. When these day-glow colors are used in conjunction with symbols, they imply similar meaning as the original colors, but with interesting differences. The suggestion is that there is something attention-grabbing about the situation that is serving as a distraction or a source of fascination. Someone close to you may be assuming an attitude that is not sincere or may present themselves in such a way as to captivate and consume the energy of others. Be wary of committing fully to the opportunity or person who comes clothed in fluorescent colors before you have deduced what portion of the situation is real and what is simulated.

Colors Can Deepen Our Understanding

Colors can enrich our recognition of the deeper meaning of a symbol, showing us how an event or issue is impacting us as well as what possibilities it holds for us. If you do not as yet recall the colors in your dreams, don't be dismayed. Learning more about the significance of colors may encourage your dreaming mind to make greater use of them and will give your conscious mind more motivation and understanding to help improve your recall of them. Some research suggests that is it normal to dream in color, but that for many of us, the details of dream recall fade rather quickly. As a result, when we look back at a dream hours later, we remember it in black and white. I believe there are also marked individual differences in the way our dreams are depicted visually. Some of us *always* dream in vivid color and are amazed when we have an entire black and white dream that looks like an old newsreel. Such dreams can imply that the pattern or story being depicted dates back to the dreamer's early history or to a time when things appeared to be limited to two choices (black or white). Others find that their precognitive dream fragments are in a hazy photo-negative style while their normal dreams are brightly and realistically colored. Because of these individual differences, it is important for you to get well acquainted with your normal dreaming style so that when variations occur, you have a good basis for detecting what they may mean to you. Sometimes clients report that the majority of a dream was monochromatic, but a single image was brightly colored. When this happens, I believe it is because the emotional qualities and potentials (represented by that color) are breaking through into consciousness more fully. When something comes alive for you in waking life, it is likely to be reflected by unusually vivid color in your dreams.

Special Contemporary Images

Few people have dreams anymore about taking a barge across the Nile or having our favorite camel refuse to walk. Today, our dreams are filled with cars, computers, airline crashes, and plastic surgery. Contemporary images operate with the same logical consistency as all symbols, and their prevalence in our dreams is a testimony to their shared as well as individual meaning. Here are some of the images you may encounter in your dreams.

Shopping Malls

Malls are associated with social customs and making choices. In dreams, malls often serve as a background when we are meeting friends or trying to obtain something that suits our needs. One key to understanding the mall imagery is that it seldom appears in dreams dealing with professional activities or the meaning of life. Instead, we find ourselves dealing with people, friends, lovers, rivals, and salespeople in these dreams. Many women have rather involved shopping dreams about trying to get just the right thing for themselves or a friend. In this way, the image represents the social milieu in which we operate. The obstacles and assistance we encounter there symbolize the real-life forces (internal and external) that play a role in the choices we make and the satisfaction we experience.

Naturally, teens have many dreams of dramatic episodes with friends at the mall. True love is won and lost in front of Gap and Baskin Robbins. Women tend to have dreams about choice and identity set in the mall. This image tells you that you're dealing with social and communication issues, trying to be true to yourself, while at the same time wishing to satisfy and please those you care about most. Pay close attention to the events that inhibit satisfying resolution in these dreams; they reflect the concerns or patterns that prevent you from letting everything fall into place.

Parking Structures

Parking structures are almost inevitably sources of confusion in dreams. They are difficult to navigate because it's tough to tell the various levels apart, and all too often there is some anxious mix-up involving a missing car. This image (made of steel and concrete) reflects the solidity of contemporary mores and pressures. We usually dream of parking structures when we're sorting through our personal preferences in light of our professional goals and drive to excel. Getting lost in a parking structure symbolizes feeling overwhelmed and disoriented by the consensual opinion of how life is supposed to go. If your car is missing, this implies that it feels as if the real you got lost somewhere along the way while you were trying to succeed and meet expectations.

This image more often is connected with career and life path issues than with personal relationships. The deceptive appearance of the circular structure seems to reflect the seductive illusions of the good life or making it. You can park where you're supposed to park, pay for your ticket, and at the end of the day, come back to discover that your car (self) has been lost. Although the structure represents the current maze of your conflict, there is nothing inherently wrong with any of these rules. They are only inappropriate to the extent that they are a mismatch with your core desires and hopes for your life.

Broken Glass

In the past five years, the image of broken glass has been appearing quite frequently in dreams. Women specifically have dreams of walking on broken glass, being surrounded by shards of glass, and most distressingly, of chewing and eating broken glass. On one level, this image conveys the symbolism of a cutting instrument, which often represents wounding words and experiences. A second dimension of the image is that of something shattered and broken. So the suggestion is that of an experience or expectation which was all right when whole, but which has turned dangerous and harmful when fragmented. My sense of this image so far is that it reflects the shattering of an expectation which has proven hurtful and threatening to the dreamer. For the most part, these dreams have been linked to difficulties in personal relationships more often than career conflicts.

A simple way to consider this image is that something has snapped or changed, and because of that you are exposed to hurt of one kind or another. If you are eating the glass, remember that taking something into your mouth represents taking in an experience. Women have told me they believe this image shows they've been trying to take something painful and swallow it, rather than acknowledge how painful it is to them. If you're walking on broken glass, consider how your direction in life is being impacted by painful forces, either because of your upbringing or due to current circumstances. The vivid horror of this image is designed to draw your attention to pain you may have been downplaying to yourself. The purpose is not to make you feel like a victim, but to encourage you to maintain a threshold of well-being in your life.

Computers

Computers are a symbol of the brain and the way we process information. Computer glitches often represent errors in thinking, outdated belief systems, or faulty logic. The various parts of the computer also have metaphorical meaning. The hard drive seems to be associated with the driven parts of the dreamer's personality, the screen with perceptions, the memory with memory, and the printer with the realization of plans.

Twilight zone malfunctions typically reflect distortions in the way we're approaching a current issue or problem. Just as we repeatedly try what is obviously not working with our computers, we tend to respond to life's puzzles and disappointments with redoubled efforts using strategies that have already proven unsuitable. Pay attention to your response in the dream, because it provides clues about how to tackle the real-life issues that are driving you crazy.

Factories

Factories and processing plants reflect the worker part of your personality. The conditions around the factory symbolize the health of your urge to contribute and create. People working in jobs that pay well but discourage their spirit often dream of hideous sweat-shop factories filled with moaning, abused workers. These dramatic images don't merely parody the job they currently hate, they suggest that sustained participation in such an environment is damaging their own generative abilities.

Pay close attention to the attributes of the factory. Is it high-tech and creepy like the Borg station on *Star Trek*? Or manic and insincere? Whatever imbalances appear, consider how they reflect the current health of your urge to contribute to the world. While we all must make the best decisions we can for family and our futures, it is wise to consider the effects of long-term exposure to conditions that erode your capacity to love your work.

Hospitals

When you dream of hospitals, the implication is that the psyche is delivering a message about some part of your life that deserves more care. Hospitals are where we go when something has happened to us and we want to heal. So dreams set in this background serve as a heads-up that you should turn your intention toward supporting your comfort and well-being as much as your responsibilities and ambitions.

The elements within the hospital that support or ignore your needs reflect factors in your life that are impacting your well-being. Brusque experts who ignore your requests usually represent your own stoic refusal to cut yourself any slack or to acknowledge your needs. Failed procedures can symbolize mistaken attempts to solve lasting issues with quick fixes. Think about what would improve the dream situation to better support your healing, and then try to translate the essence of that into behaviors and choices in your waking life.

Condoms

Aside from the obvious connection to the prevention of conception, condoms appear in dreams that deal with other relationship concerns as well. Many people refer to prophylactics as protection, and in dreams they tend to symbolize psychological protection from all sorts of vulnerability in relationships.

This image deals with emotional as well as physical protection against the vulnerability of intimate relationships. Take these dreams as a reminder to proceed toward love with caution and respect for all concerned.

Toxic Substances

Typically, toxic substances represent situations, patterns, and people that contaminate our happiness and sense of self. For some people, this means the warped opinions of in-laws who pull strings and intrude from time to time. Whoever or whatever delivers the emotional toxins into your life, there is usually a special interaction with your personal chemistry that renders the situation poisonous to you. This is not altogether bad, since it means you can work on your own reactions at the same time you work on the outside to reduce exposure and distribution of the toxic experience.

There are usually two qualities that cause us to develop sensitivities to specific experiences, rendering them emotionally poisonous to us. In the first instance, we become emotionally allergic to something due to previous overexposure to it. Just like a food, drug, or other substance, if you've already been maxed-out and made sick by a certain kind of energy in your life, you can be knocked out by a very small dose of it in the future. Don't worry about the logic of this: if you're doubled over, getting a migraine headache, or suddenly having food binges, listen to what your body and your dreams are telling you. In the second type of situation, you may be poisoned by a type of energy that is so antithetical to your own that it seems like a violation of your life principle just to be around it. Trusting people often get sickened when they're thrown in with manipulators, while extreme introverts and extroverts may wear on each other in distressing ways. Whatever the source and the interaction involved, take your signals of distress seriously and do what you can immediately to stop the trashing of your energy while you strategize about how to reduce this type of contamination from your future.

Angels

When we dream of angels, we are almost always dealing with a situation that will be supported by remembering (or exploring) spiritual faith. Many people take all dreams of angels at face value and believe they have been visited by a spiritual being sent to assist them. This makes every bit as much sense as the numerous explanations designed to argue against the existence of divine support. And ultimately, a question of such mystery can only be resolved within each individual. Regardless of what you decide, dreams of this nature possess special potential to be of immediate benefit to the dreamer. As far as I can tell, this is true regardless of whether the dreamer interprets the image as an actual visitation, or a dream symbol.

These dreams tend to provide a reminder of hope and to direct our attention to the potential for healing and change within us. These images tend to appear in relation to long-standing core issues. It is a testimony to their potency that so often dreamers derive an immediate shift in perspective, relief from emotional scars, and the ability to move forward again after having felt immobilized by troubles. As any therapist will argue, any factor that permits us to change overnight is the strongest and best medicine. I would urge you to embrace the momentum of your dream experience and let it carry you forward. The particulars of your circumstance may only fall into meaningful categories after you have moved though this passage. The image of angels always carries the energy of trust and abilities waiting to be harnessed on your behalf.

Working with Symbols

By now you have seen something of the logic you can apply to any symbol that appears in your dreams. Look at the way an item functions and where you might find it in waking life. Consider any special memories you have about an object to see if it is appearing in a dream as a symbol of something related to that memory. If you wore rhinestone high heels to the prom and you dream again of those shoes, are you proceeding with a current situation in a way that is adolescent or filled with wonder? Remember that your sense of a symbol's meaning will coincide with the plot, action, and feeling of the dream. If all this is congruent, you know you've got it right, and your subjective sense of rightness is always your best signal that you've discovered the gift within your dream.

Chapter

6

The Human Body

Dreams of illness or death were once thought to be harbingers of doom. In psychological terms, they might be considered signs of depression or memories of past trauma bubbling to the surface. I believe we dream of things happening to and through the body so frequently because the dreaming mind is disposed to use physical imagery for all nature of experiences, even thoughts, feelings, and decisions. Psychological patterns, emotions, and disappointments, as well as success and healing are often depicted in dreams as physical changes or as events impacting the body. Just as computers have default settings, so the dreaming mind appears to prefer to use the language of body symbolism to express its messages.

This is why dreams seem so preoccupied with sex, violence, elimination, surgery, and bizarre circumstances involving the body. If you think of the body as representing your whole life or your lifestyle, you'll have a better chance of identifying what your dream really means.

A Physical Picture of Lived Experience

During my college years, I had a particularly painful breakup with a young man I'd been seeing. Because the connection had been deep, it took me several months to shake the idea that all my chances for happiness had been lost. Just as I was beginning to feel like myself again, I ran into my old flame and was dismayed at the feelings that washed over me. To make matters worse, he too seemed struck by our chemistry and tried to convince me that an impromptu romantic tryst would be in both our best interests. With my last shred of willpower, I managed to decline his offer and to insist that our break should be maintained to avoid further confusion. Feeling like an addict who has narrowly escaped a relapse, I went home weak-kneed, wondering if I'd made the right choice.

That night I dreamed about being in a hospital room, recovering nicely from major surgery. Because of a serious problem, I'd had to have a head transplant, and I awoke from the surgery feeling the stitches around my neck that held on my new and improved head. I had recovered so well that I was allowed to go home, and as I gathered my belongings and moved carefully, my old boyfriend swept into the room. He came close to me and said I was looking very good since the surgery, and that he'd like to give me a kiss. Immediately my hands went to the intricate stitches at my throat, as if to shield the miraculous healing that was joining my new head to my body. "Please don't kiss me now," I pleaded. "If you do, I might lose my head."

I awoke from this dream knowing that I'd made the right choice the day before. My new head represented the new attitudes and understanding that I'd gained about the romantic disappointment, and the setting of the hospital room implied that I'd been doing some important healing. The delicate stitches around my throat showed that my newfound independence was still vulnerable, however, and that contact with my old flame (the kiss) should definitely be avoided.

Physical Images and Decisions

It is typical for recent decisions to be reviewed in dreams that provide a kind of follow-up on the course of action you've chosen. Often, as in my example of the new head, a dream will support your decision by showing in a dramatic physical way how necessary it was for your well-being. In other cases, dreams will provide graphic and disturbing images in order to temper your enthusiasm or counterbalance an attitude that could be costly because it is too extreme. It is human nature to make decisions as if our options were completely good or bad. The dreaming mind is aware that life is more complex than that and it often uses physical images to draw attention to important factors we've overlooked because they've been overshadowed by our black and white view of things.

Feet

One man who was very happy because he'd just gotten engaged dreamed of taking a walk with his fiancée and feeling a severe pain in his foot. When he looked down, he discovered he was barefoot and that there was a thorny vine growing out of the back of his heel. When he tried to pull it out, several more briars erupted out of the opening in his foot, and he and his fiancée had to sit down and consider what to do since they clearly couldn't continue their walk.

Feet often represent our foundation in life, the assumptions upon which we build our existence, and the principles we use to make decisions and move forward. In a literal sense, the feet may reflect issues with our family of origin or our early foundation. The shoes on our feet often reflect the role we are using as we stride into the next chapter of our lives; or if we are barefoot, the implication is a sense of vulnerability or lack or preparation. In some cases, being barefoot may indicate a sense of freedom or naturalness, but in the majority of dreams being barefoot is paired with walking in a setting where the lack of shoes is a handicap. When bare feet are a source of pain or difficulty, the implication is that the dreamer feels ill-equipped for the journey upon which he has embarked.

In this man's dream, his problem was reflected in two ways: he was barefoot in terrain where that was a problem and he had a mysterious, thorny vine growing out of his heel. Growths in the body often symbolize psychological patterns in our lives, emotions, or reactions that have taken on a life of their own and seem to inhabit us like a parasite. Because vines grow rapidly and can spread out of control, they sometimes represent emotional complexes. In the shorthand of dream language, his mind was saying, *before you get married, you'll want to take a look at the unconscious material from your childhood. See how it has woven through your life and how it is part of your basic assumptions about life, love, and marriage.*

This dream certainly was not a sign that the young man couldn't or shouldn't get married to the woman he loved. But it was tempering his euphoria by pointing out he should examine his assumptions and patterns before setting out on this journey. When viewed from this perspective, his dream made a great deal of sense to him. His parents had bitterly divorced when he was young and their continued barbed comments about each other had subtly infected his view of romantic love and fidelity. Although consciously he chose to believe that couples can make it, unconsciously he tended to look for signs of betrayal in his partner and to interpret innocent comments as slights or signs of cooling interest. If ignored, these patterns could spring up like twisted vines and threaten the healthy vitality of a very nice relationship. He and his fiancée decided to explore some counseling and workshops in communication to help them understand their unconscious patterns and individual needs in a relationship.

If you have a striking physical image in a dream shortly after making an important decision, you can assume that the dream, no matter how bizarre, is trying to support your success by emphasizing a certain perspective or providing information you may have overlooked.

Wounding

Perhaps because our modern culture emphasizes productivity, achievement, and success, many of us have little room to explore or express the subjective costs of our lifestyle and choices. When I work with the pain and suffering expressed in the dreams of happy, highly functioning people, I have the impression of brave soldiers struggling in battle who are ignoring their loss of blood from both minor and major wounds.

This kind of dissociation is a valuable part of coping with crisis and focusing on goals and should never be confused with mere denial or spiritual cowardice. However, when we live entire decades of life as if we are under siege, this temporary heroic effort becomes a chronic style of coping. When a short-term emergency tactic is used as a long-term life strategy, we court imbalances that may come back to haunt us. We mistake our ability to keep running hard for wholeness and we're shocked when our dreams focus on severed limbs, broken hearts, and devouring cancers. Dreams that express our wounds are not trying to sabotage or even contradict the success we've built by day. Instead, they are giving voice to the parts of the psyche that have fallen out of favor with the dominant forces of the personality. In a culture where sickness, poverty, and incompetence are the most dreaded of conditions, the vulnerable or naïve side of your nature can become a psychic pariah, exiled to forgotten outskirts of life.

Dreams tend to highlight the emotional cost of behaviors engaged in over time and to amplify the voice of the side of yourself that has, for whatever reason, been repeatedly discounted.

Being Burned

One man contacted me about his vivid dream of watching a man being executed by being burned alive. In his dream, two prisoners were herded along a trail as if marching toward a death camp. They stopped, and one of the men was given food, water, and clean clothing. The other was tied to a stake, doused with flammable fluid, and torched. However, in the magical fashion of dreams, the burned prisoner did not die, and when the flames died down he and the favored prisoner continued on their march forward. The healthy man and the charred, unrecognizable prisoner staggered arm in arm toward their destination.

The dreamer said this was one of the most disturbing dreams he'd ever had and the image of the two prisoners was so gut-wrenching he knew the dream was important to understand. With the exception of post-traumatic nightmares, dreams of torture usually express the pain of some part of the dreamer that is being sacrificed in order to experience certain benefits or privileges, or to accomplish something the dreamer feels is expected of him.

In this man's case, he was set on the fast track in a technological field and had just been promoted to a new and more demanding position when he had this dream. He was marching forward with great determination but had forgotten that his original goal had been to take a lucrative job in order to accumulate funds toward a graduate program in psychology. He really wanted to be a counselor but he had temporarily shelved the idea when his interim career had proven both consuming and lucrative. The dream revealed that his dogged march along this path was, in one sense, a kind of brave trek as a prisoner. The focus was on endurance, stoicism, and putting one foot in front of the other. But the landscape was bleak and full of hardship and there was a fundamental lack of freedom and even torment involved.

The two prisoners represented two sides of this man's personality: the executive who enjoyed special privileges and the would-be counselor who was completely burned out by the lack of human contact and spiritually meaningful activities. In a way, the part of him that wanted to be a counselor was being sacrificed so that he might stay with the company where he was making progress. In response to the dream, this man decided to investigate graduate programs that would permit him to work full time and go to school so that he did not have to sabotage his success entirely in order to allow his inner counselor to be free to live. I think this was a wise direction to move towards a resolution. While the drama of our dreams sometimes seems to cry out for a drastic change, it is more often the case that we are being asked to honor parts of our nature that have been relegated to the shadows. Many imbalances can be healed when we evaluate present actions in light of long-range consequences and expand our choices to nourish the soulful and less apparent aspects of ourselves.

Death and Birth

When a chapter in your life draws to a close, you may find yourself dreaming of deaths and funerals because death usually reflects a time of change. If something new is about to dawn, you may dream of babies, pregnancies, or recovery from illness. If you are coming out of a period of mourning, or emerging from a time of withdrawal you may dream of checking out of a hospital or meeting with doctors and nurses. Physical illness and healing are often metaphors for recovery from emotional trauma. If you dream of going to a hospital or spending time as a patient, this may be a sign that you should be giving your own well-being and needs top priority. We charge through life without acknowledging the symbolic births and deaths that are a normal part of our existence. Dreams tend to illustrate these phases with scenes of actual birth and death. If you consider the phases of endings and beginnings these dreams reflect, their meaning and gifts will become more accessible to you.

Fatal Illness

One woman told me that when she was particularly stressed by circumstances, she would dream that her doctor had diagnosed her with terminal cancer. More than once, she had physical exams in response to these dreams because they were so realistic and upsetting, but the results showed her physical health to be unimpaired. Over time, she came to interpret the dreams as symbolic messages about her tendency to let herself be devoured by her work as a helping professional. She realized that the cancer was not reflecting a physical illness but rather a psychological pattern that was taking over her vitality and choices almost like an emotional cancer. It was not literally killing her, but it was destroying her life because it consumed all her energy, and sometimes threatened to grow out of control. Without creating a major upheaval, she began to decline some invitations and cases that would have unduly burdened her schedule, and she kept in mind the responsibility she had to lead a happy life as well as to make a contribution to the world.

Certainly if you have any suspicion that a dream may be highlighting an actual physical condition that is too subtle to have come to your conscious attention, get a checkup for your peace of mind. But in most dreams, a death sentence can represent any condition that takes away your natural life, the life you were meant to live. Although vitality may seem like an abstract term, the dreaming mind sees a marked distinction between an existence and a life that is worth living.

Themes of Connection and Separation

Separating from something or someone you love may evoke dreams of losing limbs. Many people who are newly divorced, breaking up, or being forced from a job will dream of a lost arm or leg.

One woman who was coping with early retirement dreamed of losing her right arm. The right side of the body often is symbolically related to work or masculine energies. Losing her professional identity and the satisfaction she had always derived from her work was indeed like suddenly losing an important part of herself. However, as she worked with these issues in therapy and self-studies, she later dreamed of getting an artificial arm that fit her perfectly but required patience and practice to learn to use. She had learned to cope with her new life and her dream reflected her tentative but gradual acceptance of retirement. This follow-up dream showed that her diligence with her own process was paying off. Instead of trying to use willpower to overcome the anxieties and grief she felt about her change of status, the deep explorations she used were helping her to find an inner stability in the midst of external changes.

Transplants

Just as the loss of a limb may reflect the severing of a tie that leaves us shocked and bereft, so the transplantation of a limb or body part may symbolize a new arrangement in our lives. It is especially common for people in new relationships to dream of getting new feet or legs, or even a new heart or a new head. Although these images may sound gruesome, in general the dreams themselves are relatively matter-of-fact and comfortable, showing the dreamer adjusting to their new parts and testing the limits of their new abilities. If you dream of getting a new body part, you can be sure that you're going through a significant change that is registering on a deep level with the psyche. (Obvious exceptions to this interpretation are individuals who are actually in need of or awaiting organ transplant surgery. In those cases, dreams of undergoing surgery are most probably related to hopes and concerns about the future.)

Contact, Affection, Intercourse

As I mentioned in the sections on sexual dreams, intercourse is often symbolic of making a connection or uniting with a particular quality in your life. Other types of contact may also indicate a sense of growing connection or understanding. A kiss is one of the most common symbolic dream acts, often reflecting the recognition of someone's importance. In dreams, a kiss represents appreciation more often than attraction or desire. This is why you may kiss or be kissed by someone in a dream who is unthinkable or nonsensical in waking life. One man who was exploring a far-reaching course of study dreamed of kissing the late Carl Sagan. This is a good example of a dream kiss that symbolizes new understanding and appreciation. Other embraces—hugs and expressions of affection—sometimes reflect a dawning recognition of the importance of a particular person, idea, or quality in your life.

Eating as Taking in Experiences

We eat and attempt to eat all kinds of things in our dreams. You may dream of attending a fabulous banquet where you are surrounded by food but no one will let you eat, or dream of swallowing a strange object and having to rush to the hospital emergency room. The things we eat in dreams generally represent experiences we're having or are striving to have.

Swallowing Objects

Swallowing objects is usually a sign that you're trying to digest or take in an experience that isn't right for you. You don't know how to cope with it and try to break it down into something meaningful or nourishing; instead, it is an experience that just sticks in your craw. Many people report dreams of having dinner with their parents or in-laws and consuming objects or indigestible food there. This implies that there are always issues surrounding gatherings with those people and the dreamer hasn't figured out a way to be comfortable in that environment. This doesn't mean there isn't also love and affection in those relationships; the object or bad food simply represents the issues that don't go down well for the dreamer.

If this phenomenon fits your experience, you may want to plan something just before you get together to help bolster your spirits. (Try taking an emotional antacid before a spicy meal.) You will also feel better if you plan something for after the visit to bring you back to your center and help you release tensions you may be holding. Talk with friends who have a grounding influence on you, listen to a favorite tape or CD on the way home, or rent a movie that reminds you what life is all about. These psychic antidotes can go a long way toward minimizing the discomfort and disorientation you may feel at such gatherings. With distress and confusion minimized, you'll ultimately be better able to enjoy the positive side of things and will develop a centered (not a feigned) tolerance for the patterns you encounter.

Food Issues

If you're dealing with real-life food issues, your dreams of particular foods may be related to unhealthy eating patterns, cravings, allergies, or binges. It's not uncommon to dream of gathering a hoard of your favorite binge food, going to consume it, and then discovering that insects, worms, or dirt have gotten into the food. This is often an indicator that the food in question has been overdone and is not healthful for you at this time.

Another common warning dream is that of going to purchase a favorite snack food and discovering that those chips cost $59.99 or the cake is $100.00 per slice. This is the mind's way of saying, "*You're really paying a very high price for indulging in that food right now.*" If you're on a merry-go-round with a particular food or pattern, try to learn what you can about the situation by consulting a nutritionist or reading up on the topic. What you may have attributed to deflated willpower may in fact have more to do with food allergies, stress, or lack of rest. Learn about nutrition in general and your body type in particular and then make decisions about what kind of support or plan will be ideal for your lifestyle and goals.

Food Symbolism

Often when we dream of particular types of food, it has little to do with what we're eating or craving in waking life. In those instances, the food in your dream is symbolic of a type of experience you're having or trying to have.

One woman dreamed that she was ignoring all her work at the office and leaving it for her colleagues to handle because she was wandering around daydreaming and munching raw green beans. Neither of these behaviors really made sense to her, and she had never snacked on raw green beans in her life! However, the beans symbolized something new (green) and untried (raw) as well as something that had the potential to take off (like Jack and the beanstalk). From this perspective, she was able to recognize that she was neglecting some of her regular work because she was constantly ruminating about a brand new project idea. Although she managed to do her job, she was basically just going through the motions because she was very focused on her new idea. The dream helped her realize that she couldn't go on this way and that she needed to wrap up several tasks before she would really be free to tackle the new idea and see what she could make of it.

Common Food Symbols

Although any food that seems unrelated to your actual eating patterns is likely to be symbolic, there are specific food images that are most common in modern dreams. Here are the ideas most often associated with them.

Meat

Meat is associated with strength and power. Even vegetarians who are actually repelled by meat will sometimes dream of eating flesh and finding it delicious. When this happens, it usually means they are devouring a life experience that is allowing them to accept and utilize their personal power. Therapists call this owning your power. You may need to reflect on the dream's other images and overall plot to determine whether the dream is a prescription or a reflection of what is going on.

One young man who was struggling to make a decision dreamed of eating a large steak with friends. During the meal, he announced humorously, "I like steak, but I eat it rarely." He awoke knowing the dream was symbolic, because, indeed, he almost never ate red meat. The pun on rare steak suggested to him that to really get a run at the tough decision he was facing, he should tap powers within himself that he seldom used. Since meat is associated with power, he realized that his normal style of putting everyone ahead of himself on the priority list might not be the ticket for this decision. He might need instead to take a powerful stance and charge ahead with what he believed was right. He made a move that took considerable courage, and against the odds, things have fallen into place for him. In his case, the rare tactic proved to be the right medicine for the situation.

Sweets

Sweets can represent sentimental expressions of affection, but they can also represent experiences that are truly sweet and precious. We all have a need for a certain amount of innocent joy, and when our lives become too grave or serious, we may dream of trying to find sweet things to eat. Typically, dreams of sweets will either come as a signal to take time out to do the things you love, or as a warning that you are skipping the basics in life and trying only to experience the frosting.

Just ask yourself if you're focusing on the goodies in life and neglecting the basics. If so, you'll find greater satisfaction by correcting the part of life that is out of whack, and immediately feel less inclined to chase the endless list of things you don't really want.

On the other hand, if you're living life as though it is a jail sentence and not allowing yourself the lovely moments that are full of rewards, your dreams of going after sweets may be a heartfelt signal to give yourself a break. People who are hyper-responsible tend to think in extremes, and fail to realize that some minor adjustments toward a more balanced life can be made without destroying all you've achieved. Make a list of ten things you can do that would be fun, restful, and renewing that won't affect your job or relationship. You'll probably be shocked to see that you seldom, if ever, allow yourself those pleasures even though they are not only harmless, they are good for you! Go after quiet joys the way you go after the big victories, and you'll go a long way toward finding greater contentment in the life you already have.

Milk

Milk is symbolically related to maternal affection and sometimes to issues with one's mother. For some people, milk (and mother) represent uncritical affection and the kind of support that nourishes growth and success. For others, milk and maternal energy are more complex and mixed in their impact and nourishment.

One woman who was helping her elderly mother move into a retirement complex dreamed of gathering hundreds of empty milk cartons and delivering them to a recycling plant. Her relationship with her mother had been a charged and complex one. She felt it was important at this stage of their lives that she focus with clarity on her affection and responsibility toward her mother and recycle the energy from past difficulties into a form that fit their current roles and relationship.

A man told me his confusing dream about his girlfriend. He had a mildly erotic dream about being with his lover when she held him in her arms and her breasts began to drip with milk. When he awoke, he found this odd, but when I asked him what he liked about her most, he said that her personality was so encouraging and positive that he felt renewed confidence in even his most ambitious plans and goals. Her belief in him was like mother's milk because it was extremely nourishing to his spirit and encouraged him to take his business and success to the next level.

Vegetables

Vegetables often symbolize experiences that are good for us or which have special emotional nutrients. Corn is particularly associated with the harvest of positive experiences, while green vegetables are more often symbolic of new potentials. Dreams of vegetables often feature scenes of the garden or field from which the produce was harvested. In such cases, the imagery suggests the importance of following a natural cycle within a project, career, or relationship. Be conscious about whether it is time to plant, tend, or harvest.

Fruit

Fruit is associated with lush experiences that are doubly rewarding. Typically, these are activities that are easy to take, enjoyable in the moment, but are also rich with promise for the future (because they are full of seeds). Succulent fruit may have sexual connotations in some cases, but it may also represent any experience that is lush or emotionally and physically satisfying.

Bread

Bread typically represents experiences that must be created through effort, planning, and waiting. Projects, careers, pregnancies, and building your own home may all be depicted in dreams of hearty bread. Eating bread usually represents the culmination of efforts that have taken several stages, while kneading or baking bread symbolizes earlier stages of projects. The implication of bread-making imagery is that whatever you are pursuing or building right now will prove to be rewarding and nourishing.

Toilet and Elimination Themes

Just as eating can be a metaphor for taking in experiences, so elimination can symbolize not only the release of extraneous material, but also communication and self-expression.

We may wrinkle our noses at the way dreams try to convey their messages, but even our gross dreams can have something to say. Good examples of this are the dreams that involve elimination. It is logical and psychologically fashionable to assume that a dream of excrement means there's something you need to let go of in your life, as if you need to flush the emotional toilet. Sometimes the interpretation is just that simple.

One woman had a pleasant dinner with her ex-husband after a long and bitter estrangement. That night she dreamed that together they were able to unclog a backed-up toilet so that it returned to proper working order. The metaphor of a clogged toilet for emotional tangles was very clear, and combined with the new peace and communication they'd discovered that night, the dream was very easy to recognize as a kind of celebration of their progress and healing.

However, many clogged toilets and complicated dreams about lavatories are not so much about emotional baggage as about a lack of adequate outlets for creativity, talents, and self-expression. Many talented, sensitive people tend to act as informal therapists for their families and friends, and these people (as well as helping professionals) tend to dream often of toilets too full for them to use.

Other variations on elimination themes include surprise episodes of eliminating in strange places, in front of people, or during conversations. In these dreams, the image of elimination represents the expression of information or opinion that is later deemed unsuitable or too revealing by the dreamer. One woman dumped her opinion about a work conflict on her husband during dinner and he defensively rejected her tactless bombardment of suggestions. That night she dreamed of having a large bowel movement behind her chair at the dinner table. She fumbled to clean it and herself up while carrying on a conversation with her husband that she hoped seemed natural. The dream was showing that her thoughtless onslaught of improving suggestions had been inappropriate to the situation.

Overflowing Commodes or Inappropriate Elimination

In most cases, dreams about elimination either highlight the factors that are impairing your freedom of expression or they reflect the concern you may have about being too impulsive in the way you've expressed something. If you dream of eliminating in front of people or in an inappropriate fashion, it's likely that you're having second thoughts about a recent conversation. If so, you may want to bear in mind the possible impact of your words as much as you do your need to speak your mind.

If your dreams involve frustrating attempts to find a toilet that is suitable for you, it's likely that you've said yes to too many jobs and people and now find there is no time, opportunity, or outlet in which you can express your own feelings and talents. Begin to pull back from those extra commitments and explore the activities that have been calling to you. Remember minor adjustments can create major improvements in your life.

Another common theme in this area is lacking a private lavatory. This theme is common to people who are sharing housing or an office and who find the practical advantages of the arrangement fail to compensate for a lack of privacy and personal space. If this sounds familiar, you may have to make some hard choices and alter the arrangement. At the very least, explain your personal style and preferences to others and brainstorm about compromises that may allow you to feel more at home in your present circumstances.

Loss of Self, Fragmentation

Because the body often represents the self or the lifestyle of the dreamer, broken bones and other injuries in dreams can symbolize emotional pain and a sense of losing parts of yourself. When you give up or edit parts of your nature in order to fit a prescribed mold or please others, psychologists call that *fragmentation*. We all do this occasionally or in moments when it seems absolutely necessary, but when a profoundly censored nature is the basis upon which we build our lives, the psyche begins to send out warning signals about what we stand to lose by such an existence. The dreaming mind appears to be very concerned about not only your survival and health, but also your ability to grow and flourish throughout a lifetime.

If you dream of losing a hand or foot, missing a heart or brain, or having some other part of the body disappear, this is often a sign that a whole portion of your potential is being lost due to something in the path you've chosen. The common dream of losing teeth is a prime example of such warning signals. This dream appears in numerous variations, but it is always a signal to beware of just how far you're willing to go with some compromise. Don't overlook the sense of losing something personal, because what is eroding, like your teeth, may be irreplaceable.

Remember, too, that dreams are in touch with the deepest and most unique levels of your nature. We tend to evaluate choices by objective criteria we believe to be sensible and to shortchange the importance of our dispositions, talents, and spiritual hungers. When you view the bizarre physical images in your dreams as parts of your self, they begin to make more sense.

The Brain, Head, and Hair

Many people dream of things happening to their brains. Something may eat your brain, or it may be shot or impaled by an object. Things that invade, harm, or take over your brain usually represent current factors in your life that are powerfully impacting your perspective. Usually people who are quite bright have dreams of something taking over their brain, perhaps because they are most likely to find themselves working as brains for hire in settings that ultimately prove constraining to their many gifts and ideas.

On the other hand, if you dream of having brain surgery or of prying a foreign object or growth out of your brain, this is more likely to reflect a change in your own thinking. It may be that you are eliminating a long-standing block to creativity or communication or that you have decided to release the brakes on your quest for success.

The head has much of the same symbolic meaning as the brain. The head pertains not only to the intellectual faculties but also to your overall attitude, personality, and perspective. Dreams about wearing a certain type of hat or headpiece are very revealing of your attitude and where you're coming from these days. In a similar manner, dreams of getting a new haircut or having wildly tangled hair reflect the types of thoughts you're dealing with. In broad terms, orderly, organized hair tends to reflect a systematic, methodical approach to things. Wildly tangled or snakelike hair in dreams can symbolize self-critical or even hysterical thoughts. If you dream of having long seductive hair like Lady Godiva (and you have shorter hair in waking life), this suggests a recent dip into your sensual, earthy nature.

Hands and Fingers

Hands represent our ability to grasp and control our destiny. They combine autonomy with creative expression and have a very strong symbolic presence in modern dreams. Think of hands as representing authority over one's own life. To dream of losing a hand or having it damaged is a warning that this sense of authority and creative freedom is being threatened.

One woman wrote to me about a recurring dream that both her hands had been cut off. In her dream, she was reliant on her husband for everything and was frustrated because she could do little to help herself. The dream made no sense to her because in waking life she said she was completely happy with her marriage and there was no trouble or abuse involved in the relationship.

Dreams of amputation or loss of a body part sometimes reflect a sense of having lost part of ourselves. Women, whose power is still affected by so many varieties of experience and relationship, often dream of losing hands and fingers. Although this imagery is usually not to be taken literally, it should always be taken seriously because the dreaming mind is in a sense screaming to get our attention.

Hands symbolize the ability to execute varied behaviors on our own behalf. They represent the capacity we have to select and manifest all sorts of choices at any given time, to create and tailor our lives to match our vision and preferences. Losing this ability or even having it somewhat impaired is a huge price to pay. Although this woman felt her marriage was a good one, her unconscious mind was trying to tell her that an invisible but significant cost was being exacted from her. This did not necessarily mean she needed to leave the marriage, but only that she should examine it closer. Certainly every relationship and every job involve significant compromises, but dreams of severe wounds or severed body parts provide clues that on some level the sacrifice involved is not wholesome or in the interests of long-range happiness.

Fingers have a similar connotation, in that they are associated with our individuality (fingerprints) and our freedom to express ourselves in many ways. Although any damage or harm to a finger in a dream should be taken seriously, there appear to be individual symbolic associations to the specific fingers as well. In most instances the little finger seems associated with communication, the ring finger with commitment, the middle finger with sexuality and sexual relationships, the index finger with authority, and the thumb with the will.

The Heart

Dreams about the heart may be as common as dreams about the head. It is easy to understand why the heart is a symbol of romantic love, but it also appears in dreams in a larger sense. The heart can represent the dreamer's style of loving all things, not just romantic partners. It also can reflect problems with not having followed the heart in choosing a career or life path. Heart surgery can represent a change of heart in some significant way. As in other cases, if you have any reason to suspect that your dreams are signaling an actual physical problem, do get a checkup. In most cases, however, the metaphorical meaning in dreams of the heart are readily apparent.

The Liver

The gift in dreams about the liver is usually derived from a pun. That is, in dreams, this organ represents the liver as in the one who does the living. Many of us have been busy with our battles, our goals, and obsessions, and have given virtually no thought to the part of ourselves that does the living. As hard as we try, we are *not* machines, and if we go too far too long in this vein, the dreaming mind may warn us that our "liver" is in deep trouble.

The Throat

The throat often represents the ability to express oneself verbally. Dreams of injury to the throat or of strangulation are almost always connected with a current pressure impacting the dreamer's honest expression and communication. Be aware that unconscious contracts with loved ones, unspoken rules at the workplace, and mixed feelings about what you want are the most likely forces involved. Such dreams do not mean that you must speak your mind fully and completely at all times. Instead, they merely urge you to become consciously aware of the dynamics that are affecting you and to be honest with yourself about what it going on, how you feel, and what your preferences may be. Once you have everything clear in your own mind the right action in the current circumstance will be much easier to discern and you will likely find that the impossible bind is not as airtight as it seemed.

The Face

The face is the portion of the self most often seen by others and most often judged by ourselves. This should not be confused with a false self or a contrived presentation, however. The face is more than just what we choose to show the world; it is the intersection between the whole self and the world. For this reason, it is associated with psychological territory that is highly charged for most of us. In dreams, we may find something embarrassingly strange about our faces and spend anxious moments wondering how to conceal a bizarre problem. This suggests not only that we are anxious to be liked, but that in our heart we deeply want to be seen for who we are and not to be judged for what appears to be a flaw or eccentricity.

One drawback of our exceptional access to information these days is that we have grown suspicious of our own natures and tend to greet each new self-awareness as if it somehow incriminates us. In dreams, this phenomenon appears in scenes of discovering strange growths, flaws, and unfamiliar features in the mirror.

If something in a dream harms or disfigures your face, it is likely that a current situation is impacting your confidence or self-assessment. In such cases, awareness is one key to coping with whatever real-life challenges arise.

The Neck

The neck represents the interface between your thoughts and opinions and your lifestyle, feelings, and choices. Sometimes this is the place where we feel most constricted in life because we believe one thing but find another set of actions to be most necessary for survival and success. Dreams that contain imagery about the neck can indicate the need to come to terms in a deeper way with the difference between thoughts and feelings, or beliefs and actions.

Remember that when you believe your choices exist only in two extreme and mutually exclusive forms, you're probably missing a big piece of the picture. You really *can* think and feel at the same time and you absolutely can deal with richly complex conditions without shutting down or chopping off your feelings.

The Skin

Skin represents our social and personal boundaries. Dreams of trouble with the skin or even being without skin indicate that you may be feeling vulnerable or that it's time to focus on developing some better boundaries. Many dreams feature creepy things like insects burrowing under the skin. These images can mean that something upsetting has gotten under your skin or that a single incident has multiplied in your imagination until, like a nest of spiders, you feel infested with unpleasant memories and concerns about the future.

The Feet and Legs

As I've already mentioned, the feet tend to be associated with our foundation in life, the sets of beliefs, memories, and expectations upon which we stand. They also symbolize our ability to move forward into new situations and roles. In this manner, dreams of finding the right shoes or of experimenting with strange footwear can reflect our conflicts and desires about working from an identity that suits us and still allows us to grow.

Bare feet tend to reflect vulnerability, while injuries to the feet can indicate pain around early conditioning, and our ability to follow the direction in life that truly calls to us.

Legs seem particularly associated with relationships. Dreams of losing a leg occur most often when we either try to adapt to a new love relationship or when we break up. Dream surgery on legs, such as getting a leg transplant, usually happen when people become engaged or move in together. The implication seems to be a fundamental change in the sense of self.

You can tell something about the prognosis for this change by seeing how the situation works out in the dream. Even the most startling surgery or change can be positive if it seems to work well in the dream. One young woman who had split from her partner of many years dreamed of seeing a woman who'd lost her leg, sitting on a pier. Holding the leg on her lap, the woman calmly sliced off small bits of the leg and fed it to passing fish and sea lions. Although the dream sounds disturbing, both the woman and the observing dreamer felt a sense of calm and rightness about the situation. In her case, feeding the fish with the loss appears to have meant she should be unresisting and calm about what felt like a loss.

Although the dreamer was somewhat stunned by the sudden change in her life, she was able to recycle the energy (feed the fish) and move in directions that proved very positive for her. She went off to graduate school, met and married another man, and has recently had their first child.

The Body's Wisdom

If you look at the body in dreams as an image of your life and potentials, the shocking drama of many scenes will transform into a rich view into your well-being and the way present circumstances are affecting you. Don't be overly agitated by dreams that seem to present a warning: instead, start by piecing the clues together in your own mind and being completely honest with yourself. If you're in a bind at the moment that seems unalterable, begin to make a plan for how you can change things in the future. We seem to resist the kind of incremental changes that are often our best solution, perhaps because we've grown used to the tidy and dramatic resolutions presented in the movie of the week. But often awareness, clarity, and a clear strategy will set the stage for unexpected opportunities. Gather your forces, clear your thoughts, and extend your time line. You may be amazed to find that your own presence of mind has already started fate moving to lend a hand.

Chapter 7

Your Dream Home and Other Dwellings

O ften our dreams show us living in bizarre situations, or in a home very different from the one we inhabit in waking life. These settings are often elaborately detailed; although you may shake your head upon awakening, in the dream it made sense. It was simply taken for granted that you were a part of the underground railroad smuggling slaves through various hiding places before the Civil War, or that you and your family lived in a tree-house and could swing on vines like Tarzan.

Our dream homes frequently have little to do with our real live residences; instead, they say a great deal about our present circumstances, the stance we're taking toward goals or fears, and the real nature of present challenges and life lessons.

The House: Psychological Territory

There is a saying that used to be popular to convey empathy for another's point of view. The phrase was: "I know where you're coming from!" The casual phrase meant you understood what was motivating the other person, what their concerns were, and how they saw the situation. Because we are all so different, something your neighbor might shrug off could be a major upset to you. When a dream shows you living in a particular kind of home or setting, the mind is pointing out: *this is where you're coming from right now*, and also, *this is how things are affecting you*. In other words, dream homes reflect your perspective and also your experience of current conditions.

One man, who was struggling to accept an unwanted early retirement, dreamed his house was infested with termites that were threatening to destroy its entire foundation. His dream reflected his frustrations at being assailed by unwelcome conditions, as well as his sensation that the foundation of his life had suddenly become unstable and vulnerable. When he gradually switched his focus to family activities, church, volunteer work, and travel, his unwanted retirement transformed into a wonderful lifestyle and his dream dwellings began to resemble paradise as his experience and attitude changed.

Parts of the House

Many people are amazed at the detail and precision of their dreamed houses. From the placement of the toilets to the furnace in the basement, every element seems meticulously planned and often familiar, even though it bears little or no resemblance to their real-life home.

In symbolic terms, each part of the house carries special significance. The parts of the house featured in your dreams are no accident and the unique features each boasts can be especially important to understand.

The Kitchen

A great number of dreams are either set in the kitchen or they feature this room in an important way. The kitchen is like the emotional heart of the home. When we're trying to sort through feelings, interpersonal conflicts, or get clear on priorities, we may have dreams set in the kitchen. The kitchen is also a room of magic, where we create new dishes out of existing ingredients. This style of taking what you've been given and forming it into what you really want is very much like the alchemy of life—building, mixing, and healing situations by experimenting with combinations of energy and intention. If you view a disappointment differently, you may discover a hidden blessing; if you forgive an old hurt, you may reclaim the energy that was frozen by holding a grudge. Any cook knows that if you assume you have everything you need to create a desired dish limited ingredients can be stretched or substituted in creative ways.

One woman who was struggling with weight gain dreamed that she had a large fireplace in the midst of her kitchen. This suggested that her passions, emotions, and eating patterns were all getting lumped together. She was between relationships and found herself falling into the trap of eating for company, as a pick-me-up, and as a tranquilizer. Once she recognized this pattern, she was able to deliberately expand other activities and interests in her life so that she wasn't using food inappropriately and her health and energy improved.

Pay attention to the amenities in your dream kitchen because they reflect the strengths you can call upon or the way your energies are organized with respect to current conditions. If the kitchen is cramped and cluttered, you may have sabotaged yourself by taking on too many problems that belong to others. If something precious has been forgotten on the back burner of the stove, it may be time to tackle that beloved project or ambition you postponed earlier in life.

Some people are concerned by the presence of deceased relatives in their dreams, who, along with other family members, are featured gathering around the kitchen table. We'll explore in depth the questions about psychic dreams in chapter 12, but for now, understand that kitchen imagery almost always reflects the need to work through your current situation by coming straight from the heart.

You need to get clear on what is most important to you and recognize how different factors are impacting your thoughts and feelings. To summon your strength and emotional clarity, you may need to recall the unquestioning love of a grandparent or the simple wisdom of someone dear who has passed on. Assume that *all* the elements and characters in your dream kitchen are there as clues to help develop your power and happiness.

The Bedroom

While Hollywood would have us believe the bedroom is a symbol for all things sexual, in dreams this room has an even broader meaning. This room is where you rest, where you retreat from others, and where you sleep or become unconscious. In our dreams, the bedroom may certainly deal with sex, romance, and intimacy, but just as often it reflects areas in our lives that are particularly private, or issues about which we are somewhat unconscious.

One woman who was prone to tumultuous romances vowed she would begin choosing a different, more reliable sort of man in the future. She met and became involved with yet another tempestuous fellow, but set about convincing herself that this man was not at all the same as the others. The light came on however, when she dreamed about tucking a double of herself into bed and slowly hypnotizing that woman by chanting *you're getting sleepy, just go to sleep.* Her dreaming mind was trying to point out that she was in effect going unconscious about yet another roller-coaster relationship in the making. Her constant rationalizations were like the hypnotic chant she used to try and numb her awareness of what was really afoot. Anyone who has tried to change a habit or break out of a pattern knows the sensation of almost being two people; one of you is trying to break free and a second part of you is working overtime to keep things as they used to be. Just the conscious awareness of this pattern went a long way to helping this woman make choices that resulted in better relationships and the kind of lifestyle she really wanted.

When a bedroom scene is associated with sex and romance, there are usually other markers in the dream that make this clear. One man dreamed of trying to make love with his wife when all their relatives were also in the bed. Although he found this humorous, he also felt it clarified the issues that had been impinging on their intimacy for some time. A young woman who was involved with her boss dreamed there was a large picture window in her bedroom and that passersby on the street would stop to watch the couple for entertainment. Though neither of them was married, the relationship made her feel exposed and vulnerable, as if her private life was somehow on display to the world. She struggled with this sensation for a while and then transferred to another department and supervisor so that she no longer had such a vulnerable dual role in the relationship.

Keep in mind that bedroom scenes tend to either express issues affecting intimacy or remind us of factors that may have been relegated to the unconscious. Don't make the mistake of assuming that your bed of snakes reveals hideous, repressed material, however. Your dreaming mind may use a number of startling images to represent feelings, beliefs, and nuances that are not objectively horrific but which are nevertheless having a strong impact on current circumstances.

The Living Room

When we dream of the living room in a house, we're actually taking a look at the amount of room and freedom we have to relax and be ourselves.

Dream living rooms are typical for their lack of space, crowded conditions, and strange furnishings. Toilets in the living room suggest a lack of privacy; office furniture that takes up space there implies absorption with career. Some living rooms are thrown in with other areas of the house, suggesting inadequate boundaries between life activities that can, over time, leech the enjoyment from all the areas involved. Keep in mind that dreams show us these conditions because they are correctable and greater awareness about them is to our advantage. Don't assume that a trashed living room or even a coffin in the parlor means you're doomed. Think of the qualities of the room as potentials and resources within yourself and decide whether you need to make some adjustments in your attitude or approach to life.

One woman who had started a counseling practice dreamed that countless strangers wandered into her home and (like untrained puppies) left piles of excrement all over her living room carpet. The dream was letting her know in graphic terms that she was feeling like a universal dumping ground for the whole world. The reason for this feeling, the dream pointed out, was because she was taking so much of her work home and dwelling on it in the hours when she should have been living. She had been worried that she'd make a terrible mistake in choosing her career but the dream helped make it clear that it was not the work that was wrong, but the way she obsessed about it in her off hours that was the problem. After setting some inner boundaries for herself and practicing switching off in her home, she was able to adjust to the demands of the field and enjoy applying her talents.

When a living room is featured in your dream, notice the qualities that make it special or pleasant; these are the things in you and in your circumstances that are available to make life more enjoyable. If there are objects, walls, or leaks spoiling the room, consider what parts of life these represent and how you can create enough psychic space to find joy in living again.

The Basement

Though basements are becoming less common in new homes, they are still prevalent in our dreams. The symbolic basement area often has odd equipment, strange animals, or even dead bodies stored in it. Since few of these items bear a resemblance to anything in our waking lives, this area is one of the most challenging parts of the house to understand.

The basement is a mixture of psychological storage space and foundational material. It is much more than just a reference to a Freudian unconscious buried under your house. The dream basement, like those of real life, can have numerous and varied functions. This is the psychological space where we file things we have not yet made sense of but which we think might come in handy someday. It's also where we shoved the bodies of potential selves we decided weren't a match with our over-riding ambitions.

Many dream basements can reflect the metabolism and health of the dreamer. One woman with a chronic health problem dreamed of ailing animals struggling around her basement. Another with hyperactive thyroid dreamed of a raging furnace in her basement that was overheating her entire house.

Sometimes factories and assembly lines in the basement will reveal the origins of an obsession with work or success. In waking life, we sometimes store chests and possessions from past generations in the basement. Sometimes our dream basements reveal to what an extent our current attitudes are derived from early assumptions or family legends as well.

One man, who was the first in his family to divorce, dreamed that his basement was completely empty. His entire sense of past and future was deeply disturbed by the divorce and also by the way he interpreted it. He saw it as a grave failure which swept back into past generations and forward into his future, eradicating his chances for happiness. However, his dream basement did hold one important clue. In the corner of the vast, empty space was a fireplace with a steady, long-burning fire glowing softly. This suggested that his capacity to feel passion and love was certainly not lost; it burned quietly in the midst of his grief and feeling of emptiness. With counseling and hard work, he would be able to love again, and that steady flame suggested he had deep warmth to offer a future partner.

The Attic

Like the basement, the attic in your dreams may have a great deal to do with stored material. Ghosts in the attic typically represent memories that haunt us, while the jumble of old clothes and furnishings may reflect unused energy stored away through fear or discouragement. Although some people vehemently postulate that the attic in dreams represents the higher self of the dreamer (apparently because it is located upstairs), this notion rarely makes sense. It doesn't fit that our higher selves would be full of haunted specters, forbidden doors, and dusty baggage. If, however, your dream attic contains a panoramic picture window and a heavenly radiance, then you may indeed be exploring your higher self.

Whatever your dream attic contains, consider it a clue to making present conditions more comfortable and balanced. One woman who had been feuding with her sister for years dreamed that the two of them met upstairs in their mother's attic. There both sisters discovered that some spiders from the attic had at some time nested in their hair and had been running around their heads, irritating them for years. She realized upon awakening that their parent's divorce and their polarized views about what had happened to their mother afterwards had been at the root of their stubborn misunderstanding. In her own way, each woman had been trying to reduce the pain surrounding the memory by adhering to a historical view that was biased and incomplete. As siblings so often do, they had identified with very different opinions and emotional styles, living out their lives, at least in part, as though they were experiments in proving their hypotheses about history. Once she knew that their differences stemmed from choosing sides in their parent's divorce, the personality conflict that had appeared so insoluble lost its power.

The Backyard

Have you ever heard someone say they hadn't expected to find the right mate (job, etc.) right in their own backyard? In dreams, the backyard of the home generally represents the territory of your life that is taken for granted because it is so ordinary and close that you forget it's there. If something nice shows up in your backyard in a dream, it probably represents a potential that is available to you without changing a thing. If, however, you dream of a monster or a plane crash in your backyard, the implication is that there is an intrusive energy in your life that is hitting too close to home.

One woman who was trying to get a promotion dreamed that her backyard was full of rusty farm equipment, such as broken down tractors and hay bailers. To her, the backyard full of discarded junk revealed the need to let go of years of unfinished business and partially completed projects. To really commit to her career in her own mind, she needed to admit that it meant letting go of the numerous other things she'd thought she might get to someday. As she set about clearing the decks and zeroing in on what she wanted, she enjoyed renewed energy and eventually did land the promotion that she'd been craving.

The Front Porch

The front of your home is symbolically very much like your face. It is the portion of your life that is on display to others. This doesn't necessarily mean it is artificial or phony, just that this is the side of life that most people see when they look your way. This area is more important and complex for some of us than it is for others. One man who worked as a television host told me that many of his dreams take place on the front porch of his home. This makes sense in light of the fact that so much of his work life takes place under very public circumstances. The success of that portion of his energy that is out front is particularly vital to making the rest of his life work well.

If something happens on or to the front of your dream home, it is likely that you are experiencing the effects of something made more intense because it is quite public. When that is the case, you'll need to give yourself time and support not only to assimilate the experience itself, but to adjust to the sense of exposure involved.

The Bathroom

Plumbing problems in the bathroom sometimes reflect trouble in processing feelings. There isn't necessarily any grave or toxic problem involved; we all feel out of whack when the inflow and outflow of our energies and feelings are unbalanced. Flooding in the bathroom suggests a deluge of feelings that are out of character or difficult to handle. When more emotion flows through us than we are accustomed to, our habitual style is not adequate to the task of keeping us feeling all right. Take dreams of overloaded plumbing as a sign that you may be swamped right now, and just as you'd call in a plumber, it may be time to arrange for emergency support from a therapist or support person.

Another common theme associated with bathrooms is that of desperately seeking a bath or shower, but being unable to find peace and quiet enough to manage. In this sense, the bathroom symbolizes a place for cleansing, refreshment, and renewal. It is a place where a dreamer, running dry, can take a dip in the parts of life that act like water to the spirit. This kind of dream usually recurs during those stretches of life when we say yes to too many chores and postpone indefinitely those things we truly need.

Secret Rooms

There are two general types of secret rooms in our dreams. The first type is a room that has been long forgotten, and once rediscovered is found to contain many wonderful (if dusty) possessions. This room has great possibilities and the dreamer often vows to clean it out and start enjoying it again. This special room represents a neglected potential in the dreamer's life that the deeper mind is trying to coax us to reclaim. It may be time to return to college, get back into your dancing or artwork, or return to the church. If you think about the thing that keeps calling to you but you reject because it's been too long, you'll probably discover that it isn't too late after all; the right time may be now.

The second type of secret room has a more ominous quality. This is usually a room in some dark region of the house that is marked by a locked door and entrance into this room is strictly forbidden. Many people report this dream: some never go into the forbidden room, others have tense scenes in which they struggle with the lock or the forces that seal the door.

Those who go through the door usually find the room does contain something they find super scary. Although the locked door and the forbidden room are fairly universal, the rooms' contents are very individual. One man who taught positive thinking courses found his secret room contained a depressed clown with a big smile painted on his face. While one part of his mind felt he needed to evaluate a hidden depression that seeped through his life, other forces in his psyche strove to hide this fact from him in an effort to keep him working at his career of motivating others. One woman who was considering leaving her husband found her forbidden room contained a number of battered women in hospital beds. Her deep fear was that if she told her husband the marriage was over, he might turn violent.

In both these cases, the insight the room presented was difficult to swallow. But having a clearer awareness of the dynamics involved helped these people cope more compassionately and effectively with the situations they faced.

The blessing of modern psychology is sometimes a mixed one because some people who have dreams of these forbidden rooms assume they always reflect suppressed memories of abuse or tragedy. Sometimes, unfortunately, that is true. But in many cases, the forbidden room simply contains information that is time sensitive, something you could not allow yourself to think about or focus on until now. Tension between two aspects of the psyche that seem to have opposing goals is a large part of what makes this dream so charged.

If you have this dream, pursue it gently and patiently. If you are willing to see the room's contents and willing to consider how it may heal or restore your choices, you will find the tension diminishes. You will be able to move through that doorway and make use of what you find.

Windows

Windows can show up in strange places and provide unusual views in our dreams. In general, these windows represent points of view, perspectives, and glimpses of insight. One woman, who was disgusted by her younger sister's choice of boyfriend, dreamed she was standing in her sister's bedroom looking through her window and all she could see outside was a giant, phallic shaped object. The view from her sister's room was very focused on this prominent object and it suggested to the dreamer that the chemistry and physical side of the relationship was the reason the sister failed to see the dangerous side of the questionable young man she'd chosen. The dream helped the elder sister to understand what she was dealing with and to offer her advice and opinions in a more tactful and understanding manner.

When you dream of a window, ask yourself what it reveals about the perspective you have on current events or whether it seems to hint that a broader view of a current predicament might help you spot a workable solution.

Doorways

Doorways represent opportunities and potential changes. If someone knocks on your front door in a dream, this likely reflects a recent opportunity that is being presented to you. Because each new opportunity comes with both positive and negative potentials, feelings and imagery surrounding doorways are often mixed. You may want to welcome the strange man at the door because he is attractive or charming, yet also feel it is inappropriate that he should demand entrance into your home.

Unwanted changes in our lives are often depicted in dreams as intruders or strangers coming to the door. If something is happening at work that is contaminating your home life, you may have a recurring cycle of dreams about strangers barging in or menacing figures coming to the door.

Abrupt, unsettling romances also have the effect of threatening our comfort zones and women especially tend to dream of dark strangers at the door when they embark on sudden relationships. Pay particular attention to themes of home invasion, rape, and burglary when you are launching a romance. While these dreams don't necessarily mean your sweetheart is up to no good, they can sometimes provide an early warning that there are some undercurrents in the relationship that may not be nourishing to you over the long haul. In some cases, the dark, destructive stranger at the door represents a part of the dreamer's psyche that is self-critical or self-sabotaging. The dream is a warning that this element of the personality has found a viable vehicle through which to operate in the form of the relationship.

Another theme featuring doors is that of locking yourself out of the house or of being unable to enter the place you feel you belong. This scene reflects a pattern or situation that is preventing you from having access to your best talents, drive, relationships, and energy. We all have seasons in which we are locked out from our best selves for some reason. These dreams attempt to provide clues about misplaced keys, carelessness, lack of planning, or lack of faith in ourselves. Remember, this dream is showing you a pattern that can be corrected readily and with a minor change; it is for you to discern what adjustment will get you back into your own center.

Upon reflection, many people find that some type of addiction is at fault for locking them outside of themselves. This is not necessarily an addiction to alcohol or chemicals; we also get addicted to consuming relationships, compulsive work habits, distracting social habits, procrastination, and even judgments. These types of addiction require a willingness to change, to experiment with alternatives that may seem less desirable at first, but they are highly responsive to your intention.

Passages and Corridors

In the creative style of dreams, some houses magically contain hallways that seem to run the length of a football field. There are usually doors on either side and numerous rooms as well as other corridors attached. These hallways represent the way you have your choices and options arranged in your own mind. If you're feeling like your current situation is a dead end, your psychic hallway will contain a blockade of some sort or a set of guards who insist on checking your credentials. During times when too many choices are impairing your ability to make a simple decision, you may dream of wandering a hallway packed with doors and off-shooting passages so that instead of walking in a straight line, you are sucked into a kind of maze.

We view our problems, choices, and blessings with a particular mental structure, and to a great extent our mental maps have more impact on our lives than does the actual territory we face. The hallway in your dream can be an invaluable look at what you believe to be possible and necessary. Look at such dreams carefully to determine whether you may be shortchanging your opportunities or cluttering you mind with unnecessary considerations.

Homes from the Past

If you continually dream of living in a home from an earlier time in your life, it doesn't necessarily mean you are stuck in the past. The homes we live in become emblems of certain factors that were in play in our lives during the time we lived there.

One woman lived in a tiny, drab studio apartment when she first graduated from college. During those years, she felt cramped and poor, as if she had little control over her life. With her success and marriage, she was able to move into a nice home and for many years afterward her residences reflected her tastes and preferences. However, whenever a circumstance frustrated her or she felt helpless to correct some problem, she would again dream that she was still living in that tiny, dark apartment. The studio had become a symbol of frustration from outside factors that was compounded by an occasional tendency to get lost in a sense of helplessness. Our dream homes show how current conditions in our lives are affecting us by symbolizing the time in our history they send us back to. But these home flashbacks also show what set of resources and feelings we're drawing upon to respond to current conditions in our lives.

One man who was happily remarried dreamed sometimes of living in the house of his first marriage with his current wife. This dream revealed that there were times when the current relationship caused him to feel as if he were back in that first marriage. But it also showed that there were times when he responded to issues in this marriage as if he were still in the prior life. It's helpful to know where some inexplicable feelings are coming from and what buttons are being pushed. It's also important to acknowledge these reactions and feelings even when they are very different from our overall or official opinion about a current relationship. We have a tendency to discount or deny our own experiences if they are different from our predominant feelings. It's as if we're trying to remain loyal to the dominant part of our experience. But respecting the nuances of feeling that vary from the majority of our feelings will actually help those differences be digested more quickly and naturally than if we continue to try to stomp them out or ignore them.

Perhaps the most common past-home theme is that of dreaming you are still living in the house in which you were a child. We all have this dream from time to time throughout our lives. Our first residence is forever the emblem of home, family, connections, and traditions. The warm amenities, dark corners, space, and sharing that is imprinted in that home tends to be forever a blueprint in the psyche. Without question it is possible to improve and transform our experience of family systems within our lifetimes; we are in no way doomed or limited to repeat our early experiences. However, the mind does use this early home as an important reference throughout our lives and we will often find ourselves trying to work through current questions in the setting of that childhood home. Consider these dreams as golden opportunities to reflect upon early patterns, or essential beliefs about home and family. Are you running patterns from your family of origin in a current relationship or projecting the role of a family member upon an acquaintance?

One woman who had a difficult relationship with her father lived in an ongoing struggle for power with him during her early life. In later years, her husband's best friend was something of a sore point in her marriage because for some reason the man always made her want to argue with him. No matter what was going on in their lives, she always found herself getting into towering rages with this man. It wasn't until she noticed her recurring dreams about her father and her childhood home that it dawned on her what the problem was. The ongoing battle that had never been settled with her (now deceased) father was being continued with her husband's friend, who was much older than she and had a similar pedantic style of conversation. Recognition of this kind can go a long way to freeing everyone from unhappy patterns that threaten to take on a life of their own. When she finds herself feeling the visceral tug to get into an argument with this man, she takes a deep breath and thinks silently, "You aren't my father, and you don't have to act out that role in my life now." This simple statement clears her mind, returns her energy to the present context, and it also seems to free the friend to be less fatherly in their relationship as well.

Specialized Living Arrangements

Sometimes our dream homes are like extravagant Hollywood sets. You may find yourself living on a tropical island, in a medieval dungeon, or managing a station in outer space. When we awaken, the typical reaction to such outlandish lifestyles is to dismiss these dreams. Outrageous settings that bear no resemblance to waking life can seem like a complete fluke or even a mistake, as if there was a mix-up in delivery and you accidentally got someone else's dream. The truth is, when the dreaming mind has gone out of its way to set a dream in such a specific setting, you can be sure the dream is loaded with symbolic meaning.

Even the most bizarre dream home reflects the psychological territory you're living in right now. One man dreamed that he was one of a number of sewer-dwellers beneath a post-holocaust city. The few survivors struggled to stay alive, hiding scraps of food and blankets from the Gestapo-style people in power who sometimes came to check on them. It was important not to let the power-mongers know how determined they were to survive, and he acted as a kind of emissary between the dictatorship and the underground survivors. The bleak landscape of this remarkably vivid dream haunted him upon awakening from it. Like most people, his first concern was that the dream was somehow a preview of earth changes to come. However, when I told him that his dream was far more likely a reflection of present psychological territory, it began to make more sense to him.

He had loved his job at a non-profit service for many years, but his organization had recently gotten lumped into another area because it was supposedly easier to administer the program from that umbrella. The result of this change had made his department unrecognizable: all the personnel were stripped of their power and forced to do everything according to a massive book of new regulations. The focus on human service was taken away and the regime of streamlined administration was made the priority. Most new clients were turned away or offered minimized help and the employees lived in morbid fear of the new authoritarian management that had been put in place over them. Although his dream certainly dramatized this change, it did capture his subjective experience of having to accomplish things covertly (underground) while unfeeling dictators paced around doing military inspections. He eventually felt that the new regime was so antithetical to the things that had drawn him into the field that he accepted a more rewarding and enjoyable position with a different organization.

If you dream of living in a fictional setting, evaluate the qualities inherent in that situation. Are you cramped, limited, or devalued? Is there a similar flavor of experience going on now in your work setting or in your home? We dream of living in strange circumstances when something in the work life or in our home or primary relationship is exerting an unusual influence on us. The dream setting can provide a valuable heads-up about how things are affecting you, giving you a chance to plan better and set up different supports to get you through the temporary siege. If, on the other hand, your dream shows you doing a life sentence on Alcatraz, you may want to think hard about whether your present situation is really fair to you and weigh carefully whether you want to spend an extended time within that psychological territory. If there are unreasonable limits in the dream setting, ask yourself honestly whether they come from the qualities of the situation or if they stem more from your own reaction to the situation.

Remember, being honest with yourself doesn't mean you have to do anything drastic; it will simply permit you to martial your energy more effectively, and if necessary, to make a good solid plan to improve the situation over time.

Your Inner Landscape

Dream homes are usually a picture of the resources you bring to present conditions. They show symbolically the way you tend to tackle decisions and the way you have choices arranged in your mind. Strange qualities in the home or fictional settings usually represent current conditions that are impacting you in a big way. So pay close attention to the way you storm the castle walls or how you stubbornly build the igloo despite the sunny weather and melting snow. Your dream home will be like a documentary showing the interaction of preexisting beliefs, current challenges, and your recent reactions. If you don't like the formula you see, understand that you are in charge of changing the recipe for happiness. Make small adjustments but be confident in expecting big results.

Chapter 8

Cars

Just as the house in a dream reflects the structure of your beliefs and the emotional flavor of your current situation, the car in your dream says a lot about your current actions. The movement of your car is a metaphor for the way you're trying to make progress in life and the extent to which you feel in control.

One psychological theory views the car as a symbol of your current relationship, so all dreams featuring cars might be considered to be about romance or partnership. My observation is that cars have a much broader symbolism that may occasionally reflect relationship issues; but these dreams should not all be interpreted in such a narrow way. Just as you use your real-life car to get where you're going, your dream car often reflects your psychological style of trying to get what you want and avoid what you fear.

You may already have wondered why the vehicle in your dream so often is not your real car or why you are sometimes driving an army tank or a go-cart. The vehicles vary in form to reflect the current way we're approaching our goals and the powers that seem to be at our command. You may be adopting a well-armored approach to a new relationship or you may be taking off for college with an improvised approach to life that you will flesh out as you go along. Because we're often given opportunities for which we feel unprepared, many of us dream of driving thrown-together vehicles that look like glorified skateboards, with no sides and make-shift controls.

One man who had been placed in charge of a group of other commercial artists jumped at the promotion, but had second thoughts when he realized his own training and experience as an artist had given him virtually no skills for managing people. He dreamed of driving along the freeway in a rickety vehicle that had no top, bottom, or sides. In the dream, he broke into a sweat of anxiety as the traffic zoomed around him and he tried to familiarize himself with the confusing controls. This car consisted of nothing but his own chair on a platform with a gear-shifter, pedals below his feet, and a steering wheel in front of him.

The car reflected his feeling of being vulnerable and ill-equipped for his current tasks, and also showed that he was rushing himself by taking this slap-dash contraption onto the freeway. Although there was little he could do about the basic components of his predicament, the dream's manic style told him that wherever possible, he should choose to minimize the pressure he put on himself. The situation was already loaded enough without him insisting on doing everything right away and setting his expectations unrealistically high. He began to view his current feeling of crisis as a period of adjustment rather than as the symptom of a terrible mistake. When the given factors in a situation are charged with tension, it becomes especially important not to overload yourself with negative self-talk or amplified expectations. The way you frame the situation in your own mind may be the only variable over which you have control and adjusting it sensibly may be your best chance of getting a bit of breathing room.

Driving Problems

If your dream car has poor controls or missing parts this suggests that your sense of control over current conditions is somehow being compromised. For example, a woman going through her first pregnancy is necessarily taking a journey that is not entirely under her control, so she may dream of driving a vehicle that is new, different, too large, or otherwise unfamiliar and daunting.

One woman who had worked as a recruiter for years decided to begin looking for a different type of job for herself. As she embarked on her own job search, the things that had long seemed familiar to her suddenly looked different. She dreamed of driving a car that did not belong to her. It was frustrating because she had trouble finding the ignition, tuning the radio, and understanding how to shift gears. These automotive difficulties reflected the ways she experienced trouble with the job change. It was hard getting started (finding the ignition), and it was tricky knowing on what to focus (tuning in the radio). But perhaps most critical was the fact that this project involved switching gears! In order to execute this change, she had to be willing to endure the unpleasant sensation of being awkward and not having as much control as she liked.

Like most competent people, she loathed the qualities that accompany transition: slowness, methodical steps, uncertainty, and vulnerability. After the fluidity of the excellence she'd achieved in her current field, it was like going back to a manual transmission with a sticky clutch. But the dream also showed that despite the awkwardness of this new vehicle, she learned quickly, and drove with great competence. In effect, it seemed that she could afford to trust this process and rely on her resourcefulness to help her emerge into a more satisfying career field. Eventually, she accepted a position across the country in a new and exciting area that permitted her to combine both her people skills and her talents as a teacher in a way that has been richly rewarding.

Car Troubles and Your Style

The approach you have while driving your dream car reflects the style you're using to go after what you want. Are you speeding towards a broken bridge or screeching your tires around a blind curve? Daring tactics that seem dangerous in a dream can be a hint that your current approach needs adjustment if it's to carry you safely to the finish line. In a similar way, the attributes of your dream car can reflect the resources you have to draw upon and the way you're taking care of yourself.

People who are indulging in a downward spiral of overwork, poor health habits, or procrastination will often dream of heading downhill in a car that has no brakes. This exaggerated warning simply suggests that the combination of where you are in life and your current behaviors is ill-advised. A lack of brakes suggests that some force has gained momentum, perhaps without your knowing it, and so it now begins to feel as if you can't stop yourself from continuing in your present direction. Just as you would immediately get help if your car brakes really vanished, so you now need to do some serious planning to find and obtain whatever you need to alter your present habits or trajectory.

Parts of the Car

In an almost humorous way, the parts of a car have a strikingly symbolic meaning that has an understandable logic.

Battery

Many people who are overworked, overcommitted, or involved in draining relationships will have recurring dreams about their car battery going dead. In these dreams, the battery is usually so drained that it will no longer hold a charge. The person may use a number of measures to avoid slowing down their schedule, but will emerge from each place to find that once again, their car won't start. The implication is that a more fundamental change is necessary to insure that the source of the ongoing energy drain is altered. The culprit is usually an approach to work, a style of overextending social engagements, or an imbalance in a primary relationship.

Gas Tank

The gas tank is typically associated with food habits and the parts of life that nourish the spirit as well as the body. Dreams of cars out of gas can reflect a sense of having hit empty with regard to an ongoing challenge. We can sustain rationalizations skillfully sometimes for years and then, without warning, find that the next time we reach for an excuse we are just out of gas. While it's tempting to indulge in a game of blame about this type of predicament, the best response is to experience it as a wake-up call. You'll probably have a pretty good idea of where in life it feels like you have run out of gas about something, and you'll also have a pretty good idea of what changes need to be made so that your life vehicle can be refueled.

Tires

Many people dream of flat or damaged tires. Tires usually represent the sturdy buoyancy of balanced self-esteem. Like confidence, you don't want tires to be over- or under-inflated. In order to carry you forward in life, this part of your psyche should be hardy, well-cushioned, and flexible. At your best, *you* are tough, flexible, optimistic, comfortable, and able to function well rain or shine.

Bald tires in a dream suggest that you have traveled too great a distance without attention to yourself; you're probably feeling like you can't get any traction toward what you want in life and you may also feel too permeable to the things and people around you.

Nails or other punctures in the tires represent an overabundance of criticism in your life. One woman who was dating a very critical man was always dreaming of meeting her friends in the parking lot so they could have a nail-pulling party, withdrawing the various barbs that were stuck in her tires. In waking life, her friends were her greatest support and their meetings usually temporarily corrected the damage her companion had inflicted on her self-esteem. Eventually, the recurring dreams helped to convince her that the wear and tear on her was too great to continue indefinitely and she ended the relationship.

Windshield

The windshield of your car symbolizes your ability to see where you're headed and to make sound decisions based on that information. It is a combination of your ability to take in information and to evaluate it accurately. If either your access to information or your ability to make sense of your situation is compromised, it's easy to get lost and confused. Most dreams of trouble with the windshield involve inclement weather conditions obscuring the view. Sometimes, the blinding headlights of other cars mix with the elements to make it difficult to see where you're going.

As in other types of dreams, weather conditions typically are associated with the emotional climate of your current situation. Snow is connected with endings, while rain is often symbolic of sadness or a downpour of emotion.

Many people who end relationships or experience the loss of a loved one dream of getting lost in the snow. Everything looks bleak, monochromatic, and otherworldly; familiar landmarks seem to have become unrecognizable. This white landscape is an interesting reflection of the shock we feel at the end of something—that moment when you stumble to the doorway and wonder absently who drained the color out of the world. Also, in snowy conditions, it is extremely difficult to remember that this pervading coldness will eventually give way to a new beginning in the spring.

We may dream of driving in a downpour of rain when some recent crisis or change has suddenly thrown us into a bewildering flood of feelings that make ordinary decisions almost impossible. If the presence of other cars and their headlights make your vision even more difficult, this strongly suggests that the well-meaning advice of others is intruding into your own vision of things and your ability to see your own path clearly.

Finally, mud and fog tend to obscure windshields in our dreams. Fog is a combination of words (air) and feelings (water). If your dream windshield fogs, it's likely to be because of a conflict between you and a loved one or because of a conflict between what you're saying and how you really feel.

Mud is a combination between the known and the unknown elements in a situation. Dirt represents the known thoughts and logical facts in a given situation, while water reflects the emotional components. When these two elements mix to create confusion in our lives, we have mud appearing in some annoying fashion. When passing cars throw mud on your windshield, it's likely that your encounters with others are activating an internal conflict between your own thoughts and feelings. It may be tempting to blame others, but they are really only mirroring your own conflict. Although it's easier said than done, you may need to make room for both elements in your present perspective and be willing to accept the need to work through a problem that is annoyingly messy or awkward.

Headlights

Trouble with headlights suggests a lack of awareness. If your lights are stuck on high beam, you can confuse others by your insistence that your perspective is right for all occasions. If you are racing through the dark night with your headlights off, the implication is that you are somehow not seeing where you are going because you are not being mindful.

One man had a recurring dream that his father was driving his car at high speeds without the headlights on. Riding in the passenger seat, he would scream at him to turn the lights on, but his father would ignore him. In waking life, he was indeed driving himself at top speed to succeed at his late father's business and his focus was on beating the competition and "getting there." He wasn't considering extraneous things like the impact of this lifestyle upon his health or what he was sacrificing in order to achieve this level of success. It was as if the part of him that he'd gotten from his father was at the wheel and that part was not too concerned about anything but its urge to drive him hard and fast toward success.

When we are in darkness in a dream, it often means that we are working with forces about which we are largely unconscious or unaware. These elements are not necessarily unwholesome but they are largely unexamined. Once this dream made sense to him, this man was able to adjust his pace without discarding his ambition. The anxiety dreams and the tension they reflected went away.

Vandalism

A vandalized car represents the effect of a recent disappointment or trauma upon your sense of autonomy and well-being. This symbolism conveys the sense of something that has happened to you rather than something which is malfunctioning or breaking down due to your own behavior. You should look for circumstances in your waking life which could inspire dreams of vandalism. Keep in mind that dreams exaggerate and vivify internal experiences. You should be able to link your dream with a recent event that seemed to shatter your confidence. One woman had a dramatic dream that her car was trashed and turned upside down when she learned that she would not receive some funding that she desperately needed. She felt, at least at first, that her future was trashed. She was so upset that the plan she'd envisioned wasn't going to happen that for a few days she couldn't corral her thoughts long enough to design an alternative. Eventually, she did come up with a workable plan B that permitted her to continue working while finishing her education. The dream was not a final analysis of her chances for happiness; it was an expression of her temporary despair and shock.

Physical Metaphors

Some theorists believe that the car is always a metaphor for the human body of the dreamer. This doesn't seem to be the case in all dreams, but there are some connections between the way your car malfunctions in a dream and physical problems. One woman who had chronic back problems tended to have recurring dreams about her car's wheels being out of alignment; she was continuously visiting her chiropractor for adjustments and her dreams seemed to echo this theme.

Another woman who was struggling with a pattern of compulsive eating dreamed that the gas gauge in her car was broken and that no matter how full her gas tank was, it always read empty. This helped her understand that part of her problem was the sensation of being hungry all the time, when in fact she did not need to eat again.

Terrain

The car you're in, how well it functions, and the way you drive all tend to reflect your style of coping with current conditions. The challenges you meet on the road, however, reflect the outside factors in your life that are impacting your ability to get what you want.

Uphill Climb

One of the most common driving dreams is that of going up a hill that is so steep you have serious doubts about your car's ability to make the climb. In dreams, uphill inclines represent challenges usually related to achievement of some kind. We seldom realize how hard we're going to have to work until we get partway into a project, and then it's too late to back out. The only way to get out of the predicament is to climb all the way to the top and complete the thing. But partway through, you may find your energy and patience wearing thin. As you would if you were actually driving, it may be necessary to shift into a lower gear, take things at a slow and steady pace, and rest the engine if necessary.

Roadblocks

Roadblocks come in several different varieties. The blockade by officials checking identification generally reflects concerns about your own qualifications to do whatever you have set out to accomplish. Typically your ability is not in question, but you may have concerns about your official credentials and experience. While it's natural for most of us to feel uncertain about moving into territory we haven't explored before, the reluctance you feel may be unrealistically self-critical. It's best to get a reality check on the importance of these credentials by talking to some people who have already done what you are setting out to do.

Fallen trees, boulders, and other natural obstacles more often represent factors inherent in your situation that are effectively preventing you from making any more progress. One woman, who longed to return to the career she loved, dreamed that a mountain of children's sneakers and dirty laundry blocked the road she was on. She found this humorous reflection of her frustration very encouraging because none of the elements of her roadblock were really immovable. She struck a compromise by staying home with her young family but working part-time out of her home office to keep her hand in her chosen field.

The Wrong Road

Many anxiety dreams revolve around taking the wrong road and becoming hopelessly lost. Others are much like a drive in any city—you are crowded into the exit-only lane and find that you're off the freeway and down some ramp that is rapidly taking you away from where you want to go. The essential theme in these little disasters is not knowing how to get where you want to go and only being quite clear that the road you've taken is the wrong one. If you think about it, this is how many of us feel about jobs and relationships. We don't know exactly how to create what we want, but we know this isn't it. Sometimes we're close enough to have a vision of what we're after, but we feel stuck in a frustrating cycle with people and evidence telling us that we can't get there from here. Most people find that the first step in getting back on track involves getting off the wrong road. None of us want to drop something inadequate before we have what we want firmly in our sights, but sometimes it's necessary to withdraw your energy from the wrong fit before you get clear enough to find the right fit.

Spinning Out of Control

Whether you dream of spinning out on ice or having steering fail around a curve, the image of losing control indicates that some part of your life isn't going as planned. Because this image is so immediate, there is usually an undercurrent of crisis in waking life that makes this dream easy to interpret. The real-life difficulty usually lies in the contrast between current conditions in your life and the way you're approaching them.

The Vehicle That Isn't a Vehicle

Some dreams involve driving something that isn't really a car through traffic. You may be driving a small building, a bathtub, a door turned on its side, a bed on wheels, or a motorized office chair down the freeway. The interpretation of these dreams depends primarily on how well you do driving your special vehicle and how you feel about it. Remember, what you drive and how you do represent the way you're going about making progress. If you're spending all your time in front of the computer, you may dream of driving your desk down the freeway. If this works well, then your focus is probably a good one for the time being. If there's a problem with the vehicle that impairs your safety or progress, then assume the difficulty symbolizes a real-life imbalance that is working against you.

One man who had recently started his own business dreamed of driving a rough-hewn plywood truck that was so new it didn't hold together at high speeds. To keep it operational and in one piece, he had to drive slowly and stay in low gear. This dream provided him with an excellent suggestion—do not try to grow the business too quickly; take time and get a feel for it before rushing into the fast lane. If you have a strange driving dream like this, evaluate what works for you and what doesn't, and see if there is a clue about how to move effectively and safely toward what you want.

Someone Else Driving

In many dreams there is another person behind the wheel of your car or you may be riding in someone else's car. In some instances, you may be driving from the backseat or the passenger side, unable to reach the controls. All the variations symbolize the influences that are impacting your ability to move through life comfortably right now. When someone else is driving the car, this often means that a particular part of your personality or programming is at the helm. You may be driven by something you learned (particularly from a parent) or you may be accepting direction from someone close to you.

One woman who was involved with a younger man found herself agreeing to all sorts of things she was reluctant about because she didn't want to lose him. She dreamed of riding in a car with him behind the wheel while she protested at his reckless driving. The dream allowed her to acknowledge just how unbalanced their relationship had become; although she enjoyed his company, she decided that it didn't make sense to have him controlling her behavior to that extent.

One man dreamed of riding on a motorcycle behind his father. Although he had no interest in motorcycles, in the dream he was going along with his father to try and please him. This man realized that many of the activities he engaged in as an adult were in fact not particularly enjoyable to him, but he had become involved with them because they seemed appropriate and manly. He decided to take a second look at the ways he spent his free time and make sure that he was doing things he enjoyed, rather than things he felt he ought to care about.

Style, Challenges, Self-Care, and Authority

When you have a driving dream, remember that the kind of car you drive and your driving skills reflect your present style of moving toward your goals. The condition of the car often reflects the kind of care you've been giving yourself and how well-prepared you feel for your present undertakings. The challenges of the road and terrain typically symbolize the rough elements built into your present situation and the driver of the car reflects the side of life that you are placing in temporary authority. The purpose of understanding these elements is not to make you feel wrong or make you panic about the pressures you're facing. Driving dreams tell us a great deal about whether the approach we're using is going to do the job, and what, if any, adjustments need to be made in order to safely create the kind of results we truly want.

Chapter 9

Modes of Traveling: Planes, Boats, Trains, and Buses

When you travel or take a trip in a dream, you're exploring the best (and worst) ways to handle a current situation. Movement is an extremely telling metaphor because it reveals what you're striving for and how outside forces are affecting you. If you dream of riding a solitary raft down a peaceful river, the implication is that you're moving with ease along with the flow, your focus enhanced by quiet and solitude. However, if you dream of boarding the wrong bus and winding up in a dangerous neighborhood, the metaphor implies a need for cooperation with others, better communication, and clarity about your goals.

Your traveling dreams are trying to show you exactly what is keeping you from getting what you want, even if what you want is simply to feel peaceful, secure, and at home in your own skin. If your dream is fraught with frustrations or goofy mishaps, it's important to take note of the mode of transportation used, the types of challenges involved, and whether the vehicle was designed for group or solitary transport.

What the Type of Transportation Reveals

The mode of transport in your dream says something about the approach you're using to handle a current situation, and it reflects that part of you that is most deeply involved: is it your feelings, your imagination and plans, or your concentration and mind-set?

There is an obvious difference between bobbing around in a lifeboat and flying on a 747. Besides the obvious contrasts, the lifeboat travels on water, which shows that the situation you're dealing with is an emotional one, while a plane travels through air, symbolizing the realm of ideas and imagination. The environment of the transportation represents the psychological dimension that is most pronounced in your current experience, either because of your personality type or because of the particular issue involved. Someone going through a highly emotional divorce is likely to dream about boats, ships, and struggling to stay afloat on water. But the person whose idea has been shot down by management is likely to dream of a plane with a fuel leak forced to abandon its flight.

Airplanes

Because they are airborne, planes are most often associated with ideas, innovation, and speech. People dreaming about planes are often working through professional challenges or trying to determine why their pet projects and ambitions haven't yet taken off.

One woman who was trying to start her own business dreamed repeatedly of taking her seat on a plane only to have the flight aborted when a technical difficulty was discovered. In real life, she was having trouble turning a beloved hobby into a business and she'd experienced many false starts. The dream hinted that her approach was slightly passive. In real life, she also had positioned herself but hadn't yet done the necessary groundwork and promotion to have her idea launched successfully.

Sometimes dreams of planes are dealing with more personal questions such as spiritual questions or even sexual themes. But for the most part, traveling through air is associated with the realm of ideas and plans.

Boats

Traveling on water is more common when we are dreaming about romantic relationships or interpersonal conflicts. Water is associated with emotion and deep currents of feeling.

One woman who was having difficulty with a relationship dreamed of being on a cruise ship in troubled waters accompanied by her boyfriend and several dead bodies. These bodies represented the many prior relationships she'd had and then ended. (In real life, she and her current flame were definitely experiencing stormy seas and despite their sincere efforts to work through their problems, they reluctantly parted company.)

Sailing can also be a metaphor for how you feel about your life at the present: the degree of mastery and control you have and your level of satisfaction about present circumstances.

One man who accepted a new position in his company took to his new duties instinctively. He dreamed of rowing a small, one-man canoe through a beautiful, fast-moving river. Although he knew nothing about the sport, he was able to paddle and steer expertly through rapids and make excellent time. This dream showed his sense of exhilaration and surprise at his own abilities in his new job. Although there are individual exceptions, traveling on water generally reflects current emotional relationships with others and with the self.

Trains

Trains often show the kind of progress we're making by following a particular train of thought. Because they travel along the earth, trains symbolize a grounded approach that utilizes logic more often than leaps of faith. Trains also require a preexisting track to follow, so they represent our ability to move along a prescribed course with fairly specific expectations.

One woman who began working on her masters degree was dismayed by the technical requirements of the writing and found the process laborious and unimaginative. She dreamed of being trapped on a train that she could not get off; it was necessary for her to ride it the entire length of its track before she would be allowed her freedom. In waking life, she did feel as if her mind had been abducted by a steely captor and she would not be allowed intellectual freedom until she completed the course of study she had embarked upon. Although the situation was not ideal, her dream helped her cope with the subtle depression she sometimes felt during that year of her studies. It gave her greater understanding that she was not just being lazy or ungrateful for her opportunity: there was a part of her that was truly suffering and feeling cut off during the process. Understanding the nature of this feeling allowed her to be less concerned about it and to endeavor to compensate for it by completing more creative works as time allowed.

A young man dreamed of being on a train that was twisting and turning too often so the train never got anywhere. In the dream, he decided that the track was too loopy and he'd have to get off at the next stop and catch a different train if he ever wanted to get anywhere. He had been trying to make a decision by asking so many people for advice that he was encumbered by numerous contradictory ideas. This style of sorting through the problem wasn't getting him anywhere. In fact, he was beginning to feel pretty loopy about the whole thing. The dream showed that the first thing he needed to do was get off that track (change his mental approach) and then make a decision that would take him in one definite direction.

Trains frequently represent our style of thinking and logic. The track seems to symbolize the expectations and presuppositions that keep us moving in the same direction. Trouble on trains usually suggests it's time to step back, to examine your approach to make sure your thinking is current and your method is appropriate to the situation.

Common Traveling Themes

The mishaps we experience in our dream travels reflect current challenges in our efforts to achieve goals and create solutions. Glitches in the systems represent outside influences frustrating our hopes, while our own misguided or panicky reactions illustrate how we sometimes make matters worse by overreacting.

Missing Your Connection

Perhaps the most common of all traveling dreams is that of struggling to catch your plane, boat, or train, and missing your connection. This frustration dream has important implications about the way your personal style and the actions of others are affecting your ability to achieve satisfaction.

This dream is often recurring and will surface when you have something important on the line in waking life or when you feel saturated with discontent about an ongoing frustration. Many times, the connection is missed due to poor preparation, packing at the last minute, or trying to do too many things at once.

When preparation is at fault, the implication is that something in the dreamer's orientation is clogging up the works. Some people procrastinate, not about the hard work involved, but about the focus and planning required to make their efforts count. Others obsess about nonessentials at the expense of larger goals. This theme is common to very successful people who are slightly overburdened by diverse interests such as the demands of work and family. In most instances, the slapdash packing does not reflect a literal inability to handle details; it is more often a clue about misplaced attention, getting hypnotized by what seems important only to continuously miss out on what is most personally valuable.

Some versions of these dreams include being left off the passenger list, lacking the ticket or credentials to get on board, or being denied access. These themes of being thwarted by authority suggest that one of the main stumbling blocks in your real life situation is gaining the cooperation and acceptance of others. You may be in a situation where the ability to achieve your goal hinges on whether others agree that you are right for the job. Or you may be trying to decide how unconventional talents can take you to a very specialized goal more often achieved through traditional, prescribed steps.

No matter how frustrating these dreams may be, they are actually trying to help you get what you want. Look closely at what it would have taken in the dream to let you make the connection. For example, should you actually have disregarded the advice of experts and trusted your instincts about the location of your gate? Should you have taken a look at the entire city's transit map and assessed the big picture before choosing the route you would try to take? Or were you overlooking the critical element of timing, trying to board a flight that was not destined to leave that day?

When there is something you clearly should have done differently in a dream, it encourages a shift of emphasis, understanding, or action in your waking life. Look for signs that slowing down might actually be more efficient than rushing around or that being more low-key about what you're going for will make others more comfortable with your ambition.

The Wrong Bus, Train, or Form of Transportation

Many people report dreams of taking the wrong bus or train and only realizing their mistake when it seems too late. Disoriented and unable to change course, each second takes them farther away from the place they're seeking.

This dream is common to people having difficulty with an important decision. They are exploring their worst fear of going in the wrong direction and being helpless to correct the mistake. We also have this dream when we've plotted a course based on sensible information that isn't completely right for us as individuals. The bus that represents collective desires may be the obvious choice at twenty years old, but it can begin to feel like the wrong road at thirty-five. The dream of going in the wrong direction is a signal from the psyche about the need to check into your original hopes and dreams and reconnect with the person you were before you got instructions about who you were supposed to be.

We may also have this dream of the wrong direction when we're worried about making our goals acceptable to others. At certain times in our lives there is great tension between what we want, what others want for us, and our sense of being able to control our own lives. Older people often have this dream when they are wondering about their options (how to stay close to adult children and maintain fulfilling activities). Young adults may have this dream when they are confused by the urge to make their own way and their desire to stay close to the fold. For many people, this dream is also associated with spiritual issues and a slow-dawning sense of having been swept along a road that isn't in harmony with their deepest spiritual convictions or hungers.

Remember, this train or bus is probably representing an inner direction in your life and to correct the course you're going to need to consult your inner compass. Friends and experts may not be much help in resolving your confusion; your best sources are probably your heart, intuition, faith, and inner convictions.

Loss and Disaster

Dreams of group disaster can be very frightening and they often recur, making it easy for us to wonder if they might be warnings of actual events. But vehicles and vessels filled with people are usually symbolic, reflecting our experience with a social influence or a real-life group.

A woman executive dreamed of being in a bus crash that left her dazed and miles from home. She was feeling increasingly detached from the goals of her company, and her hopes of achieving satisfaction with that group were, in fact, wrecked. She had gone as far as she could with that team and now felt strongly that it was time to alter her career course. She eventually changed fields completely and is very pleased with her new profession.

Just as a car can represent your individual progress in life, a group vehicle can reflect your role within a group: as a professional, student, man, or woman. One boy who was graduating from high school felt lost because his closest friends were leaving for college but he didn't yet know what he wanted to do. He dreamed of taking an ocean voyage that hit a hidden reef and left him abandoned on a desert island. On this island was a wise old man who advised him to stop feeling sorry for himself and start assessing the elements on the island that might help him survive until help came. This dream reflected his grief at the end of an era (the collective voyage was at an end, and he felt left behind). But it also suggested that the best way to get through this transition was to take stock of what he had going for him and be practical about his future until his choices and preferences became more clear to him.

You Must Take Charge

Another common traveling dream involves being on board a ship, train, or plane when the person in charge becomes unable to steer. You may have to jump into the cockpit of the plane and make an impromptu landing or leap to the front of the bus and heroically steer around mountainous curves. This dream suggests that you've been thrust into a leadership role through no fault of your own and that you feel the weight of responsibility for making some process work well for others.

A young teacher was asked to take over a class for a colleague who was on maternity leave. She dreamed of being on a bus when the driver became unable to drive. Although she preferred to remain a passenger, it was clear that no one else on board had the courage or the sense to take the wheel, so she rushed to the driver's seat. In waking life, she would have preferred not to take on the additional class, but no one else seemed willing to help out. The nerve-racking dream reflected her anxiety about the unfamiliar coursework. It also showed her ability to react swiftly and effectively to unknown conditions. She managed her extra work efficiently without mishap.

Dreams that force us to take control sometimes reflect the structure of a recognizable situation. In other cases, such dreams seem to be goading us to action, almost like a psychological prescription that reads: *take charge as needed*. In these cases, it may be tricky to recognize just what the dream crisis represents. If nothing in your waking life looks like this, it may be that you simply need to move forward with something that is important to you. Move to the controls and captain your ship with more purposeful action.

Safe Harbor

Some dreams of traveling seem to highlight the need to reach a safe haven, such as a sheltered harbor. Whether you're coming back to Earth after a space mission or sailing ashore on a wooden craft, the implication is that it's time to have a respite from your more heroic efforts. There is a natural rhythm that encourages us to take periodic breaks from our frenetic activities, but its subtle call is often drowned out by other, louder demands for our attention. But if you're dreaming of a calm harbor or a docking bay, don't be afraid to take that sabbatical or turn down the chairmanship of that committee. By taking time to restore your energy, you'll find the next chapter of your life more exciting and less effortful.

Meeting Loved Ones

Many dreams of flights, trains, and ocean voyages involve attempts to meet loved ones from whom we have long been separated, often by death. This certainly does not mean you are about to die or that the departed is trying to come for you. These dreams capture the bewildering sensation of being separated, yet emotionally never apart from those we love. They are like motion pictures of our inner landscape, showing us journeying to meet our loved ones but always somehow missing them.

In some cases, our dreams of traveling with the departed suggest we're dealing with challenges that may best be understood by considering what those loved ones would have thought of this situation or what they might say if they were here.

One woman decided to return to finish college after her children had grown up and left home. She was uncertain about her decision because it felt somehow wrong to focus on her own personal goals after having placed others ahead of herself for so long. She dreamed of traveling out to sea on a large vessel inhabited by all the women in her family. Her mother was there, as well as her grandmother, and other relatives she had never met but had seen in pictures. There seemed to be no captain on the ship, and all the women were reading maps and trying to plot a course even though they were unfamiliar with the process. The dream was both stressful and awe-inspiring because the women were so clearly determined to find their way. This dreamer realized that part of her discomfort in returning to school was due to the fact that no woman in her family had ever gotten a college degree and she was sailing off into uncharted territory. But the dream also inspired her because of the determination of the women. It touched her to think she was going to accomplish a goal that perhaps others might have wished for but felt was completely out of reach. She decided that when she was troubled by challenges and felt afraid she would remember the generations of women whose spirits would have been pleased by her accomplishment.

Keys to Understanding Traveling Imagery

Dream journeys typically reflect the progress we're making toward desired goals or they explore our struggles with a current life challenge. Since either situation can be fraught with stress, journey dreams often contain elements that reflect frustration and anxiety. It's important to try and identify the waking life situation that is being reflected in the dream. The more turbulent your dream, the more likely it is to be reflecting a current problem. If your dream is predominantly a disaster theme, then it's likely you're exploring various levels of a current challenge. But, if the dream is more focused on the destination and there are various frustrations along the way, then the focus is probably upon your progress toward a goal and the factors that seem to challenge that progress.

Either way, it's important to note the type of transportation you're on in the dream because that lets you know if the journey is one of the emotions (water), the imagination (air), or the intellect (ground). This can be important to understand consciously because no amount of rationalizing is going to resolve an emotional journey. To get back on an even keel, you will have to work with the emotions involved. If the situation is long-standing, this may take time.

When air travel is grounded by mechanical problems, this reveals that in order to launch your plans successfully, you'll need to iron out details of a practical nature, make sure the plan is viable, and ensure that you have funding and support.

Train troubles imply a need to examine your thinking, to focus on logic and strategic plans, to make a clear decision, and follow through with confidence.

Buses often reflect the way our decisions are influenced by collective expectations. Problems on a bus imply the need to identify what is most important to you, and if necessary, to summon the strength to go your own way even if it seems to oppose the status quo.

Remember that the trials and challenges you face in the dream symbolize the real-life impediments and emotions that are slowing you down. Perhaps most importantly, consider the reactions and solutions that the dream calls for to resolve the story it presents. What actions would improve your dream journey? The necessary ingredient to solve a dream dilemma is often a symbolic prescription for the action or position to take in waking life that will be most helpful to you.

Chapter 10

Water and Other Dream Settings

Water is a contender for the most popular, thought-provoking dream symbol. Even people who aren't familiar with dream interpretation will notice when they dream each night about floods, lakes, and tidal waves. All that water is too much of a coincidence and too persistent to be random. But the symbolism of water is often misunderstood because it has different connotations depending upon the form the water takes in the dream.

Traditional interpretations of water suggest that it always represents the unconscious mind, the collective unconscious we may all share, or deep repressed feelings. My theory about water is that it has a somewhat different meaning in a dream depending upon how it appears and what form it takes. The beauty of morning dew upon a flower is quite different from the horror of an approaching tidal wave. Both may be connected with the feeling aspects of life but the interpretations of the images are quite different. In order to understand the water in your dream, it is necessary to look at the form of the water, the tone of your dream, and your relationship to the water.

Bodies and Forms of Water

When water in some form is featured prominently in your dream, you know that the feeling, creative, and unpredictable dimension of life is having an impact on you. The symbolic nature of water is very much like its real-life qualities: fluid, life-sustaining, and relaxing. Showers, bathtubs, and inviting pools tend to represent this restorative aspect of water energy. However, when you have too much water energy in some situation you can feel flooded by emotion or drama and over-whelmed by a sense of having no control over a force that is sweeping through your life. Tidal waves, backed-up sewers, and leaking basements tend to represent this overdose of feelings that can accompany unwanted changes or deep uncertainty. Water in natural settings such as rivers, lakes, and the ocean tends to represent life situations of epic proportions that can initiate us into deepened emotional maturity.

Traveling on a River

Rivers can symbolize the flow of our lives in much the same way that a high-way or path can represent the road of life. This is particularly probable when you dream of traveling down a river in some kind of craft or boat. This type of river dream can provide a reading on how you're handling the particular phase you're in and whether your skills and responses fit the challenges you're facing. Typically, this type of dream is either exhilarating or frighten-ing. You either feel ready to deal with the rapids, the twists, and the current, or you're falling out of the boat, losing passengers, and narrowly escaping death. This type of dream is common to people who are bright, capable, and who enjoy using their brains and abilities to handle life. They can be all the more frustrated when the powers that usually serve them well are not suited to the particular condition they're dealing with or when their sense of con-trol over their fate is being battered by a rocky passage.

One woman who had just started graduate school dreamed of traveling down a beautiful river in a rapidly moving rubber raft. Although she was frequently doused in the rough sections of the river, she retained her balance and generally enjoyed pitting her skills against the toughest parts of the river. This dream seemed to be saying that although she was in for some real challenges ahead, she would not only be able to handle them, but would actually relish the chance to test herself. Her subsequent experiences in school bore out that theory; she not only succeeded in her studies but also found the work very stimulating and exciting.

Crossing a River

Another common image is coming to a river that must be crossed before you can go further. The necessity to cross a river is often symbolic of a phase that you must move through prior to achieving the goal you're after. In some cases, the crossing represents something you must face (inwardly or outwardly) in order to digest and get past a recent painful experience. After separating from a spouse or partner, many people dream of coming to a river they must cross and feeling confused about how to manage it. This implies that they are not only suffering a loss but that a great deal of what they're experiencing is an initiation or a preparation for what they will do next.

Others dream of coming to a river when going through a change such as becoming a professional, starting their own business, or moving away from their hometown. This type of image signals that you may be moving through a phase where you must stay positive even though you don't feel adequately equipped for what you're facing. If this fits, then it is a good time to reach out for support and reconnect with inspiring ideas and people.

When I had compiled the information for this book I was confused about which publishers to approach. I dreamed of reaching a river that had no bridge, so I would be forced to swim across. I held a wicker basket of precious paperwork that I desperately wanted to keep dry as I crossed the water. I laid the basket on the shore and jumped into the water, which unfortunately was over my head. After thrashing about unsuccessfully, I wound up sitting on the embankment stymied about how I was to make this crossing carrying the basket.

When I awoke, I realized this crossing reflected the next hurdle in the process (finding the right publisher). Since the dream made it fairly clear that I was not making much progress with solitary efforts, I determined to ask friends who were authors for their suggestions. Fortunately, one friend was working with an outstanding editor and a very positive publishing company that he recommended to me. I contacted them about the project and they decided to publish the book. They formed the bridge across the water so that the information could complete the rest of its journey into the world.

Encountering a Stream

Streams may represent a stream of information, ideas, or influences in your life. This is more likely to be the case if there are creatures—living things or fish—in the stream. If you are walking along the flow or beside the stream, you may be trying to follow a project or teaching in this time of your life.

The difficulty or pleasures involved in your progress sometimes reflect your level of satisfaction or frustration with this process. Concealed hazards along the stream don't mean you're on the wrong track, but they may serve as a heads up that the assignment you've tackled is laden with some unexpected complications or hassles. When a stream is magical, pure, or enchanted, it is likely that you're connecting with someone or something that is reminding you of essential truths and what it feels like to flow with life in an easy fashion.

A woman who was recovering from a death in the family and turmoil among her relatives found some solace in her dream of sitting by the bank of a sparkling stream. The sound of the water flowing along made her feel pure inside, as if all her tortured emotions were being washed clean. Birds sang gently in the background and a soft breeze lifted her hair. Although there was very little action or story to the dream, it was almost like a therapeutic treatment that she absorbed. Something inside her felt able to relax better after that dream—the very memory of it soothed her. She felt gently reconnected with the flowing quality of life, reminded of the sweet wholesome things she'd temporarily lost track of during her family's crisis. Some dreams of water are like that, presenting us with a scene or experience that is like medicine for the spirit.

The Peaceful Pool

Pools are often symbolic of a time to refresh and renew yourself. People dream of pools when they need to dip back into more pleasurable activities or reconnect with a sense of peace following a taxing period in their lives. When your time in the pool is refreshing and blissful, it is likely the dream is affirming your need and right to take time for yourself. If the pool has some exotic problem, contamination, or unwholesome conditions, this can reflect a tricky problem that is stirring up mixed feelings and draining vitality.

One young college student dreamed of taking a swim in a pool full of strange objects: there were seeds, beer bottles, gum wrappers, and old clothes floating in the water. All these objects made it hard—even dangerous—for her to swim and she felt confused and frustrated by the clutter. In waking life, she had become swept away by the party scene and understandably her studies and concentration began to suffer. She wanted to be with her friends, but her cluttered lifestyle was beginning to weigh her down. She realized some shifting of priorities was necessary if she wanted to accomplish her real long-term goals.

Taking a Bath or Shower

Baths and showers represent fresh starts and renewal. Usually dreams of showers and baths involve frustrating incidents where you can't find the shower, lose your belongings, or never make it to the bathroom because there are too many demands on your time. Some people have this dream pretty regularly when they fall prey to multiple pressures and postpone their own wishes for too long. It's a good idea to interpret these dreams as reflecting a need for time and activities that feed you, as well as a need to start fresh with the challenges and demands you already have. Step off the treadmill and do what you can to reorganize priorities so that you aren't living continuously under siege.

The Ocean

The ocean is associated with the unconscious elements in life, things that are very fertile and powerfully alive but which are a bit foreign to our everyday perspective. An ocean voyage implies a passage through sides of life that are mysterious to you. Being swept into the sea implies that recent experiences have launched you right into a hands-on struggle with the most baffling feelings and challenges you've known. This doesn't mean you're doomed by any means, but you may expect emotions to be on the surface and perhaps to feel more in crisis than your objective circumstances would seem to warrant.

When your relationship to the sea is a positive one, the implication is that you're enjoying this passage despite its mystery and uncertainty. Artists and mystics often have dreams of struggling with the ocean that are as beautiful as they are demanding. If you dream of coming to the edge of the shoreline and gazing out to sea, it is likely you are dealing with a situation that has brought you to the very edge of all that seemed certain. You may now be considering the vistas of possibilities that were previously unknown to you. This image is essentially a positive one since it shows you moving to your edge with a sense of wonder and interest. An open mind and heart will be your strongest allies at this threshold in your life.

Puddles, Mud, Swamps

Mud is a mixture of the things we know (earth) and the things we feel but aren't sure about (water). So in our dreams, mud is the perfect image for those situations that trip us up and slow our progress precisely because they evoke mixed feelings that are usually in conflict with our thoughts and opinions. A variety of images carry this symbolism including quicksand, mud puddles, eroded paths, and mucky swamps. Whenever you find a mixture of soil and water you are likely seeing an image of mixed emotions in conflict with thoughts. This can be useful to consider consciously since you can then stop waiting for the situation to make sense or come clear to you. You are going to have to proceed for the time being without the clarity you'd prefer. The nature of this situation is likely to be complex and paradoxical. Though your powers of logic may not solve the problem itself, they can help you orient effectively and realistically toward this slippery situation.

Rain

In most instances, rain carries the quality of sadness. Often, this is a subtle background effect in a dream that is easily overlooked. The rain is most likely to reflect sadness when the individual drops are felt or seen. Rain that overflows a container suggests a welling up of feeling or the sense that something is getting to be too much. If this fits, then acknowledging your feelings can go a long way toward making you more comfortable and balanced. There are times, however, when the rain is not so much poignant as simply natural, and part of the cycle of life.

A woman who was interested in moving overseas had a dream of driving a convertible car when it began to rain. The rain fell so hard and fast that soon it began to fill the car's interior and she was forced to pull over, open the car door, and let some of the rainwater out. In real life, she had been offered a wonderful promotion if she would move overseas, but the man she'd been involved with off and on for years would not agree to move with her, nor would he agree to get married if she stayed and declined the position. Although disappointed by this, her connection to the man felt very deep and she was overwhelmed with grief at the thought of moving away and ending the relationship. The convertible car, representing her desire to change, was flooded and detained by her powerful emotions. Although the situation was difficult and painful, the dream helped her to assess the choice differently; she did not want to stay stalled by the side of the road, bailing out water for the rest of her life. She decided to accept the position overseas, and once the decision was made, she felt strongly that she had done the right thing for herself.

Leaks

When something in your dream springs a leak or takes on water, this suggests that feelings previously kept on the sidelines are now coming to the forefront. This doesn't mean your emotions are out of control or that you're falling apart. But change or disappointment can stir up feelings of long duration that may seem irrational or unconnected to what you're going though. During such times, it's easy to be frustrated with many aspects of your life that seemed fine before or to suddenly feel as if nothing you do ever works out. Don't give in to that feeling. The sudden belief that everything is wrong or you're doomed to failure is a sign that one facet of your life is triggering some old issues. The cumulative effect can make your life (which seemed fine last week) look like a complete mess.

A woman who was going through a divorce dreamed that a leak in her kitchen quickly began to flood her whole house. To make matters worse, the water mixed with some old containers of Kool-Aid so that the leak that swept through her house stained everything a bright orange. In real life, her divorce triggered feelings she'd had since childhood about being abandoned by a man, partly because her father had abandoned her and her mother when she was little. Although the divorce was relatively amicable, she felt swamped with the hopeless fear that all men are untrustworthy and that for some unknown reason she was unlovable. The old Kool-Aid in her dream symbolized these old issues which mixed with the water of her current pain and suddenly became visible in a dramatic way. The dream's stain helped show how and why it suddenly felt to her as if her whole life was hopeless, when objectively it was only one brief marriage that had not succeeded.

If you're dreaming of leaks flooding the home, the implication is that you must tackle one thing at a time and resist the panicky illusion that everything is lost or everything is wrong. Your best tactic is to address the current difficulty and observe how it may be connected with other layers of feeling and memory. Be tough and practical with the objective factors in your situation and flexible and tolerant of your own feelings and needs.

Keys to Understanding Water Imagery

In symbolic terms, the element of water is associated with feelings, with the fluid, ever-changing energy of life. It is something without which life cannot be sustained; and in dreams of hunger for water, bathing, or soaking, it is the expression of a need that is very natural and very fundamental. For an artist, water might be the opportunity to express his art; for the religious person, water might be found in returning to the church. For people of deep feelings, water is the permission and space in which to live like a feeling creature rather than like a machine striving for efficiency. Symbolic water, like its real life counterpart, has the ability to make us clean, refreshed, and ready to start life anew. You might think of dipping into this water as letting your soul take a drink, whatever that means to you. In order to feel healthy, productive, and whole we seem to need the right balance of water energy in our lives.

When the water in your dream is desirable and appealing, this is almost always representing the nourishing aspects of fluid feelings, experiences, and people in your life.

When dreams present water that is formidable or contaminated, this often represents the swelling feelings that can seem to swamp the decks during unexpected transitions or disappointments in our lives. When that happens, the energy of water is taking us over and our coping strategies become vital to our survival and the maintenance of a solid perspective. Just as you might respond to an actual flood or emergency, you need to seek high ground and supportive people and let them know you need to tune into some stability and enduring perspectives in the midst of your storm.

Water that is mysterious, unfathomable, or oceanic may represent the unconscious regions of the psyche. Don't make the mistake of assuming this is territory filled with pitfalls or pathology. Instead, realize that it is unsettling primarily because it looks unfamiliar to us and because it operates with different laws than our conscious logic. This is also the region from which intuition, emotion, art, and innovation spring.

The Symbolism of Your Dream's Setting

There are two main reasons why the setting of your dream is worthy of attention. First of all, the setting is often a vivid clue about the topic of the dream. Scenes in a home are likely to express issues about relationship and family, while dreams taking place at work settings tend to explore work-related themes. This rule of thumb is certainly not ironclad, but it should be a reference point for beginning to examine a dream.

The second thing to consider is that the setting of your dream is often a metaphor for the real-life situation you're struggling with, whether the forces are external such as your work demands or internal like an inner conflict.

The City

Many action-packed dreams are set in a modern city. It may or may not resemble the town where you live, but the crowded streets, lights, and big buildings are almost like a generic modern city.

Cities are associated with the social aspects of our lives, the way we connect with people, and the give and take of communication. Whether you live in town or in the country, you derive a great deal of your identity and understanding of life from your contact with others. When we have a dream set in a city, this is the mind's way of exploring the beliefs, feelings, and issues associated with being a social animal.

War Zone

Battlegrounds typically represent the point of conflict in the dreamer's life. It may be that you have an ongoing conflict with your spouse and the dream of living on the edge of a war zone accounts for that setting because emotionally, that is a picture of your experience.

More often, however, the war zone is a picture of an internal battle that is being waged between different regions of your own psyche. You may have strong feelings in one direction and an equally strong belief or opinion in another. The price of this conflict, like the price of war, can at times be very high and quite painful.

Caves

Although few of us explore caves in waking life, it's very common to dream of camping or resting in a cave. This represents a place of sanctuary where outside forces cannot penetrate. It's a psychological haven you may need to retreat to for some reason; many people need to find a kind of center during transitions and upset. After pulling their energy back for a time, they are able to emerge with renewed strength and certainty.

The Forest

In every life there are times when we're lost, confused, or ejected from the tidy arrangement that made us feel secure. When that happens, we take our turn walking in the wilderness, trying to find certainty and looking for something new to hold on to. When that happens, we dream of being in the forest. This image seems to be deep, symbolic shorthand for moving though territory that is unsatisfactory, insecure, and unsettling. As many stories and parables attest, it's only human to rail against this fate and to try and make it to safety as soon as possible. But there is something important about our time in the forest. It takes as long as it takes and embracing the process seems to be the fastest way to get through it. It is the best way of ensuring that we emerge wiser and better for the experience.

The Seashore

The seashore is symbolic of the place we come to when we've exhausted the known possibilities and can no longer pretend we're going to be able to out-smart this particular situation. At the end of the day when we're out of excuses, explanations, blame, or anger, we reach an edge in our conscious-ness. There really is nothing left to think about the situation and no possi-ble angles to work. This is the threshold to new territory and even a new dimension of experience. The land symbolizes everything that we've tried to stand on and the water is a symbol for a whole new, unlimited potential. When resistance, fear, and staying stuck are done, we dream of reaching the seashore and seeing how unlimited the choices really are. This image usually comes in dreams before we consciously know we're through the worst of it, so take it as a harbinger of hope, growth, and change.

The Jungle

The jungle is a metaphor for tough, confusing situations. Like the forest, it is a place where it is easy to get lost, but the jungle is more about intense frightening passages than the transforming time in the forest. The jungle appears in many dreams about work pressures; it's very much like the atmosphere of trying to get a job done (or reach a goal) while numerous dangerous creatures and pitfalls surround you. Jungle dreams almost always include an important strategy that serves to improve the situation or reveal a counterproductive pattern that keeps you in the quicksand.

Prison

Various types of jails and prisons are common dream settings and they reveal the times in our lives when someone or something is reducing our sense of freedom. For men, the combination of rules at work and expecta-tions at home combine to create many dreams of being well-adjusted in prison, having cell-block barbecues with the other prisoners, and making the best of a life sentence. For women, more frequently dreams of imprisonment deal directly with primary romantic relationships and the sense of loss of autonomy that may accompany layers of well-intended compromise. It's critical to evaluate the degree to which loss of the experience of freedom is self-enforced and to be honest with ourselves about the causes and costs of feeling imprisoned.

On Stage

Regardless of your lack of theatrical experience, you may occasionally dream of being onstage to give some kind of performance. When a dream is set onstage before an audience, this suggests we're working through a question that pertains to the way we are seen by others. It's typical of new employees to dream of being onstage expected to perform but never having been given their lines. This suggests we're concerned with pressures to perform mainly because we fear so many others will be watching. Whatever the plot of these dreams, their setting onstage is a clue that the issue is exacerbated by concerns about being on display to others.

High School

So many dreams are set in high school that this may be one of the most frequent of all contemporary dream settings. In general, high school settings tell us that we're dreaming about social concerns, even if the real-life situation that gave rise to the anxiety is related to work. Whether it's a lost classroom, unprepared exam, or a confusing locker we're dealing with, the primary worries in these dreams center around our own competence and how it may reflect on us in the eyes of others. We don't want to look foolish, to draw attention to our mistakes, or fail to fit in. These are dreams of quiet torture and tension in which we sweat it out alone and try to conceal the areas where we have questions, confusion, or are in need of help. In high school dreams, asking for help or giving away our plight is like a fate worse than death. This irrational hierarchy in which fitting in is so much more important than finding out what we need to know is perhaps the reason why so many anxiety dreams dive back into high school. Perhaps this is one of the psychic imprints for this particular error in thinking. Dreams set in high school reflect our insecurities and social fears.

The Mall

The mall is a social marketplace where we make choices and try to find a balance between being true to ourselves and fitting in with others. Dreams set in the mall almost always have to do with making choices juggling these two urges. It is not surprising that teens and young adults have the most dreams set in this area because in early years these forces seem mutually exclusive and harmonizing them seems almost impossible. When more mature adults dream of the mall, they are usually involved in trying to make decisions and choices as well.

A Place from the Past

Many recurring settings are unique to the dreamer. You may spend a surprising amount of dreams in your hometown or a place you lived years ago. Dreams take historical snapshots of our first experiences and use those settings as symbols of a particular quality or feeling. Just as your first love is often the star of dreams about current loves, so the first place you felt independent, connected, betrayed, or frightened may appear in future dreams.

My mother lived in Chicago until she was twenty-two and had trouble learning the route of the elevated train downtown. Once, she got on the wrong train and felt anxious about finding her way home. To this day, when she feels overwhelmed about making a decision with too little to go on, her dreams are set in downtown Chicago near the train station. That setting is the imprint for feeling anxious about which way to go.

The place you used to live holds some special significance, and although you may not be aware of it consciously, your deeper mind has it tagged as the first experience of some kind. If you're curious, make some free-association notes about what overall first experience you had in that setting. Decoding this kind of psychic labeling can make your dreams more clear and useful to you. If you're stumped, here are some sentences to complete.

This place was where I learned to: _____

That was the first time I ever really felt: _____

The biggest thing I learned about myself during that time was: _____

That was an important time for me because: _____

Keys to Understanding the Setting of Your Dream

Remember the setting of your dream may be a prime clue to what part of your life the dream is focusing on. Look for shades of your work or living situation to determine if this is about your professional or personal life.

When the setting is less familiar, consider how it may reveal the psychic territory or emotional climate of a current concern. You may need to summarize the setting in one word in order to recognize this factor. The jungle you might describe as dangerous, the war zone as conflicted, and the ghetto as disenfranchised. These labels can help you get a handle on the variables involved in current challenges and sometimes they will provide important clues as to how best to respond to them.

Settings from your past may be imprints—memories of hallmark events or passages in your life. Making mental notes about how you would summarize these times will help you recognize what you're going through and why you may be feeling or reacting a certain way.

Chapter 11

Animal Imagery in Dreams

Whether you're rescuing an abandoned kitten or scrambling up a riverbank to escape the jaws of an alligator, the animals in your dreams are likely to be images you remember for years to come. Certain animals are extremely prevalent in modern dreams and have relatively universal associations, although many of the things they symbolize may surprise you.

One prevalent theory about animal symbols is that they always represent aspects of the dreamer. Although this theory has great validity in some cases, I believe that it does not always lead to a correct interpretation. I've discovered certain markers in dreams that indicate whether an animal is a part of the dreamer's personality or psyche and when it represents a person or force in their life. Folkloric interpretations suggest that certain animals are bad luck while others are more benevolent. My dream studies suggest that the rigidity of these notions doesn't fit with the rich variety in our contemporary dreams.

We must look at the nature of the creature as it is presented to us and notice our reactions toward it and feelings about it. In this approach, the image and our reactions to it flesh out the meaning of the symbol and should be considered together before attempting to translate the meaning of the animal. That being said, there are certain animals that are in the majority among modern dreams; they are the most prevalent animal symbols. Their presence is suggestive of certain predictable conditions in the dreamer's life, and for this reason, I've included the most typical explanations of their meaning for your consideration.

It's important to note that all animal images have both positive and negative potentials; they may represent the worst danger in your life or the noblest aspect of your spirit. The interpretation of the image depends upon the tone of the dream and the light in which the animal is presented. Since our concern is with contemporary dreams rather than historical mythology, I'll present the animals that appear most often in our dreams today and share the interpretations of these images that have most often been fruitful.

Lions

Positive Potential: In its positive aspect, lion energy is valiant and courageous. It moves against the odds and carries one forward into victory. The phrases we use to describe this energy are "lionhearted" or "she fought like a lioness." When dreams are highlighting this potential, the lion will be imposing and beautiful, but not generally threatening. This may be a reminder to call on reserves of courage within yourself or to reconnect with people in your life who make you think of this kind of brave heart.

Negative Potential: In its negative polarity, the lion can depict shame-based energy that will do almost anything to avoid an encounter with the unadorned self. It is pride turned upside down and eating us alive. This is the kind of drive that compels us to have the latest car and the right clothes because the self we dress up this way is propping up our sense of security. This energy leads to chronic compensation for a self that is quite likable to begin with. It can also lead to compulsive behaviors and a sense of being secretly afraid. In some cases, the lion may represent a person who is frightening or intimidating you. This is likely to be a person who has significant appetites and possibly a ruthless side to their nature. When dreams are reflecting this type of dynamic in your life, the lion will be on the loose, terrorizing you or taking over in some way.

Elephants

Positive Potential: The elephant is an emblem of enormous strength and power. This strength is connected with original or old intentions and motivations. This is not the achievement you were taught to desire by outside influences; it is the core ambition or urge you possessed even before you learned what was stylish or rewarded by society. When the elephant appears in a dream, it may serve as a reminder to harness early ambitions or natural inclinations at this time in your life. It is a signal to ride forward using a brand of wisdom that is not sensational or glamorous, but which is related to your very essence. Think of the elephant as often an emblem of the original self, the person you were born to be. I ask clients, "If you were hit on the head and lost all memory of your identity and had to start life over with just your natural inclinations and disposition, who would you be?" We keep so much of the original self in storage that when it emerges and requests our attention, it is quite often huge and overwhelming, like the elephant. When dreams present the essential self in the form of the elephant, it is often a magical, highly friendly, and benevolent creature.

Negative Potential: Negative dreams about elephants are rare, but they usually show that the original self has been lost or violated in such a way that some other pattern has been made to take its place. Sometimes we cultivate an inflated sense of importance to compensate for feeling separate from our best selves. In other cases, we become engaged with problems that actually consume our attention for years and save us from having sufficient time to notice how lost we've become. When dreams point to these patterns, the elephant may seem fat and unattractive, unhealthy, or neglected. In a few cases, elephants may be enraged and attacking in dreams, suggesting that unconsciously this central aspect of the spirit is frustrated with its containment.

Turtles

Positive Potential: The turtle appears in dreams when we are in some way focused upon the body. Turtles represent the power to protect yourself, and to move at your own pace. Since they enjoy both air and water, they also represent the capacity to think clearly and feel deeply at the same time. When dreams remind us of these abilities, the turtles in our dreams are fascinating and often mysterious.

Negative Potential: Turtles frequently appear in the dreams of people who are dealing with chronic health issues. These turtles are often ill, neglected, or confined in some way. It is not necessarily a sign of illness, but seems strongly related to the struggle to feel at home in the body and to make peace with physicality. When the turtle is wounded or has been contained, there is reason to wonder if you are struggling to resolve a question about body image, being safe in your body, or other psychic scar tissue related to body questions.

Mice

Positive Potential: A single mouse may symbolize an approach to things that is quiet, diligent, and detail-oriented. Such an approach is highly valuable if you're in the midst of a project that requires focus and meticulous accuracy. This method also requires the ability to narrow your field of attention and deal with one element at a time. The mouse in your dream may symbolize these qualities in you and encourage you to recognize and use them or it can symbolize someone you know who values this style.

Negative Potential: The negative polarity of a mouse is the way that small things can evoke exaggerated worry and fear. If you reacted with fear or panic toward the mouse, it's possible you're letting something extremely minor ruin your peace of mind. Several mice tend to represent pettiness, smallness, and the way that small worries can eat away at something and do significant damage. If the mice in your dream seemed like pests or problems, you may feel better if you can expand your view and look at the big picture instead of fretting over minor problems. If you are surrounded by mice in the dream or they've gotten loose somehow, this implies that you may be letting yourself be seduced by preoccupation with detail and postponing a necessary change.

Rats

Positive Potential: On the positive side, rats are the ultimate survivors. People who have been orphaned or who grew up with tough conditions may dream of rats long after they have carved out excellent lives for themselves. The rats in this case may be depicting the strength and stubbornness that carried them to safety. Because this survival trait is associated with hard times and desperate measures, it can be relegated to the shadow or unrecognized part of the personality. Later, when signs of the rat emerge, they can bring unsettled feelings and inexplicable concern. If this fits you, then owning and understanding the positive as well as the negative aspects of this energy can help you integrate and appreciate all your strengths and abilities. Your rat energy can be like an inner warrior that will step forward and defend your territory, your business concerns, and your family when necessary.

Negative Potential: Rats often represent something in ourselves or another that we dislike or feel disapproval toward. They symbolize fierce greed, aggressiveness, and the ability to invade almost any territory. You may have seen a side of a loved one or friend that shocked you recently or felt something you did or said was strangely cruel or selfish. This does not imply that either you (or your loved one) is a rat. Anyone can be shocked to see a starved, desperate, ruthless side of themselves surface and try to grab what it wants. Suspending judgment can help you look at recent events with objectivity and honesty.

Squirrels

Positive Potential: Squirrels represent the bustling energy of everyday concerns. This energy can be immensely productive and focused, permitting you to nest in a new home quickly or finish projects in record time. To others this pace may seem frantic or silly, but once you're in gear it's best if they just step back and let you go to it. Squirrels also have an innate sense of timing, so if you flip the switch inside and go into this mode, it's best to trust it and go with the flow.

Negative Potential: In the negative polarity, squirrels can reflect an empty whirlwind of busyness. We all sometimes slip into automatic pilot at a very fast pace and focus on getting things and relationships without really considering whether we truly want them. We get stuck in a hoarding cycle. If this sounds like you, calm down a bit and take time out to reflect on what's worth your energy and emotion at this point in your life.

Badgers

Positive Potential: If the badger in your dream is impressive but not attacking you, it may represent your own qualities. If you are fighting for a cause or defending your family or home, you may be startling others with your fierceness. But as the badger would agree, it might be entirely called for in this instance. You also don't necessarily have to be ferocious or threatening to enlist your badger energy. If you've ever dealt with a company that refused to issue a refund for a return, you may have courteously hounded them until you obtained satisfaction. In your own way, this determination, resistance to discouragement, and tenacity are examples of positive badger energy.

Negative Potential: When they are menacing, badgers represent power that has an edge of intimidation. The badger may depict someone you know, like the boss who rules with domination when reason isn't on his side; or it could highlight your own tendency to fall back on personal power to get your way. If the badger is attacking or bothering you, it probably represents someone who is giving you a hard time right now and causing you some hurt feelings.

Fish

Positive Potential: Schools of fish glimpsed beneath the surface often represent unconscious material or truths about the self. People doing powerful personal growth or therapy sometimes dream of recognizing beautiful fish beneath the surface of the water. While many people dream of beautiful fish, some people envision different settings and fish. Don't worry if your fish don't look so good or the water is polluted. This doesn't mean your unconscious is dirty, but rather that the phase you're in may be painful and tough at the moment. This is a time for patience and gentleness with yourself.

Negative Potential: Fish in a bowl, pool, or aquarium typically represent aspects of the self that enjoy emotionally nourishing situations. If you dream of fish needing your care, it is likely you're a creative, sensitive person who has somehow gotten into a lifestyle that cuts you off from the things you love or from creative self-expression. This dream tends to recur in variations until some steps are taken to make the emotional climate you live in more supportive.

Frogs

Positive Potential: Because they undergo such dramatic changes in form, frogs are often associated with transformation. If you're entering a new phase in your life or emerging from an ordeal, you may be feeling like a whole new person before too long. Don't let details or uncertainty wear you down. The vastness of this change may have an up side because it's going to catalyze a whole new life. Frogs that lead or guide you in a dream (especially those that can talk) reflect a side of yourself that is very basic and trustworthy: your instincts and intuition. This dream may be a clue that you can think all you want about a current problem or question, but your best bet is simply to follow your instincts.

Negative Potential: In some humorous dreams, frogs represent men who did not turn out to be princes. If you have a collection of frogs, or you're bringing home another frog on Friday night, you may see a pattern. Instead of rubbing salt in a wound, though, this dream could be a suggestion to give the search a rest and focus on enjoying your life and friends in other ways for a bit.

Rabbits

Positive Potential: Rabbits represent quick responses and the need to take action. Rabbit energy in this form can help you sense danger and steer clear of predatory people.

Negative Potential: If you or someone near you has recently become frantically busy out of worry, the rabbit may reflect this pattern. Avoid judging yourself or anyone about their fears, but keep in mind that the urge to rush right now may be misguided and counterproductive. Strive instead for a sense of steadiness and some more relaxed rhythm to your efforts. By pacing yourself you'll be less likely to make a slip that could worsen the situation and you'll maintain your health and energy so you can stay the course.

Dogs

Positive Potential: Dogs are associated with love and loyalty. When you dream of a dog that is hurt, injured, neglected, or confined it is very likely a symbol for part of your own nature. This is particularly probable when the dog in the dream is your own dog in real life. The dog in need of help or care represents your own need to be loyal to yourself or to get yourself out of a situation where you are being hurt in some way.

Dogs are also emblems of the masculine elements in life, and for this reason they sometimes symbolize a man in your life or the way masculine factors are effecting you. Women often dream of picking out a puppy or trying to find the dog they want to bring home when they are selectively dating and looking for a man to become involved with. Problems between cats and dogs in dreams suggest a tension between masculine agendas and feminine needs.

Negative Potential: In cases where wild or mean dogs are threatening, these animals usually represent aspects of a situation (or sides of someone close to you) that are bothersome. Examples are the wild side of your partner or the elements of a current situation that make you feel vulnerable.

Uncontrollable factors that come with the territory need not be a concern, but if you're worried about addiction or other serious conditions it may be time to get support and bring your worries out into the open.

Cats

Positive Potential: Cats are associated with feminine qualities, characteristics, and energies. The cat in need of care, feeding, or rescue typically represents a side of the dreamer that is not being supported by present circumstances. If your need for freedom, unconditional affection, or tenderness is being neglected, it may be time for you to begin supporting this aspect of yourself. If you are in a relationship that neglects these needs, you may assume the dream is highlighting that deficiency. You may also assume that your real task is not fixing the relationship, so much as it is taking steps to begin taking your own needs more seriously.

Negative Potential: Wild, unruly, or vicious cats tend to represent someone in your circle who has a mean streak. That person is likely to be female, but if not, it is probably the female aspect of that person that is given to hostile episodes.

Pigs

Positive Potential: Pigs that are depicted in a pastoral setting may be associated with family ties and relationships. If you're confused about a situation involving a relative or family ties, the difficulty may be arising because you are so close to different factions and you have conflicting sets of expectations to uphold. This may be a situation where you'll have to settle on what you think is best and adapt to a compromise that isn't completely perfect but upholds what you believe is right.

Negative Potential: Pigs that appear in an unfavorable light are typically associated with someone you know who has recently been greedy, selfish, or insensitive. The image of the pig may be highlighting the attributes that disturb you in the other person in a way that helps you understand the problem better.

Kangaroos

Positive Potential: Kangaroos represent special agility and strength. When presented in favorable scenes, this type of energy suggests that your ability to bob and weave may be of service in a current situation. In other words, you are equipped to do something that few others could manage. If this seems to fit, it is time to rely on your special powers to get things done quickly and to tackle things in your own way.

Negative Potential: Kangaroos are associated with exotic situations that bring with them unexpected attributes. You may be dealing with a group of people making impossible demands or a faction at work that has swept in full of eccentric ideas. In some way, if you're dreaming of kangaroos, it's like your world is a bit upside down at the moment or you've fallen into the clutches of some odd characters. Just behave with whatever dignity you can muster and wait for the whole thing to blow over.

Whales

Positive Potential: Like the elephant, the whale is a symbol of the original self, the being you were before all the bruises, misunderstandings, and disappointments in life cut into you. The whale surfaces in our dreams to show this being is still alive and whole, emerging again in the present. You may be returning to your faith, emerging from a dark passage, or regaining stability after divorce or addiction. Whatever the particulars of your circumstance, the sighting or encounter with a whale is a reminder of power and hope. It offers assurance that a huge force within you remains unscathed and is available as a resource from which to draw strength, healing, and sound judgment.

Negative Potential: Although negative whale dreams are rare, they usually show menacing and large creatures that impinge upon swimmers or boaters in a threatening way. These scenes reveal that some problem, habit, or misunderstanding is taking on huge proportions in your life. It's time to get straight with yourself, acknowledge what is going on, and think about changing course. If you need help because this is something that defies your ability to handle it alone, then set about finding the right person, group, or resource to set a solution in motion.

Snakes

Positive Potential: Some snakes are associated with initiations of power in the psyche. They appear as a single snake you have to pass in order to proceed or the snake you have to befriend or embrace despite your fear. Be aware that you may be in for some changes and that you'll be walking through issues and barriers that have stopped you in the past but will not stop you now.

In some dreams, snakes are associated with the boundary between life and death, matter and spirit. If you have recently lost someone or have been contemplating mortality for some reason, your snake dream may reflect this. This is certainly not a sign of death, but rather an emblem that spiritual issues are of importance to you right now.

Negative Potential: Snakes often represent troublesome situations that are intimidating and disturbing. This is most common if you've dreamed of a pit of snakes or piles of them on the floor around you. These situations have layers of complexity that make it especially hard to deal with them in a straightforward way—or to avoid them. One of the secrets to handling these snake pits is to be conscious of your own fears and issues. If your buttons are getting pushed or someone is intimidating you or using your moral standards to manipulate you, get as clear as possible in your own mind and heart about what's going on. Consciousness is your best weapon and medicine here.

Some snakes do have sexual implications. A single snake in the bedroom or a single powerful snake may indeed represent a man in your life or masculine energy that is creating power issues in the relationship.

Pythons

Positive Potential: Clearly the python is a snake, but because its symbolism is so specific it should be evaluated differently from other snake imagery. Although positive dreams of pythons are rare, this snake does embody the power to dominate a situation by having a potent grasp on it. If the python in your dream is a pet or clearly a benevolent presence, it is likely to be a reminder of your power to wrap yourself around a challenge and successfully prevail.

Negative Potential: Pythons can represent situations or people who put the squeeze on you. If the person is a loved one or a romantic interest, you may be torn between wanting to please them and feeling they don't give you enough room to breathe. Every person or situation has a down side. When that down side is a feeling of pressure or being suffocated, it's hard to put your feelings into words—or even to understand the sense of panic you've been feeling. Relationships that have a terrific sexual charge often come loaded with jealousy and possessiveness, too. Regardless of what (or who) your python represents, be careful. If you have to choose between your well-being and this consuming attachment, vote for your own life. If the python represents a situation, take your needs for greater freedom seriously and assume your inner voice is telling you the absolute truth about what is good for you and what crosses over the line.

Octopus

Positive Potential: As a sea creature, the octopus carries the energy of emotion and multiple ways to hold or connect. In their positive form, these creatures reflect emotional depth and the ability to send your energy in myriad directions without losing your center.

Negative Potential: The octopus represents a person or situation that has multiple ways to hold or influence you. You may be dealing with something you'd like to create or move toward, but find to your surprise that you can't quite make it happen. Think about the fears you have under the surface and evaluate whether they may be tripping you up. There's no need to panic about this—awareness is your solution. The more honest you are with yourself, the less those tentacles can hold you back.

In some cases, the octopus is associated with one's mother; the rules, expectations, hopes, and even hostility toward her can run surprisingly deep and affect situations that seem unrelated on the surface. See if familiar issues with Mother may be involved in your present circumstance. If this makes sense to you, then realize your awareness is the key to greater mobility and freedom. This has, of course, less to do with your actual mother as a person than with the feelings and shoulds that are inside you. Take your time, keep choosing wholeness and freedom in large and small ways, and learn everything you can about these issues in books, tapes, and discussions.

Horses

Positive Potential: Horses often symbolize a side of the self that is spirited and in need of stimulation, movement, and life itself. A damaged, shackled, starved, or overly confined horse suggests that you're being hobbled by a restrictive condition or choice you've made. The suffering horse is a desperate symbol designed to make you take your own needs seriously and begin choosing what makes you feel alive and authentic.

In some cases, horses are specifically representing the part of you that is like a workhorse and has been placed in harness. If you have enslaved your vitality consistently for too long without reward, you may have some very desperate horses in your dreams. The cure is likely to evaluate how you can make a living with something that enlivens rather than deadens you. Sometimes small changes are significant enough to turn the tide so you can breathe again.

Negative Potential: Because horses are closely associated with vitality, they sometimes reflect your body. If you're living like a machine and never letting up, you may dream of exhausted horses that have been run into the ground by unfeeling riders. Though you live in your body, you are also its caretaker. A threshold of well-being can be regained if you will take reasonable and compassionate care of it.

Deer

Positive Potential: Deer represent the quality of gentleness that is without aggression. This harmless aspect is capable of extreme tenderness and understanding. It also requires the care and protection of other sides of your nature in order to remain safe and secure. It is not wise to lead with this side of your nature, but instead to be protective of it and share it with those who are worthy of its light and tender presence. The deer in your dream is most probably an emblem of this aspect of your own nature, but it may also represent someone who is very dear to you.

Negative Potential: When deer are too vulnerable or naïve, they can easily become victimized. You must evaluate whether this is the right time to share your deer energy with others or if you should be more respectful of the deer qualities in someone you love.

Bears

Positive Potential: Occasionally bears represent an inner force of power and strength ready to be tapped. If you are facing something that seems bigger than you can handle, your dream of a benevolent bear can be a signal that normally dormant powers are being gathered in preparation. When you need to take action, you may be surprised by the forces at your disposal.

Negative Potential: Bears often appear in dreams as symbols of men with dominating or frightening characteristics. This is particularly true if the bear in your dream is menacing or chases you. Women with painful incidents in their history are particularly prone to dreams of being chased by a bear. This implies that in current relationships and interactions, the specter of an old wound may be causing them to be less than comfortable. The bear in your dream is not necessarily a comment on a current partner or friend, but is a reminder that domination, force, and bullying are things you cannot tolerate.

For men, a bear may represent the single overwhelming challenge faced while growing up. Economic struggles, someone who undermined your confidence, or overly macho friends may have been a burden that strongly impacts your view of the world. In one sense, whatever you do battle with today has a flavor of that old challenge about it. In such cases, the dream may recur periodically whenever you are pitted against negative factors. This need not be problematic. Knowing what drives you allows you to make keener, more intelligent choices to fulfill your goals and to discern whether they are in your best interests.

Owls

Positive Potential: Owls are associated with unusual powers of discernment and wisdom. They reflect the ability to be perceptive and to deeply comprehend the meaning of those perceptions. Owls are also associated with the ability to decipher mysteries. The owl in your dream is likely a symbol for the part of you that is highly intelligent and somewhat psychic. This symbol suggests you may be involved in studying unconscious material or things that are typically hidden from view.

Negative Potential: Owls sometimes appear as symbols of the end of an era, the passing of a loved one, or a metaphorical death of some kind. They are not predictors of death but they may appear in dreams when you are digesting changes that involve any kind of ending or letting go. If you are losing something at this time, the appearance of an owl suggests that you will do well to let go with as much grace and understanding as possible. By releasing our endings, we move more smoothly into the new beginnings that follow.

Peacocks

Positive Potential: This bird symbolizes great beauty and emotional depth. Because the tail feathers include a variety of colors, the implication is of a broad range of understanding and feeling.

Negative Potential: Peacocks typically represent pride in appearance or accomplishments. This bird is likely to represent someone in your immediate circle who is showing off or unconsciously positioning themselves to be admired. This may explain why that person is irritating to you or what has been making you uncomfortable in their presence. If you suspect the bird reflects a part of your nature, it may be useful to know when and where you've been bragging or displaying your accomplishments. There is nothing inherently wrong with showing your stuff as long as it is not an unconscious drive that controls you without your knowledge.

Wolves

Positive Potential: The positive polarity of the wolf is very common in dreams. This is the symbol of loyalty to the passion for life. It is the vital part of the psyche that needs freedom, solitude, and authenticity. Many women dream of wolves with luminous eyes that seem to be guides or totems. These wolves appear when you need a reminder to stay with your quest, to feed your freedom, and to return to the part of you that is authentic and not domesticated.

Negative Potential: Wolves that are frightening symbolize some kind of devouring tendency. This could be anything from a sexual appetite to an addiction of some kind. The wolves in your dream may represent someone or something in your life right now that seems beyond your control. Or they may reflect the part of yourself that keeps you running to feed its cravings. The appetite for possessions or the craving for new, different partners may be part of the wolf motif. If you suspect this is an aspect of your personality, be aware that you have choices about how to respond. If an addiction or compulsive pattern is at play here, get help or at least learn more about how it operates. If you think the wolf is someone else, be cautious about which vulnerable spots you expose to the wolf's appetite.

Spiders

Positive Potential: In their positive aspects, spiders represent the feminine capacity for weaving successfully, for creating something beautiful and intricate where nothing existed before. Spider energy is also connected with patience and the inevitability of success through skill.

Negative Potential: Spiders represent small things that evoke big fears. A dream featuring scary spiders reflects current challenges that are bugging you because they're associated with personal fears. Try not to take them as seriously as you have been. Because you're dealing with something that is, for you, emotionally loaded, be on the lookout for overreactions on your part and a tendency to worry more than you need to.

A big, hairy spider or a spider in bed with you is sometimes an indicator that your current relationship is touching a sexual wound or fear. This is not a sign your partner is trouble, but that intimacy is triggering your fears about being vulnerable or exploited. Steady yourself by confiding in your partner if appropriate and observe the trend of your spider dreams. They should subside and possibly disappear as your confidence grows.

Sometimes spiders are associated with one's mother or the mother figures in your life. When mother-in-laws visit or mother energy is somehow thrust upon you (with all its blessings and frustrations), you may dream of spiders cropping up. This doesn't imply that mothers are creepy, but simply says that the threads that influence us are extremely strong even if they are not always visible.

Rarely, spiders appear in dreams when there has been a death in the family or when some kind of death is an issue in your life. These are not harbingers of death but they do reflect the discomfort and fear that arise when we are forced to walk through that territory. This is a time to take extra care of yourself and to be careful about making drastic decisions. Stability, not change, should be your goal for the time being.

Crabs

Positive Potential: In their positive aspects, crabs symbolize the ability to cultivate a homey energy in varied circumstances. The person who makes the office feel like a family or team atmosphere is using crab energy. The public servant who truly cares about individuals and families is coming from a crab perspective. Have you ever noticed that some people get married and almost immediately their life blossoms into a family atmosphere, while others marry and are like two single people who have become roommates? Crab power is the energy of making a home.

Negative Potential: Crabs represent the part of the psyche that is resistant to change or letting go. This is the side of us that is afraid of losing what we have and so may hang back instead of taking a chance. Yet this tendency also permits us to build homes, make lasting connections, and dig into a niche we find, so we may be stubborn about evaluating when and where we're misusing this power. If you are bitten or pinched by a crab it is likely that part of your current situation involves a resistance to change—in yourself or another. If this fits you, then your task is one of respecting the need for security (or what appears as security) while still setting the stage for continued progress.

If you've been dealing with someone recently who is irrationally crabby, take time to offer subtle reassurance that nothing will be lost by the actions you're taking. Once that person knows their status quo isn't being threatened, they will be more able to relax and accept what is happening.

Wildcats

Positive Potential: Wildcats are associated with feminine elements of life that are untamed and may be fierce or irritable with hunger. A snarling wildcat may symbolize a part of your nature that has long been neglected and wants what it wants. This will usually be in the nature of a love affair, an adventure, or some emotional experience. This is not a craving for an emotional connection of cloying sweetness but of vital aliveness. As long as you are not being pushed into some kind of addictive pattern, you may want to listen and consider the needs of this wild thing because they may be things that will also feed your soul.

Negative Potential: Some wildcats are simply images of a woman who has been hostile or volatile with you recently. The boss or visiting bigwig who snarls at everyone without cause may appear as a vicious wildcat in your dreams. Be aware that some of her anger may in fact stem from her neglect of her own inner cat. You'll have to guard against sudden ambushes, but inwardly, spare a grain of compassion even as you keep a low profile.

Ravens

Positive Potential: Ravens are symbols of the mystical side of life. Although folklore pairs them with death and morbid tales, they appear in dreams more frequently when psychic abilities are opening up or when the dreamer is a student of transpersonal awareness. You'll need to summon a kind of spiritual courage right now to avoid being thrown by the emergence of so much material. If you're experiencing an ending, keep in mind that a beginning or birth is just around the corner. Allow yourself to lean into what's happening in your life right now and trust that at its core some healing truths are being uncovered.

Negative Potential: Ravens can also represent the flurry of activity that can accompany an ending or change. The people who try to benefit from a misfortune can sometimes appear as ravens in dreams. So, too, can people who derive energy from recounting tales of woe, even though their stolen energy is an unconscious process and they're unaware of the real urge behind their interest.

Dinosaurs

Positive Potential: Dinosaurs represent experiences, feelings, and patterns that date back to your early history. In their positive aspect, dinosaurs represent exciting discoveries about the past that have powerful implications for the future.

Negative Potential: If you're wrestling with a relationship or striving toward a goal, be aware that one of the things influencing you may come from the distant past. This doesn't mean you're trapped by your past; rather it suggests that being aware of this element can give you an important advantage. If you're willing to let go of things that have held you back before, you'll be capable of taking a significant leap forward now. You may also be able to understand something in yourself in a much deeper and more comprehensive way than ever before.

Bluebirds

Positive Potential: Bluebirds are associated with pleasant feelings and positive experiences. They are primarily symbols of good times and happiness. They also represent the power of positive thinking because birds are symbols of thought and spirit. If you are happy now, the bluebird almost certainly reflects that condition. However, if you have not been well or content lately, the bluebird may be a reminder to get a grip on your attitude and try to become more positive in your outlook. Finally, because the blue color is associated with personal truth, you may find that doing what you believe to be right, combined with a positive attitude, is the best medicine for your present situation.

Negative Potential: Negative images of bluebirds are quite rare, but because of their upbeat associations they can sometimes warn of the cost of chronic denial. If you are too busy selling others on how great your life is, it can prevent you from recognizing and correcting the things you would like to change.

Vultures

Positive Potential: Although vultures in the sky usually signal the remains of a dead animal, a vulture in your dreams is not necessarily as morbid as it seems. Vultures often appear with positive attributes, or are capable of taking apart something that seems ruined. This is a reminder that the remains of a situation or memory can often be transformed into knowledge or power. Some dream vultures are actually therapists, turning the past into nourishing fuel for the future.

Negative Potential: Vultures represent situations and people that are focused on the past, sometimes dissecting it with unrelenting determination, other times seeming to be fueled by it. These may be people who veer off into the past no matter what topic is brought up, or people who seem to devour the details of other's misfortune as if fueled by them.

Eagles

Positive Potential: Eagles are emblems of strategic intellect and the ability to make wise decisions. The eagle in your dream likely reflects these capacities in yourself or in someone near to you. The eagle suggests the power available by using the intellect to scan the big picture, identify what you want, and swoop in to get it.

Negative Potential: In some dreams, eagles come in and devour helpless animals or precious things. The implication here is that the scalpel precision of the intellect is gone awry and, like a buzz saw, is devouring the tender side of life or relationship. If you've ever been around an erudite person who ripped you to shreds with rhetoric, you know the destructive power of the negative eagle. If you suspect that this element in yourself is becoming overblown, take time to engage in activities that get you out of your head and into your heart and body. You don't have to abandon your intellectual gifts, just restore life to the other sides of yourself for greater balance.

Parrots

Positive Potential: Parrots are birds of great intelligence, sensitivity, and devotion. They represent a verbal disposition and quick thinking. If the positive potentials of the parrot are trusted and allowed to merge with the verbal skills, the result transcends glibness and becomes a genuine and very moving expression.

Negative Potential: Parrots are associated with the tendency to repeat what we've heard or been taught. All of us know what it's like to be with someone whose conversation seems to be a series of tape recordings on different topics. Bring up a topic and they will spout their prerecorded message. The parrot in your dream may be reflecting someone near you with this annoying trait, or it may be warning you to evaluate things for yourself before you begin sharing them with others.

Seagulls

Positive Potential: Seagulls are associated with the ability to understand change and transformation. This quality is common to people who are either older or who are soulful in some way. The gull suggests patience with situations involving uncertainty or lack of control. People with this quality are good at accepting strange events, things that would unsettle the average person. The presence of this bird suggests that (whether you know it or not) this quality of acceptance, grace, and understanding is one of your strengths. If you're dealing with something that's been consuming your energy or triggering control issues, take a deep breath and begin to let go. If you can't let go completely, then just begin to unhook what has been pulling your strings. The gradual freeing of your energy will go a long way toward bringing a satisfactory resolution to things.

Negative Potential: In their negative form, seagulls represent wasted potential. Think of them swirling and screaming above some litter in the park, eager to sample a bite. This is a symbol of higher potential sidetracked in the pursuit of what is convenient or trendy.

Doves

Positive Potential: Doves are indeed emblems of peace and symbols of fulfillment. Doves may represent creative works that you have undertaken, things you promised yourself, or the potential for a special kind of happiness. Doves are also emblems of integration. After an interior battle or inner conflict has been waged, doves may represent the wealth of possibilities open to you now that your creative impulses are no longer blocked or detoured.

Negative Potential: Although negative dove imagery is rare, they can represent cloying sentiment or passivity carried too far.

Hawks

Positive Potential: Hawks represent the capacity for swift action and sound judgment. The hawk's appearance in your dream suggests that a broader perspective will help you with a current situation. Look at things for the long-term or from a higher viewpoint and apparent obstacles may prove illusory. If you've been paralyzed by indecision or are too worried to act, the hawk suggests that swift, bold action may be helpful. This doesn't imply aggression toward others, but it suggests taking action in a way that lets you move toward what you want.

Negative Potential: If the hawk was scary or too predatory in your dream, the implication is that you may have too much of this tendency operating in your present situation. Either someone else involved is coming on too strong or you yourself are letting the hawk energy be dominant in your personality. If this approach is inappropriate for the situation, this power can do more harm than good. In that case, moderate your predatory instincts and maintain your keen perspective.

Foxes

Positive Potential: Foxes are associated with keen intelligence and good survival instincts. As with any animal, this may represent a side of your own nature or someone close to you. Foxes that are disarmingly wise or even crafty are more likely to represent a side of your own nature that will stand you in good stead with present challenges. Because the fox is predominantly associated with the ability to avoid harm, this image may be a cautionary one. You may be in a situation where keeping your cards close to your vest is a good idea. It is all right to plan and quietly be watchful until the time is right to make your move.

Negative Potential: Generally, foxes that are unsavory in some way represent that side of someone you're dealing with. There may be some sleight of hand going on; so look twice at all offers before saying yes. Foxes, like the coyote, are associated with the archetype of the trickster. That is a symbol for the kind of situation that is especially tempting to you but is actually a form of enchantment. You could fall under the spell of something that is not ultimately good for you. Try to keep your perspective and avoid getting carried away.

Weasels

Positive Potential: The weasel represents the capacity to be extremely flexible and subtle. The symbolism suggests that flexibility is more important than bravado in your current situation. Be creative, plan quietly, and don't boast of successes or ambitions right now. Keep one eye on the door and have a plan for getting out of the present situation quickly if necessary. Weasels have a bad reputation, but when this animal appears in a positive form in your dream, it may be a signal to focus on the outcome you're going after rather than the impression others have of you. The implication is that this set of traits is somehow favorable to you right now. You may need to be extremely diplomatic, tactful, and circumspect in current negotiations. It is fine to draw upon these traits in ethical ways to protect your interests as long as you don't allow this mode to possess you.

Negative Potential: If the weasel in your dream is unpleasant or suspicious, it's likely that someone you're dealing with has an agenda they haven't told you about. Pay particular attention to any loopholes in contracts or agreements you may be considering that would allow the other party to let you down. When in doubt, take precautions that might seem unnecessary under most circumstances and play it safe. If you're relying on someone to support their half of the agreement out of their good nature, temper your trust with some safeguards and consequences should they fail to come through. If you have everything in place, including a back-up plan, then you can relax about the situation and let the chips fall where they may. Avoid going off into emotional tangents about the situation or getting lost in judgments about others. People who become possessed by their weasel energy are often largely unconscious of the ethical and moral implications of their actions. Becoming attached to judging this phenomenon or feeling victimized by it is a trap that will bind you to them and drain your strength.

Crocodiles

Positive Potential: When crocodiles appear in dreams as impressive, beautiful creatures, you are being reminded of their positive potential as a resource to call upon. Crocodiles are obviously powerful, and much of their strength comes from knowing how to do one or two things extremely well and in being comfortable with who they are. This may be a time when you should lie in wait for an opportunity and avoid showing your strengths to passersby. Timing is very important in your current situation and you should focus your energy toward being ready to seize the moment when it comes.

Negative Potential: Crocodiles represent hazards that lurk beneath the surface of a seemingly harmless situation. This could be a bad temper in someone around you or a pitfall built into some new deal or territory you're exploring. If you're dreaming of a crocodile, some part of your intuition has already detected a potential problem on your turf. Keep a watchful eye out for telltale signals and incongruities and be ready to defend yourself or duck. Your brain may not be able to keep up here, but your instincts are already tracking the situation. Tune into your body, trust your reactions, and you'll respond effectively to whatever comes up.

Alligators

Positive Potential: Although positive dreams of alligators are extremely rare, they can let you know that in certain cases, making a nuisance of yourself may be the right thing to do. In psychological shorthand, alligators represent problems that come on suddenly and consume all your attention while they're around. If you're involved in a conflict or are trying to figure out the right strategy to use, positive alligator energy may be a good resource. This doesn't mean you need to try to intimidate anyone or get into attack mode. But it does suggest that being all over a problem and using energetic follow-through may bring about a swift victory.

Negative Potential: When you're pitted against an alligator in a dream, it means you're dealing with a situation that has severely rocked your sense of balance. Alligators represent problematic situations that are intense but usually not of long duration. The alligator in your life could be an assignment, a new responsibility, a job layoff, or an interpersonal problem. Whatever this situation is, it has shaken you a bit. It may be strictly business, but somehow it probably feels more personal than that. You need to decide whether you're going for containment (minimizing the problem), wrestling (taking it on no matter what), or recruiting reinforcements (enlisting others in the cause). Discussing the situation and seeing if others can at least support your efforts may be a good place to start.

Monkeys

Positive Potential: Monkeys sometimes represent the traits of high energy, intuitive leaps of thought, and extreme mental agility. If yours is a charming monkey or one in need of attention, this may be a sign that you've been working beneath your capacity or somehow holding back your brightest self. It may be time to take the first steps toward that thing you've always wanted to do.

Negative Potential: Monkeys often represent minor problems or ideas that grab hold and won't let go. If you've been obsessing about a work project or feel consumed by the need to make a decision, the monkey is probably representing that pattern. You may be convinced the problem is extremely serious, and perhaps it is, but your own obsession may be a big part of what's throwing you off balance. If you really can't rest until you get this resolved, then do what you must to get help or sort things out.

Buffalo

Positive Potential: Buffalo represent great strength, power, and purpose. If they appear in a dream in a favorable light, the implication is that returning to something you've always loved and trusted may be in order now. Go back to your roots, your faith, your early certainty, and let it nourish you. Try on the concept that nothing in your life was wasted and nothing was mistaken. Look at the crossroads in your life for the gifts they bring and spend time mentally collecting and appreciating those gifts. If your dream featured a magical or blessed buffalo such as a white buffalo calf, then you are definitely being reminded of a special capacity within yourself that is now being presented with a window of fulfillment. This is a time to reach for the magic.

Negative Potential: In some cases, buffalo appear as symbols of intimidating power; there may be a stampede or a wall of creatures that will not let you pass. Being aware that something is taking your power by bluffing you is sometimes enough to halt the process. Now is the time to let your own strength start to build up again, especially if you've been through an ordeal or change. Your task is to focus on systematically doing every good thing you can to build up your strength. There may be times when courage fails you or you're tempted to doubt yourself. Don't give up. The only antidote to falling sway to this force is to prepare beforehand something you can mentally return to when you're feeling shaky. Write down an affirmation or an uplifting quote that you can read whenever you feel uncertain or arrange a couple of friends to act as supporters so that you may call them for a booster shot if those doubts begin to creep up on you. The more you refuse to be buffaloed by this problem, the sooner it will leave you alone.

Bats

Positive Potential: Bats represent the unknown, unfamiliar elements in current experience. They can reflect the surprising side of someone's personality or the potential for magic and mystical events. When bats are likable or seem more mystical than scary, you are being reminded of the positive potential of this image. This is a time to court your psychic abilities and to lean into your sense of fate and destiny. Believe in yourself and retain an open mind about meaningful coincidences. If you see something that those around you fail to recognize, don't doubt your perceptions, but also don't feel obliged to convince anyone about what you know. Magic moves on its own continuum and if you're traveling that wavelength in some part of your life right now, it behooves you to concentrate on learning all you can and respecting the opportunity to grow.

Negative Potential: If the bat in your dream was scary, you may be picking up mixed messages from someone or getting involved in something that is against your better judgment. You don't have to abandon your sense of adventure entirely, but if you're getting signals to be careful, listen to them. Remember that bats straddle the energy of day (conscious thought) and night (unconscious processes and mysticism). There is nothing more alluring than energy that blends these two dimensions and you may feel almost powerless to resist a seductive force in your life. If you must take the initiation of visiting the shadows, then do so knowing the hazards involved. And, if possible, take at least one objective friend into your confidence so that you have someone to throw you a life raft if you seem to be getting out too far from shore.

Insects

Positive Potential: In their positive aspect, bugs represent the power of small things to create large results. If your dream features industrious ants or other insects getting a job done, you are being shown a strategy for accomplishing what may have seemed like a daunting task. You need to focus on details, make sure you do all the small things right, and avoid looking at the mountain and thinking how big it is. Also, this is a time to work in harmony with others. Lean into the existing team and let others do their jobs, and don't hesitate to enlist others in your plan. If you're the type who usually does things alone, this is a good time to learn about the power of asking for help and asking for what you want.

Negative Potential: Bugs usually represent people, situations, or behaviors that drive you crazy! In themselves, these things aren't important but they have a tendency to get under your skin and create big reactions. One way to adjust the situation is to take your feelings seriously and quit trying to brush them aside. This person, group, or outing may not be for you.

In some dreams, ants or termites appear to be taking something apart or breaking it down. This suggests you may be in a phase of ending something and that you'll need to finish the disintegration of the last thing before you launch into something new. Take the time to explore and digest what's happened recently. By absorbing the ending phase, you'll be more capable and refreshed when the next phase opens up.

If the bugs in your dream were in your food or had invaded or contaminated something, it's time to take stock. Consider whether your health habits and relationships are wholesome and nourishing for you. Just be sure, whatever you decide, that you're being honest with yourself and taking the best possible care of your health and happiness.

Ants

Positive Potential: The positive aspect of ants is their amazing capacity for work and accomplishment. They are testimonies to the power of intention, organization, and persistence. When ants appear in a dream in a positive or neutral light, the implication is that this humble but powerful motif may make a difference in your life. If you're being diligent and industrious, this may be a part of yourself that you take for granted or even find boring. Don't underestimate this power, though. It is usually the force behind impressive success and achievement.

Negative Potential: The negative aspect of the ant is the robotic work syndrome. Endless overtime or a compulsive approach that never wavers can actually gobble up years of life before it's noticed. If the ants in your dream were bothersome or repugnant to you, it is possible you're feeling the need for some variety and change of pace.

Bees

Positive Potential: In their positive aspect, bees represent fertile and productive thought processes. This is a time when you can produce far more than you might have thought possible by harmonizing with the efforts of others and going with the flow. You may not always get along with family members or your team at work, but right now it's time to jump on the bandwagon and take advantage of group energy. You may be able to do several things at once without losing track or missing a beat. Just make sure you are staying on a harmonious wavelength and moving quickly because it works, not because you're pushing the river.

Negative Potential: Bees are often symbolic of busy thoughts or frantic internal chatter. The words and ideas that buzz around in your mind sometimes make it hard to think calmly or tune into what you really want. The noise and sting of bees represent this cycle of worry, internal instructions, and conflicting expectations. Bees also are strongly associated with the collective. That is, the expectations absorbed from family, friends, and social influences. It is typical to dream of bees when you're going through an experience that is highly laden with expectations from your social or family group. Weddings, college selection, funerals, and childbirth are examples of situations that bring with them intensification of group expectations. There may be little you can do to change the nature of what you're going through, but you can take steps to quiet your inner chatter and realize you're going to have to settle on reasonable compromises rather than perfection in some areas.

Hornets

Positive Potential: Positive dreams about hornets are rare. If you do dream of hornets in a positive or neutral scene, it suggests that you are about to benefit from your reputation without having to get involved in a conflict. Just as people steer clear of hornets' nests without thinking twice, you may find someone steps around an argument to avoid triggering a conflict. Stay the course, keep your balance, and the situation should work out favorably without the need for a confrontation.

Negative Potential: Hornets represent people and situations that bring with them a threat. Generally, the threat is not deadly or terribly serious but it is something that would be terribly painful, like sadistic criticism, confrontation, or hostility. The hornets' nest is a symbol of trouble waiting to happen, often something that has been quietly building without your awareness. An example would be someone jealous of you who has been seething with envy for some time and may burst out with hostile words when you least expect it. Another possibility is a pocket of anger or negativity that you've been carrying for a while.

If you've noticed a tendency to be short with people lately, it may be time to consider what's bothering you and whether you can release it. Because hornets usually nest in high places, look for the problem in some opinion you hold about yourself or how people should behave. Even if you are technically right, it may be to everyone's advantage if you let go of your agenda and concentrate on keeping your own mental field clear and healthy.

Occasionally, a hornet will represent your own busy thinking and irritability running amok. If you've been driving yourself on all fronts and feel like something is building up to a blowing point, try to calm down. Choose to tackle one thing at a time, get some exercise, rest, and relaxation even if you feel you can't afford the time. You'll save time and trouble in the long run.

Slugs

Positive Potential: Slugs seldom appear in dreams in a positive light. When they do so, it is often to highlight our human prejudice against something that we do not understand. In a culture that values speed, beauty, and dryness (denial of emotion), a creature that represents the opposite of these values is automatically looked on with disfavor. Consider whether you have been denying the nature of someone in your life or some part of yourself that needs to move slowly right now. If so, acceptance is the best medicine to support movement through this passage, as well as the awareness that this is not going to be tidy or controllable. Emotions are going to ooze out at unpredictable and inconvenient times; just let that be the way things are right now.

Negative Potential: Slugs are associated with sticky, unpleasant problems that you'd prefer not to have to address. These conditions are lingering and tend to be resolved with aggravating slowness, and only through conscious attention and awareness. Try to overcome your reluctance to handle the situation and let go of your wish that it would just go away or somehow become easy or more appealing. If you're waiting to get in the mood to handle this forget it, that's never going to happen. Just put aside your doubts and proceed with diligence and care. The situation will prove easier and less painful than you fear but only once you let go of the wish for it to disappear.

Hippos

Positive Potential: Hippos are powerful creatures who do not necessarily need to dominate in order to succeed. When you dream of hippos in a positive light, this suggests you have the power to make a difference or to have things go your way even if you don't think of yourself as a dynamic leader. Your strength lies in your ability to enjoy both air and water; you can make dazzling conversation while at the same time you understand deep feelings in a way that few others can. You hold a space in which others can discover which feelings are most impacting their thoughts or learn new concepts that can heal and uplift emotions. Your strength is in accepting your unique nature and in leading by sharing those qualities rather than trying to become what you believe might be more fashionable.

Negative Potential: If the hippo in your dream was irritable or threatening, this implies that either you or someone near you is feeling out of balance. Most of us have experienced issues with weight, food, or health that rise up out of nowhere when we've failed to understand a deep feeling that lies under the surface. This is a time to be honest with yourself about all levels of your current experience and own those aspects even while you remember that you are all those things and more.

If you feel the cranky hippo may be representing someone else in your life, try to understand that they are feeling far worse about things than you may have realized. This isn't a time to show you are right about some disagreement or to say I told you so. This is a time to support them by honoring the entirety of their experience, even if they are unconscious of it themselves. If you create psychic room for the bigness of their feelings, they will not feel so unacknowledged and confused. Grant them the right to be having the experience they're having and the tension will soon transform into something that feels more useful to all concerned.

Dolphins

Positive Potential: Dolphins symbolize your sense of connection with others and sometimes with the world. Dolphins spring up in our dreams when we are engaging in activities that increase a sense of connection. It is ironic that some dreams of dolphins happen during relative low points in our lives. But these dreams tend to leave us with a positive feeling the next day. During times of change, loss, and sadness we may be upset or confused but we may also gain a keener sense of compassion and empathy. In other cases, a course of study or a single moment of clarity may open doors that let us feel at least briefly that we are all connected and valuable.

Negative Potential: Dolphin dreams almost never show these creatures in a malevolent light; but sometimes the dolphins are in danger or it is unclear whether you are being approached by a dolphin or a shark.

Since sharks represent separation, it's likely that you're involved in a situation of heightened emotion where it isn't clear whether a relationship or connection is going to blossom or be severed.

If you dream of a dolphin in danger, this implies that some important connection is being threatened or that your ability to communicate honestly is being impaired by outside factors. Try not to panic and just keep being yourself. There is something magical about dolphin energy and if you protect it, it will reemerge unscathed, even if the form (or relationship) must change. Remember that dreams about dolphins indicate connections, so even their negative potential suggests bonds with others.

Sharks

Positive Potential: In their positive aspect, sharks reflect power and efficiency in harmony with a strong life force. If you put aside natural human fear of these creatures, their sheer capability to survive and do their thing is incredible. The shark is true to its nature and relentless in pursuing its goals. If the shark in your dream seems beautiful or more inspiring than frightening, it's likely you are being reminded to trust your instincts and strive toward what you desire.

Negative Potential: Sharks typically represent fears that arise in specific situations. You may be interviewing for a new job, sensing trouble in your romance, or taking a stand against a circle of friends with a different code from yours. Sharks represent fears that have intense impact on us but which tend to be invisible in most situations. Like the fin or shadow of a shark in the water, you can't be sure what you've just seen or why your heart clenched with panic for a second and then returned to normal. Most shark dreams not only express hidden fears—they send up a flag that these issues cannot be ignored.

There are usually conflicts involved that have to do with a wish for autonomy and individuality versus a wish for union and security. You may be taking steps in your life that create a sense of independence or separation from what is familiar. Thus the shark represents the fears you have about what it may mean to be on your own in a new way.

If you're sailing over shark-infested waters with your lover, you may be sensing some things in the relationship that compromise your individuality. In that case, the sharks reflect your conflict between wanting more respect or freedom and your desire to stay in the warm place you've found. The real-life choices may not be so extreme and uncompromising but the conflict that pushes and pulls you tends to have these two polarities. The one guarantee with such dreams is that in order to resolve this situation you are going to have to trust your own take on things and then have the courage to support what you decide. No matter what choice or direction you go for, you'll find that courage is that passport that takes you through.

Flies

Positive Potential: Although flies are seldom featured positively in dreams, they can represent the ability to move quickly without getting caught up in the machinery of a cumbersome plan or requirement. If the fly in your dream seems positive, this suggests that your inclination to do things in your own way isn't as far-fetched as you may have been told. Have a back-up plan in place, but experiment with the departure from tradition you have been considering.

Negative Potential: Flies typically appear in dreams as signs of emotional contamination. Their appearance suggests that a current problem or project is made difficult by the presence of unstated but powerful influences. You may be responding to someone else's agenda or feeling confused by conflicts that are not yet conscious and clear. You may also be reacting to limiting ideas that are without foundation but which spread a sense of hopelessness or frustration throughout your plans. If this fits your situation, take a step back and assess what is going on. Once you identify what is making things seem hopeless, confused, or impossible, you then have a choice about how or to what degree you respond to it.

Centipedes

Positive Potential: Centipedes reflect the power of modest beginnings and activities to take us farther and higher than expected. Although dreams seldom feature this creature in an admirable light, when it does happen, the implication is that you should return to your roots for inspiration and energy. Ultimately, it's going to be very hard to stop you from getting what you want and if life is going to throw out barriers, then so be it. You aren't going to be the one to short-circuit success by holding yourself back from trying. Go ahead and crash the party, and if they ask you to leave, fair enough.

Negative Potential: In their negative light, centipedes symbolize beliefs with numerous effects. Often these are ideas adopted in early life that stay with us in various ways into adulthood. The numerous legs of the creature represent the variety of ways that limiting beliefs and self-criticism can move with us into each stage of life. Interestingly, these beliefs and ideas are seldom actually true. On a positive note, the appearance of a centipede in a dream alerts you to the existence of such patterns and indicates they may be inhibiting your progress in some important way right now. Don't underestimate your power to roust these thoughts out and cast them aside. They are quite small in comparison to the overall force of your intelligence and spirit.

Embracing Animal Imagery

The animals in our dreams are particularly potent messengers of change and healing. When the animals are presented in their negative potential, we're alerted to the nature of the threat we're dealing with in waking life and gain a quick sense of the best strategy to use.

When dream animals need our help or appear in their positive potential, we can learn the lesson of a lifetime about our deepest nature or most essential needs. Here are a few rules about getting the most from your dream animals:

1. *Remember that hostile, threatening animals tend to represent a troubling person or problem in your life.* The real-life situation or person is probably not as dramatic or scary as the dream animal, but don't be confused by that. You are being shown something important about the nature of the situation, the threat it presents, and how to protect your interests most effectively.
2. *Dream animals in need of rescue or care almost invariably represent a part of yourself that has been neglected or abandoned in favor of needs that seemed more*

important. Make it a priority to give yourself what has been missing and understand that the type of animal reveals the type of change you need to make. For example, kittens need love and tenderness. Birds need freedom to let their thoughts soar, and horses need health care and less work, just as fish need an environment where emotion is a given. Dogs need loyalty and permission to do what they love. The action you need to take is a combination of what the specific animal needed in the dream and the general needs and type of environment that species of creature would require in real life.

3. *In special cases, it may be necessary to live with the image of the dream animal for a while before you feel you have uncovered all it has to offer you.* Accept that process and work with it. If you have a general idea, that is enough to start moving your energy in a particular direction and to set the exploration in motion. Remember, the creature was selected because it most aptly depicts something important and it was selected by your own deeper mind. There is no conspiracy of secrecy or confusion involved and you are not being shown something you aren't ready to understand. Just keep your intention to understand open and receptive, and you'll be rewarded by understanding the kind of transformation you need and the best approach for creating it in your life.

Chapter 12

Psychic Factors

ny provocative subject has the potential to goad us into making extreme
judgments. In my opinion, there are two great mistakes that are often made
regarding psychic dreams. The first mistake is to dismiss the existence of
psychic elements in dreams. The second mistake is to overemphasize psychic factors
to the point that unnecessary worry is generated or faulty decisions are made. Both
are a kind of superstition. They are what psychologists call polarized views and any
researcher will tell you that extreme prejudgment is not conducive to clear percep-
tion or valid discovery.

In addition to avoiding extreme views, to understand the psychic side of dreams,
we must resist the impulse to deny all psychic abilities as either too far-fetched or as
something that only a few extraordinary individuals possess. I've observed that these
types of dreams are far more common than the current literature would suggest and
it seems likely that this capacity is a natural type of intelligence that does have certain consistent qualities.

When I first began working with dream psychology and interpretation, I bent
over backwards to avoid the topic of psychic phenomena appearing in dreams. I
believed the psychological aspect of dreamwork was the most useful and reliable
avenue through which to explore our dreams and that preoccupation with mystify-
ing phenomena was just another cop-out—a way to avoid the often difficult matter
of interpreting our dreams.

The search for meaning and the receptivity to accept gifts are still the corner-
stones of my explorations, but through my own experiences and those of my clients,

I've come to appreciate that the dreaming mind easily and often transcends the laws of everyday thinking. Dreams can bridge the gap between space and time, connecting us with the experiences and feelings of loved ones far away. But they do this in a variety of ways, and as with other kinds of dreams there appear to be individual tendencies towards particular types of extraordinary dream phenomena. Some people believe they have had many precognitive dreams over the course of their lives. Others cannot recall a single precognitive dream but say they have experienced dreams that showed what was going on with a loved one who was on the other side of the world at the time. Learning about the possibilities, as well as recognizing the kinds of experiences you have already had, will help you feel at home with these abilities and ready to benefit from them whenever possible.

From my research and work with dreamers, I've observed seven types of psychic dreams that appear most prevalently in English-speaking countries. (It is certainly possible that there are more psychic dream experiences in addition to these.) See if you recognize any of these descriptions from your own life.

Future Snapshots

Have you ever noticed an element from a dream appearing in your waking life a day or so after you had the dream? Many people get very excited when this happens, understandably so, because the connection often can't be denied. This is particularly notable when some unusual sight such as a seventy-year-old woman in a gold jumpsuit is in your dream. If you ride the train home from work the next evening and sit next to that elderly woman in the gold jumpsuit, you're going to be thinking pretty hard about the nature of reality on that ride home. But what really happened here? Did your dream come true?

Actually, what seems to have happened is that your dreaming mind borrowed a striking visual image from daily events to include in your dream just the way it normally does. Striking images arise in dreams because they are memorable, current, and usually because they strike a symbolic chord that is relevant to your situation. If you'd had the dream *after* riding home next to the golden-clad grandma, you'd simply think that image was included in the dream because it was a recent event. But the dreaming mind tends to borrow imagery from a day or two into the future as easily as it does from a day or two in your past.

I have these dreams myself several times a month and have people report this experience to me very frequently. Over the years I've come to call these events future snapshots because they are like little still portraits of a scene in your future. There may or may not be anything of vital importance to the item or person. You'll have to evaluate that on a case-by-case basis. Some people are prone to this kind of experience and I suspect that people who regularly record and recall their dreams may be more aware of the process. Others find that once they become familiar with the concept, they notice just how often it happens. I tend to dream of new people the evening prior to a conference or class. Almost invariably, those people turn up at the class the next day and I get to meet them again in waking life. However, there do not seem to be any life-changing connections to these encounters. The dreaming mind evidently picks up interesting new faces to include in the dreams and I then get to see them when the first day of class begins.

If you notice future snapshots, here are a few things to keep in mind.

1. *Be sure to consider the symbolic relevance of the item included in your dream.* The more unusual it is, the more likelihood there is that it was included in your dream precisely because it stands for something in your psyche. The item itself may not be that important but it may represent something that you should think about.

2. *Before you leap to the conclusion that your dream came true, try to consider whether an entire event or sequence came true or whether you simply saw an item that appeared in your dream.* Certainly this does not discount the transcendence of time that apparently occurred. It is important for future reference to understand whether you tend to have many precognitive dreams that come true in their entirety or whether you are prone to have normal symbolic dreams sprinkled with future snapshots that are part of their imagery.

3. *If you are prone to future snapshots, try to get used to the phenomenon and accept that this is a normal part of the way dreams operate.* It's not necessary to imbue this process with extraordinary significance every time it occurs or to think that you are destined to foretell the future, like it or not. Nudge the edges of your idea of normalcy outward a bit to include this truly normal and natural part of the dreaming process.

Precognition and Warning

In contrast to the fragments of imagery we've just explored, precognitive dreams include entire stories or sequences of events that later transpire in waking life.

The population seems divided into three categories with respect to this phenomenon. There are many people who say they have never had a dream that came true or reflected future events. There are those of us who have had a single highly memorable event of this type, and there are those who say they have precognitive dreams on a fairly regular basis.

Some researchers claim that the average person will have at least one hundred and fifty thousand dreams in a lifetime. Regardless of whether this estimate is precisely accurate, it appears clear that we have a great many dreams over the course of our lives. If you have never had a dream come true, it seems reasonable to assume that the odds of a dream you've just had coming true are lessened. However, if you are one of the people who have a precognitive dream every few weeks, then the likelihood of any given dream being precognitive is increased. Knowing more about your own tendencies in this area can help you know what to expect and give you peace of mind when you are concerned that a particularly troubling dream may come true.

Types of Precognitive Dreams

There are different types of precognitive dreams. Some seem related to the planning functions of our minds. These allow us to visit potential futures and give our choices a run through to learn about cause and effect. Other precognitive dreams allow us to preview important crossroads in our lives or to visit the scenes of physical danger to which we will later be exposed.

I believe that all precognitive dreams arise in the interests of supplying us with greater information and resources to better handle future choices. It seems possible that our survival mechanism and our psychic abilities are closely linked and that when we are asleep our lack of conscious denial of these abilities allows them to operate more robustly than they do when we are awake. It also seems likely that the shift in consciousness that permits us to create dreams operates in such a way that it easily moves through the boundaries like space, time, life, and death that appear insurmountable during waking life.

Probable Futures

In examining the precognitive dreams in my own life, I've noticed that many times they deal with possible courses of action that lie ahead. When I was younger, attending college in the Bay Area of California, I longed to take ballroom dance lessons with a particular instructor who lived in San Francisco. But I lived in the suburbs, an hour and a half away, and it seemed an impractical and expensive hobby to take up. So I put aside my hunger to study dance seriously and avoided calling about the lessons.

However, one night I dreamed of flying over the Bay Bridge and visiting this instructor in the prestigious studio where he taught in the city. The teacher showed me in and then suggested that we go upstairs to a smaller, more quiet studio for my first lesson. I followed him up some stairs and we emerged into a lovely, small studio with mirrors and ballet bars all around. The floor was covered with black and white tile and the sun streamed in the old-fashioned windows. We worked with the fox-trot and the rumba for the first lesson and it was completely fascinating to me.

The next day, I felt a new resolve. I'd enjoyed my dream lesson so much, I felt I just had to meet with this teacher and see if he would accept me as a student. A week later I drove into the city to meet him. I'd forgotten about the dream that had prompted me to call until the teacher suggested that we go into a quieter studio to go through my first lesson. He then led me to some stairs and we came out in a sunny room on the second floor. It was the room I'd seen in my dream, surrounded with mirrors and ballet bars, with a floor covered in black and white tiles. Also true to the dream, the instructor chose to start me out with the simple steps of the fox-trot and rumba.

I studied dance with that instructor for three years, and found it one of the most enjoyable and important experiences of my life. I believe the dream was showing me a possible future, something that would happen if I followed my instinct to take up dancing seriously. However, I was free to choose what my future would hold. Many precognitive dreams operate in this fashion, showing us a possible future that will unfold if we go in a certain direction. It may be that many of our dreams offer this service, but when we choose to go in another direction, we do not then experience the event of our dreams.

Visiting an Important Juncture

Some dreams appear to zero in on an important crossroad in life, a decision, crisis, or opportunity that will be especially important to us. One man dreamed of living in an unusual setting on the water, in a dwelling that was half boat and half house. He saw the place in amazing detail, including the color of the walls and the view from his living room. The day after the dream, he was haunted by the memory of this home and he made a chalk drawing of the living room. He wanted in a small way to continue to feel the subtle sense of well-being that this strange setting had given him.

Fifteen years later, long after he had forgotten the dream, he moved to the Northwest and had the opportunity to rent a charming apartment on the top floor of a huge boathouse on the Columbia river. When he saw the apartment, he immediately recognized the pale yellow walls and the dramatic view of the river from the living room. Knowing that this place would bring him special renewal of energy, he rented the apartment without hesitation. For many years he lived there, his drawing framed and hanging on one wall. That home had a special significance to him because it was from there that he drew the energy to write several books and become a well-known public lecturer. No matter how busy his schedule became, he always found peace and refreshment in his home on the water.

These types of dreams seem to show us important junctures in life, frequently long before we arrive there in waking life. I believe these life previews help to set us up to recognize the importance of our actions at these points, and provide us with a better sense of the most beneficial choice to make.

Warning Signals

When people talk about precognitive dreams, they often think first about warning signals. It's especially easy to worry about a dream of death or disaster because it seems impossible to determine whether your dream has psychic elements until they play out in waking life. I've only had the opportunity to work with a handful of warning dreams, and in each case the dream did not indicate a fate that was closed or sealed. Instead, each dream presented such a memorable experience that when the waking life events began to unfold as foreseen, the dreamer recognized the situation and was able to completely alter the outcome of the events.

One woman dreamed repeatedly about being attacked in a parking lot by a man armed with a knife. Years passed and nothing happened, until she was involved in breaking off a romantic relationship with an unstable fellow who chased her when he saw her at the grocery store. Although she managed to get back to her car and quickly lock the doors, he came and pounded on the windows and pulled out a knife. She drove away quickly, got the police, and eventually the situation was resolved. After that incident, the recurring dreams of the knife attack stopped. She felt that the dreams helped her react quickly to that threat even before the man had drawn a knife and, in a sense, set her up to escape.

If her dreams were a function of her survival mechanism psychically sensing a life-or-death threat in her future, they did their job by getting her ready to respond. It was also a relief to this woman to understand that she could alter the outcome of the situation, because in her dreams, she had been caught by the man in the parking lot and stabbed.

Another woman dreamed of having a horrendous car accident and running into an animal on the road. She awoke sickened by the memory of the broken glass and the screams of the dying animal. Although she tried to analyze the dream, it made little sense to her and she had almost forgotten about it. But a year later, she was driving late at night on an unfamiliar country road in the rain, when something about the scenery struck her as familiar. She was puzzled, since she'd never taken this route before, that it should seem so familiar. Then she instinctively remembered the dream and braked the car as she rounded a curve. She slowed as much as possible and was barely moving when her headlights revealed a horse standing in the middle of the road. She stopped and stared at the horse, knowing that this moment was the scene of the accident in that dream. She pulled over and used her car phone to report the loose horse, who was soon returned to its pasture.

In this case as well, we see that the terrible crash did not actually have to happen. Perhaps the moment of meeting the horse on that road was part of her future, but the collision in the dream did not occur because she recognized the situation. This process appears to be a rather effective gift that nature has bestowed on us. These precognitive dreams help us handle danger more quickly in those split seconds that can make such a difference.

If you have a dream that you believe may contain a warning, remember that you may have the ability to change the outcome of events by virtue of the warning the dream has provided. It may not even matter if you don't keep the dream uppermost in your mind because the sense of familiarity will help to trigger your reaction to avoid harm when the time comes.

Empathy and Telepathy

Have you ever had a headache for no reason and later found out that it was because someone you were with had a terrible headache and you seemed to pick it up somehow? Over the years I've encountered several people with this kind of strong physical empathy who experience the pain and sometimes the emotions of others quite regularly. The dream state seems to heighten this effect and it is possible for your dreams to set you in a scene that is actually being experienced by someone close to you.

One woman dreamed that she was hemorrhaging badly and had to be rushed to the hospital. She awoke and tried to make sense of the dream but didn't make much headway. She had undergone a hysterectomy many years earlier and wasn't clear what the dream was trying to indicate. Later that day, it all came clear, however, when her son-in-law phoned her to report that her daughter had been rushed to the hospital that morning because she had to undergo an emergency D & C procedure to stop her from hemorrhaging.

This is a good example of empathic dreams. The events, feelings, and experiences seem to happen to you but you are actually picking up the experience of someone close to you. In most instances, these dreams seem to happen within families, between married couples, and sometimes among close friends. In more rare instances, professional colleagues may experience these dreams as well.

I recommend that you always assume these dreams are for and about you first, but if they do not seem to be related to your life or experience, then keep your mind open to the possibility that you may be picking up the experience of a loved one. Empathic tendencies are very pronounced for certain individuals and within certain relationships. If you already know you are prone to these dreams, then you can avoid confusion and recognize the pattern more quickly.

Shared Dreams

About one in one thousand people reporting on a dream describe having had a dream the same night that someone close to them experienced the very same dream. This makes for interesting breakfast conversation when one person begins to recount a weird dream and the other excitedly interrupts to finish the story. This phenomenon called shared dreaming is startling to experience, particularly if you have never heard of it before. I hear stories most often of spouses having identical dreams on the same night, but also of siblings, close friends, and parents and children reporting this occurrence.

In my experience, shared dreams do not seem any more or less important than any other dream but they do force us to question how such a process might occur. In some cases, empathic influences seem to play a part so that the husband is having a dream and the wife tunes in, experiencing it as though it were happening to her.

Other people have what some researchers call mutual dreams that involve group activities which others remember the following day. One husband and wife reported to me an involved dream about crossing a bridge together and overcoming a series of challenges to reach the other side. The following morning each remembered the obstacles involved, their joint efforts in tackling them, and their dialogue with one another about strategies they might use.

In future years, we may discover the dreaming process has an almost holographic element involved. Perhaps our adventures are sometimes more than imaginary movements. Maybe they actually take place on another frequency or in another dimension. If that is so, then we would tend to meet our loved ones, friends, and colleagues on that dream wavelength at times. Now that we are all more likely to recount and explore our dreams, it makes sense that we will have greater numbers of people remembering their shared adventures.

Parting Visions

Perhaps no psychic dream is more provocative and emotionally compelling than a good-bye vision of the recently departed. This is, without question, the type of dream about which I am asked most often in interviews. It is also the psychic dream most often reported in our database. To my surprise, most people who have had a dream of saying good-bye to a loved one are convinced that the experience was real in some spiritual way; they believe they actually were visited by the dead and received a message.

Many psychologists and doctors feel these dreams are the product of a grieving mind reaching for any kind of (even temporary) relief from the pain of losing someone. While there is a thread of logic to that argument, I've come to believe that most of these dreams of reassurance from the newly departed are indeed messages of love from those who have crossed over.

One woman lost her mother after a long battle with cancer. She and her husband had spent a long year caring for her ailing mother and after the struggle was over and they returned to their routine, her husband suggested they take a trip to give themselves a breath of fresh air and a change of scenery. The woman agreed and made reservations a month ahead of time for a lovely stay in New England, a place they had often promised themselves they would visit one day. Yet as the time for the trip approached, the woman felt too depressed to travel and she also felt guilty for having made the arrangements so soon after her mother's death. She wanted to cancel the plans but it would mean the forfeiture of some non-refundable fees.

As she struggled with this question, she had a vivid dream in which her mother appeared at her bedside one night. "Lou, stop your nonsense!" the mother declared. "You get yourself together and go on that trip and enjoy yourself! I'm fine and I'll be seeing you again, don't worry. In the meantime, get on with your life and enjoy what you can!" This gruff but loving message was so unmistakably the voice of her mother that the woman never questioned the message. She announced to her husband the next day that she felt her mother would have wanted them to go on their trip after all. They enjoyed their holiday in New England and found it shook them out of the emotional low they'd suffered all during the past year of her mother's illness. Years after the incident, the woman remains convinced that her mother did visit her that night and that everything about that dream was unlike her normal dreams.

There are several hallmarks of the parting vision or good-bye dream that are very different from other kinds of dreams. It can be helpful to make note of these differences

1. *Realistic setting.* The dreams are usually set in the dreamer's bedroom. You are lying in bed when a vision of the loved one comes into the room, stands or sits nearby, and talks to you. This is rather unusual, since the majority of dreams do not take place in the bedroom with you lying there asleep.
2. *Lack of dreamlike plot.* There is no plot, no story, and no action to the dream. The loved one comes in and talks to the dreamer, and that's it. This too is unusual. It's very rare for a dream to consist merely of someone coming into a realistic setting and talking to you.
3. *Sensation of visitation.* Dreamers feel overwhelmingly that their experiences were quite real. There is a palpable sense of having been with the deceased the night before. Think of all the times you've dreamed of movie stars, celebrities, or other people far away. Yet upon awakening, you do not insist that those people actually visited you the night before.
4. *Impact on the dreamer.* Many of the people who describe these visions say

they felt significantly comforted by them, or were able to make a decision they'd been avoiding prior to the experience. As any therapist will attest, getting people to change is not an easy business. There is reason to suggest that an experience of this nature that creates an overnight change is more real than imaginary.

5. *Convincing elements.* In some cases, the personality of the deceased is so recognizable and so real that the dreamer has absolutely no doubt that they have been visited. Others have noted that often these parting visions come to a child or someone who is asked to recount the experience to family members so that others may not grieve so severely.

6. *Reassuring tone.* In my experience, dreamers who are struggling with powerful feelings and upsetting circumstances or trauma usually have dreams arise from the psyche that are a swirl of emotion, confusion, and pain. This is the soup that is brewing in the individual and the dreams around this time reflect those elements bubbling beneath the surface. It is unusual therefore to have a glowing dream that everything is all right or that death is only a doorway, given those circumstances. In my opinion, these uplifting visions are unlikely to have arisen from the mind and emotions of the grief-stricken individuals who have them. It seems to me more likely that these messages of reassurance do come from an outside source.

There are certainly other dreams about the dead that are symbolic or a normal part of the grieving process. Dr. Patricia Garfield has made a wonderful contribution to the study of dreams about grief in her book *The Dream Messenger*. If you have lost someone you love, you may want to refer to her work in this area. However, if your dream contains several of the hallmarks I've noted above that distinguish it from a symbolic dream or one processing excess emotion, it may be that you have indeed received a message from someone you love.

Dream Assignments

Because I hear so many dreams, I've come to notice the unusual factors that make certain anomalous dreams stand out. One type of dream that is unlike others is what I call the assignment dream. These are dreams about working at a particular kind of spiritual job while you sleep. For the people who have these dreams, they are a routine occurrence.

In effect, the dreamer will frequently find himself working at a spiritual task, almost like being an EMT or member of the Peace Corp, in their non-physical form while they sleep. Several evenings a week or month are devoted to helping the newly deceased cross over to the other side, helping children overcome challenges, helping with healing of various illnesses, or helping crops to grow healthfully.

Most people have one type of task they do sometimes throughout a life-time and this dream task may be related to their waking life job or it may be quite different.

One woman who was a writing teacher told me that she helps people cross over many times in her dreams. Another told me he helps coordinate meetings and teaching consortiums in his dreams. I often counsel other people in their dreams to help them make sense of something that has just happened, or to explain something about the nature of dreams while they're happening. It didn't occur to me that these experiences might have some type of reality until I had so many students over the years tell me about these experiences when they, too, remembered them.

If you have not had dreams of this nature, the idea may sound incredi-ble. Yet it seems possible that if we are nonphysical beings whose conscious-ness may explore, teach, and grow in nonphysical ways when we sleep, there may be some of us who are involved in some type of service that takes place through the dreaming state.

There is no need to glamorize or dramatize this occurrence. In fact, the people I've spoken with who believe their dream assignments are real are very understated about them and accept them as part of life. This phenome-non is only one portion of our dreaming experience and in future years we will learn more about how this takes place and what we can learn from it.

Unborn Children

One of the most stunning types of psychic dreams I've been told about is that of receiving a message from an unborn child through a dream. I was on a radio program in Seattle when I was first told about this, and as amazing as it may seem, the grandmother who phoned in was so unmistakably cred-ible that I knew she was telling us a true story.

The caller said that over the years she'd been hoping against hope ≠that her daughter would become pregnant. The young woman and her husband had been trying for some time without success. One night, the caller had a dream about meeting a lovely young woman named Stephanie, who introduced herself and said that she would be born next year as her granddaughter. The dreamer said that was impossible because there seemed to be some kind of fertility problem. Stephanie nodded and laughed, hugged the dreamer excitedly, and explained that the situation was resolved, and that when she woke up she would learn that her daughter was, at long last, pregnant.

When she woke up the next day, she was bemused about the dream but decided not to mention anything to her daughter about it because it was bound to be a painful reminder of her situation. But that afternoon, as the dream predicted, the daughter excitedly called the mother with the wonderful news that she was pregnant!

Eight months later, the daughter had a lovely little girl and her mother was there at the delivery. She held the little girl and quietly said, "Hello Stephanie, welcome home!"

Since that time, I've heard several more stories of this type, some including scenes of the child's appearance as a youngster which later came true or of the personality of the child that seemed to have been confirmed.

If we are spiritual beings whose consciousness is not limited by physical form, then it follows that we may indeed be able to communicate across the boundaries of space, time, and physicality. Perhaps these dreams are best judged by their content, rather than by the barriers that do not seem to stop them.

Embracing the Psychic Elements in Dreams

The dreaming process is a function of human consciousness that offers us different recourses than we have while we are awake. We have greater access to subtle impressions, memories, emotional truths, and spiritual awareness while we are dreaming than we do during our busy daytime lives. This other side of our intelligence also seems to permit us the luxury of heightened psychic processes, undaunted by cluttered thinking or disbelief. It isn't necessary to believe we are connected across space and time in order to have these experiences. But if we keep an open mind at the same time we determine to learn the truth, we will be less inclined to dismiss the vastness of our own potentials out of loyalty to trendy skepticism or fear of seeming odd.

Getting to know your own dream profile will be of immense help in quickly identifying which dreams are truly unusual because they stand out from your normal dreaming patterns. If you have a psychic dream or a parting vision, you will probably feel altogether different from the way you do about a normal dream. Your subjective sense of the nature of your own experience is a wonderful truth detector. Avoid being unduly upset or frightened if a dream seems to transcend the norm. Do what you can to respond sensibly to potential warnings in the same manner you use to lock doors and wear safety belts.

We seem to be at a stage of learning about dreams where we suspect that some of our dream experiences are quite real in a transpersonal sense. Until all the questions surrounding these processes are answered, we will have to be content with trusting our own knowing and continuing to intelligently question both the history and the horizon of our dreams.

Dreams by Category

Dreams Listed Alphabetically

About the Author

Gillian Holloway holds an M.A. and Ph.D. in psychology and is dedicated to helping us all understand and benefit from our dreams. Her first book, *Dreaming Insights,* is widely used by teachers around the world as a guide to dream analysis. The popularity of German, Spanish, and Chinese translations of this book attest to a global fascination with dreams.

At home in the Pacific Northwest, Dr. Holloway teaches courses in dream psychology and intuition at Marylhurst University and leads private dream study groups. A popular media guest, Dr. Holloway has appeared on nationally syndicated radio programs such as Art Bell's *Dreamland* and television shows like ABC's *20/20.*

Dr. Holloway writes a weekly advice column in *Woman's World* magazine titled "What Your Dreams Mean," which answers fascinating questions about what our dreams reveal. Her award-winning website, www.Lifetreks.com, is one of the most respected Internet resources on the study of dreams. A member of the Association for the Study of Dreams, she strives to increase awareness of the power of dreams to enrich and balance hectic lives.